Q-SAILING SHIP "MITCHELL"

This was one of the most famous of all the Q-ships and rendered splendid service The dummy deck house on the poop concealed the after gun (see p. 67).

Frontispiece.

Q-SHIPS AND THEIR STORY

BY

E. KEBLE CHATTERTON

The Naval & Military Press Ltd

Published by

The Naval & Military Press Ltd
Unit 5 Riverside, Brambleside
Bellbrook Industrial Estate
Uckfield, East Sussex
TN22 1QQ England

Tel: +44 (0)1825 749494

www.naval-military-press.com
www.nmarchive.com

*In reprinting in facsimile from the original, any imperfections are inevitably reproduced
and the quality may fall short of modern type and cartographic standards.*

TO
ADMIRAL SIR LEWIS BAYLY,
C.V.O., K.C.B., K.C.M.G.,

COMMANDER-IN-CHIEF OF THE IRISH COAST DURING THE STRENUOUS YEARS OF THE SUBMARINE CAMPAIGN, WHO BY HIS ENCOURAGEMENT AND DEVELOPMENT OF THE Q-SHIP SERVICE DID SO MUCH TO THWART THE OPERATIONS OF THE ENEMY AND TO PROTECT OUR MERCANTILE MARINE

PREFACE

THE wonderful and brave story of ships and men here presented needs but the briefest introduction. The deeds will forever remain one of the most glorious chapters in the chronicles of the sea. No excuse is offered for adding another volume to the literature of the war, for the subject is deserving of greater attention than has hitherto been possible. Lord Jellicoe once remarked that he did not think English people realized the wonderful work which these mystery ships had done in the war, and that in these vessels there had been displayed a spirit of endurance, discipline, and courage the like of which the world had never before seen.

To few naval historians, I believe, has it ever been permitted to enjoy such complete opportunities for acquiring authentic information as is here presented. Unquestionably the greatest sphere of Q-ship operations was off the south-west coast of Ireland, owing to the fact that the enemy submarines from the summer of 1915 to 1918 concentrated their attacks, with certain intervals, on the shipping in the western approaches to the British Isles. It was my good fortune during most of this period to be at sea patrolling off that part of Ireland. These Q-ships were therefore familiar in their various disguises at sea or in harbour at Berehaven and Queenstown during their well-earned rest. Throughout this time I kept a diary, and noted down much that would otherwise have been forgotten. Many of the Q-ship officers were my personal friends, and I have enjoyed the hospitality of their ships. Valuable data, too, were obtained from officers of merchant ships who witnessed Q-ships engaging submarines.

A considerable number of authentic manuscripts has been examined. By the courtesy of commanding officers I have been lent documents of priceless historical value, such as copies of official reports and private diaries, plans, sketches, photographs, and so on. All this information has been further augmented by personal conversation, correspondence, and valuable criticism. I submit, therefore, that with all these sources of information available, and with knowledge of much that has been published from the German side, it is possible to offer a monograph that is at once accurate in detail and correct in perspective.

'With respect to single-ship actions,' wrote James in his monumental Naval History a hundred years ago, 'the official documents of them are also very imperfect. The letters are generally written an hour or so after the termination of the contest, and, of course, before the captain has well recovered from the fatigue and flurry it occasioned. Many captains are far more expert at the sword than at the pen, and would sooner fight an action than write the particulars of one.' That statement is true to-day of the Q-ships, and it would have been negligent not to have availed oneself now of the calm and considered version of the chief actors in the great mystery-ship drama while they are still alive. Although the time for secrecy has long since passed, nothing has here been included of a confidential nature that can be of assistance to enemies past or potential. In one instance, for political reasons and in the interests of the service, I have made a certain omission. Those concerned will recognize this and understand : the rest will not notice it.

Among those who have rendered me the greatest assistance in regard to information, advice, criticism, the loan of manuscripts, illustrations, and in other ways, I desire especially to return thanks to Admiral Sir Lewis Bayly, C.V.O., K.C.B., K.C.M.G., and Miss Voysey, C.B.E.; to Captain F. H. Grenfell, D.S.O., R.N., Captain Gordon Campbell, V.C., D.S.O., R.N., Captain W. C. O'G. Cochrane, R.N., Commander Godfrey Herbert, D.S.O., R.N., Commander Stopford C. Douglas, R.N., and to Lieutenant G. H. P. Muhlhauser, R.N.R.

E. KEBLE CHATTERTON.

March, 1922.

CONTENTS

CHAPTER		PAGE
I. The Hour and the Need		1
II. The Beginning of Success		13
III. Q-Ship Enterprise		26
IV. The Story of the 'Farnborough'		39
V. The 'Mystery' Sailing Ships		52
VI. The 'Mary B. Mitchell'		67
VII. More Sailing Ships		77
VIII. Submarines and Q-Ship Tactics		92
IX. The Splendid 'Penshurst'		109
X. Further Developments		132
XI. The Good Ship 'Prize'		143
XII. Ships and Adventures		158
XIII. More Sailing-Ship Fights		177
XIV. The Summit of Q-Ship Service		192
XV. Life on Board a Q-Ship		213
XVI. Q-Ships Everywhere		228
XVII. Ships of all Sizes		242
XVIII. The Last Phase		255
Index		273

LIST OF ILLUSTRATIONS

Q-Sailing-Ship *Mitchell*	*Frontispiece*
	TO FACE PAGE
An Early Q-Ship (*Antwerp*)	6
Q-Ship *Antwerp*	6
Commander S. C. Douglas, R.N.	8
Commander G. Herbert, D.S.O., R.N.	8
Q-Ship *Antwerp*	12
Gun's Crew of Q-Ship *Antwerp*	12
Q-Ship *Redbreast*	22
Q-Ship *Baralong*	22
Q-Ship *Baralong* (Two Illustrations)	28
Officers of Q-Ship *Farnborough*	42
Captain Gordon Campbell and Lieutenant C. G. Bonner	42
Q-Sailing-Ship *Mitchell*	68
Q-Ship *Penshurst*	114
Q-Ship *Penshurst* (Two Illustrations)	116
Q-Ship *Penshurst* (Two Illustrations)	120
Captain and Officers of Q-Ship *Penshurst*	124
Men of Q-Ship *Penshurst*	124
Q-Ship *Tulip*	138
Q-Ship *Tamarisk*	138
Q-Ship *Candytuft*	174
Q-Ship *Candytuft*	176
Q-Sailing-Ship *Fresh Hope*	188
Q-Ship *Record Reign*	188
Q-Sailing-Ship *Rentoul*	190
Midship Gun of Q-Sailing-Ship *Lothbury*	190
The Master of the Collier *Farnborough*	192
Q-Ship *Farnborough*	192
Q-Ship *Farnborough*	194
Q-Ship *Farnborough*	196

LIST OF ILLUSTRATIONS

	TO FACE PAGE
S.S. *Lodorer*	196
Q-Ship *Pargust*	198
Q-Ship *Sarah Jones*	198
Q-Ship *Dunraven*	200
Bridge of Q-Ship *Dunraven*	202
After the Battle	204
Dunraven Doomed	206
Q-Ship *Dunraven*	208
Q-Ship *Dunraven*	212
Q-Ship *Dunraven*	214
Officers and Crew of the Q-Ship *Dunraven*	216
Q-Ship *Barranca* (Two Illustrations)	220
Q-Ship *Barranca* (Two Illustrations)	222
Q-Ship Transformation	234
Q-Ship *Barranca* at Sea	234

DIAGRAMS, ETC., IN THE TEXT.

FIG.		PAGE
1.	Action of *Baralong* on August 19, 1915	21
2.	Action of *Baralong* on September 24, 1915	27
3.	Action of *Margit* on January 17, 1916	34
4.	Action of *Werribee* on February 9, 1916	37
5.	Action of *Farnborough* on April 15, 1916	45
6.	Action of *Helgoland* on October 24, 1916	63
7.	Action of *Salvia* on October 20, 1916	99
8.	Action of *Saros* on November 3, 1916	103
9.	Action of *Penshurst* on November 29, 1916	110
10.	Action of *Penshurst* on November 30, 1916	113
11.	Action of *Penshurst* on January 14, 1917	118
12.	The Humorous Side of Q-Ship Warfare	127
13.	*Farnborough's* Farewell	196
14.	Action of *Pargust* on June 7, 1917	201
15.	The Great Decision	208
16.	Letter from the First Lord of the Admiralty to Captain Gordon Campbell	210

'The necessitie of a Historie is, as of a Sworne Witnesse, to say the truth (in just discretion) and nothing but the truth.'

SAMUEL PURCHAS *in* '*Purchas His Pilgrimes*,' 1625.

Q-SHIPS AND THEIR STORY

CHAPTER I

THE HOUR AND THE NEED

ALL warfare is merely a contest. In any struggle you see the clashing of will and will, of force against force, of brain against brain. For the impersonal reader it is this contest which has a never-ending interest. A neutral is just as keenly entertained as the playgoer who sits watching the swaying fortunes of the hero in the struggle of the drama. No human being endowed with sympathetic interest, who himself has had to contend with difficulties, fails to be moved by the success or disaster of the contestants in a struggle of which the spectator has no part or lot. If this were not so, neutral newspapers would cease to chronicle the wars of other nations, novels would cease to be published, and plays to be produced.

Human nature, then, being what it is, man loves to watch his fellow-man fighting, struggling against men or fate or circumstances. The harder the fight and the nearer he is to losing, so much the more is the spectator thrilled. This instinct is developed most clearly in youth: hence juvenile fiction is one mass of struggles, adventures, and narrow escapes. But the instinct never dies, and how few of us can resist the temptation to read the exciting experiences of some entirely fictional character who rushes from one perilous situation to another? Is there a human being who, going along the street, would not stop to watch a burglar being chased over roofs and chimney-pots by police? If you have once become interested in a certain trial at the law courts, are you not eager to know whether the prisoner has been acquitted or convicted? You despise him for his character, yet you are fascinated by his adventures, his struggles, his share in the particular drama, his fight against heavy odds; and, contrary to your own inherent sense of justice, you almost hope he will be acquitted. In a word, then, we delight in having before us the adventures of our fellow humanity, partly for the exciting pleasure which these arouse in us, but partly also because they make us wonder what we should have done in a similar set of circumstances. In such vital, critical moments should we have played the hero, or should we have fallen somehow a little short?

The following pages are an attempt to place before the reader a series of sea struggles which are unique, in that they had no precedent in naval history. If you consider all the major and minor sea fights from the earliest times to the present day; if you think of fleet actions, and single-ship contests, you cannot surpass the golden story of the Q-ships. As long as people take any interest in the untamed sea, so will these exploits live, not rivalling but surpassing the greatest deeds of even the Elizabethan seamen. During the late war their exploits were, for very necessary reasons, withheld from the knowledge of the public. The need for secrecy has long since passed, and it is high time that a complete account of these so-called 'mystery ships' should be published, not merely for the perpetuation of their wonderful achieve-

THE HOUR AND THE NEED

ments, but for the inspiration of the new race of seamen whose duty it will be to hand on the great tradition of the sea. For, be it remembered, the Q-ship service was representative of every species of seamen. There were officers and men of the Royal Navy both active and retired, of the Royal Naval Reserve, Royal Naval Volunteer Reserve, and men from the Royal Fleet Reserve. From warship, barracks, office, colony, pleasure yacht, fishing vessel, liner, sailing ship, tramp steamer, and elsewhere these seafarers went forth in unarmoured, slow-moving, lightly-armed vessels to perform the desperate adventure of acting as live-bait for a merciless enemy. It was an exploit calling for supreme bravery, combined with great fighting skill, sound seamanship, and a highly developed imagination. The successes which were attained were brought about by just this combination, so that the officers, especially the commanding officers, and the men had to be hand-picked. The slow-reasoning, hesitating type of being was useless in a Q-ship; equally out of place would have been the wild, hare-brained, dashing individual whose excess of gallantry would simply mean the loss of ship and lives. In the ideal Q-ship captain was found something of the virtues of the cleverest angler, the most patient stalker, the most enterprising big-game hunter, together with the attributes of a cool, unperturbed seaman, the imagination of a sensational novelist, and the plain horse-sense of a hard business man. In two words, the necessary endowment was brains and bravery. It was easy enough to find at least one of these in hundreds of officers, but it was difficult to find among the many volunteers a plucky fighter with a brilliant intellect. It is, of course, one of the happy results of sea training that officer or man learns to think and act quickly without doing foolish things. The handling of a ship in bad weather, or in crowded channels, or a strong tideway, or in going alongside a quay or other ship—all this practice makes a sailor of the man, makes him do the one and only right thing at the right second. But it needed 'something plus' in the Q-ship service. For six months, for a year, she might have wandered up and down the Atlantic, all over the submarine zone, with never a sight of the enemy, and then, all of a sudden, a torpedo is seen rushing straight for the ship. The look-out man has reported it, and the officer of the watch has caused the man at the wheel to port his helm just in time to allow the torpedo to pass harmlessly under the ship's counter. It was the never-ceasing vigilance and the cool appreciation of the situation which had saved the ship.

But the incident is only beginning. The next stage is to lure the enemy on, to entice him, using your own ship as the bait. It may be one hour or one day later, perhaps at dusk, or when the moon gets up, or at dawn, but it is very probable that the submarine will invisibly follow you and attack at the most awkward time. The hours of suspense are trying; watch has succeeded watch, yet nothing happens. The weather changes from good to bad; it comes on thick, it clears up again, and the clouds cease to obliterate the sun. Then, apparently from nowhere, shells come whizzing by, and begin to hit. At last in the distance you see the low-lying enemy engaging you with both his guns, firing rapidly, and keeping discreetly out of your own guns' range. Already some of your men have been knocked out; the ship has a couple of bad holes below the waterline, and the sea is pouring through. To add to the anxiety a fire is reported in the forecastle, and the next shell has made rather a mess of the funnel. What are you going to do? Are you going to keep on the bluff of pretending you are an innocent merchantman, or are you going to run up the White Ensign, let down the bulwarks, and fire your guns the moment the enemy comes within range and bearing? How much longer is it possible to play with him in the hope that he will be fooled into doing just what you would like him to do? If your ship is sinking, will she keep afloat just long enough to enable you to give the knock-out blow as the inquiring enemy comes alongside? These are the crucial questions which have to be answered by that one man in command of the ship, who all the time finds his bridge being steadily smashed to pieces by the enemy's fire.

> 'If you can keep your head when all about you
> Are losing theirs and blaming it on you;
> If you can trust yourself when all men doubt you,
> But make allowance for their doubting too;
> If you can wait and not be tired by waiting . . .'

then, one may definitely assert, you have in you much that goes to the making of an ideal Q-ship captain and a brave warrior. As such you might make a first-class commanding officer of a destroyer, a light cruiser, or even a battleship; but something more is required. The enemy is artful; you must be super-artful. You must be able to look across the tumbling sea into his mind behind the conning tower. What are his intentions? What will be his next move? Take in by a quick mental calculation the conditions of wind, wave, and sun. Pretend to run away from him, so that you get these just right. Put your ship head on to sea, so that the enemy with his sparse freeboard is being badly washed down and his guns' crews are thinking more of their wet feet and legs than of accurate shooting. Then, when you see him submerging, alter course quickly, reckon his probable position by the time you have steadied your ship on her course, and drop a series of depth-charges over his track. 'If you can fill the unforgiving minute with sixty seconds' worth of distance, run'; if you have acted with true seamanship and sound imagination, you will presently see bits of broken wreckage, the boil of water, quantities of oil, perhaps a couple of corpses; and yours is the U-boat below, my son, and a D.S.O.; and a thousand pounds in cash to be divided amongst the crew; and you're a man, my son!

That, in a few phrases, is the kind of work, and shows the circumstances of the Q-ship in her busiest period. As we set forth her wonderful story, so gallant, so sad, so victorious, and yet so nerve-trying, we shall see all manner of types engaged in this great adventure; but we cannot appreciate either the successes or losses until we have seen the birth and growth of the Q-ship idea. As this volume is the first effort to present the subject historically, we shall begin at the beginning by showing the causes which created the Q-ship. We shall see the consecutive stages of development and improvement, the evolution of new methods, and, indeed we may at once say it, of a new type of super-seamen. How did it all begin?

Turn your attention back to the autumn of 1914. It was the sinking of the three *Cressys* on September 22 by U 9 that taught Germany what a wonderful weapon of offence she had in the submarine. Five days later the first German submarine

THE HOUR AND THE NEED

penetrated the Dover Straits. This was U 18, who actually attacked the light cruiser *Attentive*. But it was not until October 20 that the first merchant ship, the British S.S. *Glitra* in the North Sea, was sunk by a submarine. Six days later the French S.S. *Amiral Gantcaume*, with Belgian refugees, was attacked by a German submarine. A month passed, and on November 23 the S.S. *Malachite* was attacked by U 21, and after being on fire sank. Three days later the S.S. *Primo* was sunk also by U 21. It was thus perfectly clear that we had before us a most difficult submarine campaign to contend with, and that merchant ships would not be immune. On the last day of October H.M.S. *Hermes* was torpedoed off Calais, and on November 11 H.M.S. *Niger* had a similar fate near Deal.

What was to be done? The creation of what eventually became known as the Auxiliary Patrol, with its ever increasing force of armed yachts, trawlers, drifters, and motor craft; the use of destroyers and our own submarines formed part of the scheme. But even at this early stage the Q-ship idea came into being, though not actually under that name. Officially she was a special-service ship, whose goings and comings were so mysterious that even among service men such craft were spoken of in great secrecy as mystery ships. This first mystery ship was the S.S. *Vittoria*, who was commissioned on November 29, 1914. She had all the appearance of an ordinary merchant ship, but she was armed, and went on patrol in the area where submarines had been reported. It was an entirely novel idea, and very few people knew anything about her. She never had any luck, and was paid off early in January, 1915, without ever having so much as sighted a submarine. The idea of decoy ships suggested itself to various naval officers during December, 1914, and their suggestions reached the Admiralty. The basic plan was for the Admiralty to take up a number of merchantmen and fishing craft, arm them with a few light quick-firing guns, and then send them forth to cruise in likely submarine areas, flying neutral colours. This was perfectly legitimate under International Law, provided that before opening fire on the enemy the neutral colours were lowered and the White Ensign was hoisted. Seeing that the enemy was determined to sink merchantmen, the obvious reply was to send against them armed merchantmen, properly commissioned and armed, but outwardly resembling anything but a warship. Thus it came about that on January 27, 1915, the second decoy ship was commissioned. This was the Great Eastern Railway S.S. *Antwerp* (originally called *Vienna*), which operated in the English Channel. She was placed under the command of Lieut.-Commander Godfrey Herbert, R.N., one of the most experienced and able officers of our submarine service. The choice was a happy one, for a submarine officer would naturally in his stalking be able to realize at once the limitations and possibilities of his opponent. It was a most difficult task, for the U-boats at this time were still very shy, and only took on certainties. Neither in boats nor in personnel had Germany yet any to spare, and there were periods when the submarine campaign fluctuated. Thus, day after day, week after week, went by, and *Antwerp* never had any chance. The enemy was now beginning to operate further afield, and at the end of January, 1915, for the first time, a U-boat made its way up the Irish Sea as far as off Liverpool, and then, on February 18, was inaugurated the German Submarine

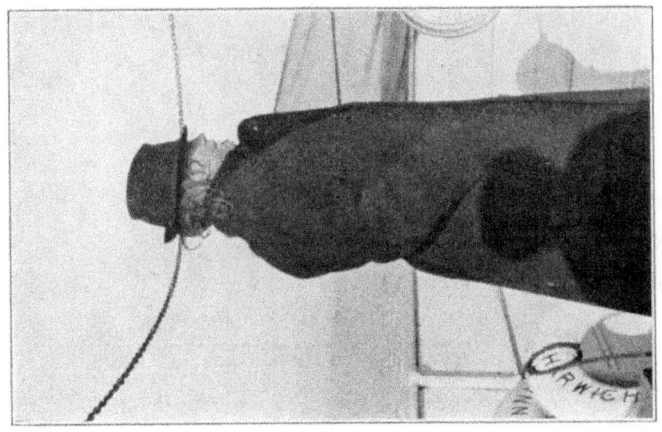

COMMANDER S. C. DOUGLAS, R.N.
When serving in the Q-ship "Antwerp," wearing a false moustache and disguised as an English commercial traveller.

COMMANDER G. HERBERT, D.S.O., R.N.
Taken on the bridge of the Q-ship "Antwerp," disguised as a Dutch pilot with a wig.

To face p. 8

THE HOUR AND THE NEED

Blockade. Shipping began to be sunk in various places, but the western end of the English Channel was now a favourite zone, especially in the neighbourhood of the Scillies; and it was with the hope of being taken for a merchant ship that *Antwerp* had come out from Falmouth and made her way westward. Thus, on March 12, we see her, about three o'clock in the afternoon, twelve miles north of the Bishop Rock Lighthouse. A submarine[1] was sighted steering in a northerly direction for a steamer on the horizon. Here, at length, was a chance. Twenty minutes later, *Antwerp* came up to a sailing ship, and found she had on board the officers and crew of the Ellerman liner *Andalusian*, which had been captured and scuttled 25 miles W.N.W. of the Bishop Rock. *Antwerp* continued her chase, and got within four miles of the *Andalusian*, still afloat, but then the submarine dived and was never sighted again. So *Antwerp* was never able to sink a submarine, and she was paid off on April 5, 1915.

During the summer of 1915 there was a small steamer called the *Lyons*, which one used to see in various naval ports, and under various disguises. Her primary object was to carry naval stores from one port to another, but it was always her hope to fall in with a submarine. I remember seeing her one day alongside Pembroke Naval Dockyard, painted a certain colour and with one funnel. A little later I saw her elsewhere with a different coat of paint and a dummy funnel added to her, so that she resembled an ocean-going tug. *Lyons* also was unable to entrap the enemy, and terminated her decoy-ship period at the beginning of November of the same year.

[1] This was U 29, which on March 18 was sunk in the North Sea by H.M.S. *Dreadnought*.

Thus the war had gone on for several months, and an apparently sound idea had failed to produce a single good result. All kinds of shipping were being sunk, and yet the German submarines somehow could not be persuaded to attack these disguised ships. How was it? Was there something in the disguise which gave the steamers away? Was it purely hard luck? We cannot say definitely, but the fact remained, and it was rather disappointing. Of course the idea of disguise had been employed almost from the very first days of the war; for, in August, 1914, Admiral Jellicoe had requested that the armed trawlers, though commissioned, should not be painted grey like other warships, but retain their fishing numbers and funnel markings just as in peace-time. In the early summer of 1915, a number of disguised armed trawlers were also sent out to the Dogger Bank in the hope of catching an unsuspecting submarine, who might think they were fishing. The idea had been further developed by a clever scheme involving the co-operation of a disguised armed trawler towing a submerged British submarine. This began in May; on June 23 it was the means of sinking U 40, and on July 20 it brought about the loss of U 23; but a few months later this idea was thought to be played out, and came to an end in October, 1915, though it was eventually revived in the following summer.

Another variation of the decoy-ship principle at this time was that employed by Admiral Startin, who was in charge of the naval base at Granton. In view of enemy submarines having recently held up neutral merchant steamers in the North Sea, he disguised two big trawlers so as to resemble small neutral merchant ships. This was in July, 1915. So successfully was this done that one of them actually deceived British destroyers, who took her for a Danish cargo steamer. The next development was further to disguise them by adding a false deck cargo of timber, boats, and other details, so as to resemble closely a Norwegian cargo ship, with Norwegian colours hoisted at the mizzen, two derricks placed on the trawler's foremast, and Norwegian colours painted on prepared slips of canvas placed on each side of the hull amidships. Those who were at sea in those days will recollect that it was customary for neutral ships to have their national colours painted on each side of the hull in the hope that the enemy would not mistake the ships for Allies'. Thus cleverly disguised, the two Granton trawlers *Quickly* and *Gunner* went into the North Sea, armed with nothing more powerful than a 12-pounder, Admiral Startin being himself aboard one of the ships. A large submarine was actually sighted on July 20, and at 1,000 yards the enemy began the action. *Quickly* thereupon lowered her Norwegian flag, ran up the White Ensign, removed the painted canvas, replied with her 12-pounder, and then with her 6-pounder. A fine, lucky shot was seen to strike the submarine, and much smoke was seen to issue. Although the enemy made off and was not sunk, yet it showed that it was possible to fool German submarines by this disguise. The decoy-ship idea was not merely sound in principle, but it was practicable and was capable of being used as a valuable offensive weapon. Most of a year had passed since the beginning of war, and there were no decoy ship results to show except those which had been obtained by British submarines working in conjunction with disguised trawlers. However, just as the seaman often finds the dawn preceded by a calm and followed by a breeze, so it was to be with the decoy ships.

The dawn of a new period was about to take place, and this was followed by such a wind of events that if anyone had dared to doubt the value of this specialized naval warfare it was not long before such hesitation vanished. Disguised trawlers had in the meantime been further successful, but there were obviously greater possibilities for the disguised merchant ship, the collier and tramp types especially. But this all depended on three things: First, the right type of ship had to be selected very carefully and with regard to the trade route on which she would normally in the present conditions be likely to be found. For instance, it would have been utterly foolish to have sent a P. and O. liner to cruise up and down the waters of the Irish Channel or an Atlantic liner up and down the North Sea. Secondly, having once selected the right ship, much depended on the dockyard authorities responsible for seeing that she was fitted out adequately as to her fighting capabilities, yet externally never losing any of her essential mercantile appearance. This meant much clever designing, much engineering and constructive skill, and absolute secrecy. Thirdly, the right type of keen, subtle, patient, tough officer had to be found, full of initiative, full of resource, with a live, eager crew. Slackers, 'grousers,' and 'King's-hard-bargains' were useless.

Q-SHIP "ANTWERP"
Showing the collapsible dummy life-raft which concealed the two 12-pounders.

GUN'S CREW OF Q-SHIP "ANTWERP"
Gun's crew of "Antwerp" ready to fire on a submarine. The sides of the dummy life-raft have been collapsed to allow gun to come into action.

CHAPTER II

THE BEGINNING OF SUCCESS

WE turn now to the northern mists of the Orkneys, where the comings and goings of the Grand Fleet were wrapped in mystery from the eyes of the world. In order to keep the fleet in stores—coal, oil, gear, and hundreds of other requisite items—small colliers and tramp steamers brought their cargoes northward to Scapa Flow. In order to avoid the North Sea submarines, these coal and store ships used the west-coast passage as much as possible. Now, for that reason, and also because German submarines were already proceeding in earnest, via the north-west of Scotland, to the south-west Irish coast, ever since the successful sinking of the *Lusitania*, it was sound strategy on our part to send a collier to operate off the north-western Scottish coast. That is to say, these looked the kinds of ships a suspecting U-boat officer would expect to meet in that particular locality.

Under the direction of Admiral Sir Stanley Colville, a handful of these little ships was, during the summer of 1915, being fitted out for decoy work. One of these was the collier S.S. *Prince Charles*, a little vessel of only 373 tons. In peace-time she was commanded by her master, Mr. F. N. Maxwell, and manned by five deckhands, two engineers, and two firemen. These men all volunteered for what was known to be a hazardous job, and were accepted. In command was placed Lieutenant Mark Wardlaw, R.N., and with him went Lieutenant J. G. Spencer, R.N.R., and nine active-service ratings to man the guns and use the rifles. She carried the weakest of armament—only a 3-pounder and a 6-pounder, with rifles forward and aft. Having completed her fitting out with great secrecy, the *Prince Charles* left Longhope in the evening of July 21 with orders to cruise on routes where submarines had recently been seen. Proceeding to the westward at her slow gait, she saw very few vessels until July 24. It was just 6.20 p.m. when, about ten miles W.N.W. of North Rona Island, she sighted a three-masted vessel with one funnel, apparently stopped. A quarter of an hour later she observed a submarine lying close to the steamer. Here was the steel fish *Prince Charles* was hoping to bait.

Pretending not to see the submarine, and keeping on her course like a real collier, Lieutenant Wardlaw's ship jogged quietly along, but he was closing up his gun's crews behind their screens and the mercantile crew were standing by ready to hoist out the ship's boats when required. The German now started up his oil-engines and came on at full speed towards the *Prince Charles*. It had just gone seven o'clock and the submarine was 3 miles off. The collier had hoisted her colours and the enemy was about five points on the bow when a German shell came whizzing across. This fell 1,000 yards over. Lieutenant Wardlaw now stopped his engines, put his ship head on to the Atlantic swell, blew three blasts, and then ordered the crew to get the boats out, in order to simulate the movements of an ordinary merchant ship in the presence of an attacking submarine.

THE BEGINNING OF SUCCESS 15

In the meantime the enemy was approaching rapidly and fired a second shot, which fell between the funnel and the foremast, but landed 50 yards over. When the range was down to 600 yards the enemy turned her broadside on to the collier and continued firing; and this was now the time for the Q-ship's captain to make the big decision. Should he maintain his pretence and continue to receive punishment, with the possibility of losing ship and lives in the hope that the submarine would come nearer? Or should he reveal his identity and risk everything on the chance of winning all? This was always the critical moment when the Q-ship captain held in his judgment the whole fate of the fight, of the ship, and his men.

Lieutenant Wardlaw, seeing that the enemy could not be enticed to come any nearer, took the second alternative, and opened fire with his port guns. The effect of this on the German was remarkable and instantaneous; for her gun's crew at once deserted the gun and darted down into the conning-tower. But whilst they were so doing, one of *Prince Charles's* shells struck the submarine 20 feet abaft the conning-tower. The enemy then came round and showed her opposite broadside, having attempted to dive. She now began to rise again as the collier closed to 300 yards, and frequent hits were being scored by the British guns. By this time the surprised Germans had had more than enough, and were observed to be coming out of the conning-tower, whilst the submarine was settling down by the stern. Still the British fire continued, and when the submarine's bows were a long way out of the water, she took a sudden plunge and disappeared. A large number of men were then seen swimming about, and the *Prince*

Charles at once made every effort to pick them up, fifteen officers and men being thus saved out of thirty-three.

So ended the career of U 36. She had left Heligoland on July 19 for a cruise of several weeks via the North Sea, and, up till the day of meeting with *Prince Charles*, had had a most successful time; for she had sunk eight trawlers and one steamer, and had stopped the Danish S.S. *Louise* when the *Prince Charles* came up. It was not until the submarine closed the latter that U 36 saw the Englishmen clearing away some tarpaulins on deck, and the next moment the Germans were under fire, and the captain gave orders to dive. By this time the submarine had been hit several times, and as she could not be saved, she was brought to the surface by blowing out her tanks. The crew then took to the sea, and the engineer officer opened the valves to sink her, and was the last to leave. Inside, the submarine was wrecked by *Prince Charles's* shells and three men were killed, the accurate and rapid fire having immensely impressed the Germans. Thus the first Q-ship engagement had been everything that could be desired, and in spite of the submarine being armed with a 14-pounder and carrying seven torpedoes, the U-boat had been beaten in a fair fight. Lieutenant Mark Wardlaw received a D.S.O., two of the crew the D.S.M., and the sum of £1,000 was awarded to be divided among the mercantile crew.

Another of the ships fitted out under similar auspices was the *Vala*, who commissioned on August 7, 1915. She was of 609 tons, and could steam at nothing better than 8 knots. In March of the following year she was transferred from Scapa to Pembroke, and her career was long and eventful.

THE BEGINNING OF SUCCESS 17

In April of 1917 she was in action with a submarine, and she believed that one shell hit the enemy, but the latter then submerged. One day in the middle of August *Vala* left Milford Haven to cruise between the Fastnet and the Scillies, and was last heard of in the early hours of the following day. She was due to arrive at Queenstown, but, as she did not return, the Q-ship *Heather* was ordered to search for her in the Bay of Biscay. For a whole week there had been a series of gales, and it was thought that the little steamer had foundered in the bad weather, but on September 7 the German Government wireless announced that 'the U-boat trap, the former English steamer *Vala*,' had been sunk by a U-boat.

Besides the *Vala* and *Prince Charles*, three other Q-ships were fitted out in the north. These were the *Glen Isla*, of 786 tons; the *Duncombe*, 830 tons; and the *Penshurst*, 740 tons, and they all performed excellent work. But before we go any further we have to consider still another novelty in naval warfare, or rather a strange revival. Who would have thought that the sailing-ship would, in these days of steam, steel, and motor, come back in the service as a man-of-war? At first it seems almost ludicrous to send sail-driven craft to fight against steel, mechanically propelled vessels. But, as we have seen, this submarine warfare was not so much a matter of force as of cleverness. It was the enemy's unimaginative policy which brought about this reintroduction of sail into our Navy, and this is how it all happened.

During the summer of 1915 German submarines in the North Sea had either attacked or destroyed a number of neutral schooners which used to come across with cargoes of pit-props. One used to see these fine little ships by the dozen arriving in the

Forth, for the neutral was getting an excellent return for his trading. It annoyed the enemy that this timber should be able to enter a British port, and so the submarines endeavoured to terrorize the neutral by burning or sinking the ships on voyage. It was therefore decided to take up the 179-ton schooner *Thirza*, which was lying in the Tyne. Her purchase had to be carried out with great secrecy, lest the enemy should be able to recognize her at sea. She was an old vessel, having been built as far back as 1865 at Prince Edward Island, but registered at Whitstable. She changed her name to *Ready*, and began her Q-ship service at the end of August, 1915, when soon after midnight she sailed down the Forth. Armed with a couple of 12-pounders, having also a motor, carrying a small deck cargo of pit-props, and suitably disguised to resemble a neutral, this schooner, manned by a hardy volunteer crew, used to pretend she was coming across the North Sea, though at first she never went many miles away from the land. Under the various aliases of *Thirza, Ready, Probus, Elixir*, and **Q** 30, this old ship did splendid work, which did not end until Armistice. We shall have occasion to refer to her again.

Who can avoid a feeling of intense admiration for the men who, year after year, were willing and eager to roll about the sea in a small sailing ship looking for the enemy, well knowing that the enemy had all the advantage of speed, handiness, and armament? Even the motor was not powerful, and would give her not much more than steerage way in a calm. The submarine could always creep up submerged, using his periscope but now and then: the schooner, however, was a conspicuous target all the time, and her masts and sails advertised her presence from the

THE BEGINNING OF SUCCESS 19

horizon. These Q-ship sailing men deserve much for what they voluntarily endured. Quite apart from the bad weather, the uncomfortable quarters on board, the constant trimming of sheets and alteration of course off an unlit coast, there was always the possibility that some U-boat's crew would, after sinking the schooner, cut the throats of these British seamen. The Q-ship crews knew this, and on certain occasions when U-boat prisoners were taken by our ships the Germans did not conceal this fact. Life in these sailing craft was something quite different from that in a battleship with its wardroom, its cheery society, and a comfortable cabin to turn into. In the latter, with powerful turbines and all the latest navigational instruments, bad weather meant little inconvenience. After all it is the human element which is the deciding factor, and the Q-ship service certainly wore out officers and men at a great pace. It is indeed difficult to imagine any kind of seafaring more exacting both physically and nervously.

But the Navy pressed into its use also sailing smacks, and sent them out to sea. This began at Lowestoft in August, 1915. In that neighbourhood submarines had been doing a great deal of damage to the local fishing ketches, so it was decided to commission four of these smacks, arm them, strengthen their fishing crew with a few active service ratings for working the gun, and let the craft resume their fishing among the other smacks. With any luck at all a German submarine should come along, and then would follow the surprise. The original fishermen crews were only too delighted to have an opportunity of getting their own back, and these excellent fellows certainly were afforded some good sport. So well did the idea work that within a very few days the smack *G. and E.* engaged one submarine, and the *Inverlyon* sank UB 4. During the same month the smack *Pet* fought a submarine, and on September 7 *Inverlyon* had a fight with another.

And still the Admiralty were not over optimistic as to the capabilities of the decoy ship, and had to be convinced of the real worth of this novel idea. However, an incident happened on August 19 which was so successful and so significant that it entirely changed the official mind, and all kinds of craft were suggested as suitable decoys. Some thought that oil-tankers would have made ideal bait: so they would, but such ships were few in number and too valuable. Others suggested yachts, and actually these were used for intelligence work in the Bay of Biscay. Many other schemes, too, were brought forward, but they were not always practicable, or had to be discarded for particular reasons.

In March, 1915, the Admiralty had taken up the S.S. *Baralong*, a typical 'three-island' tramp, as a decoy. For nearly six months she had been cruising about and had already steamed 12,000 miles, but during the afternoon of August 19 she was at last to have her chance. This was an historic day in the submarine campaign, for in that area between the south-west coast of Ireland and the western end of the English Channel eight British steamers were sunk, including the 15,801-ton White Star liner *Arabic*. It is quite certain that there was more than one submarine operating, and they had reaped a good harvest on the 17th. In the hope of falling in with one of these U-boats, the *Baralong* found herself in Lat. 50.22 N., Long. 8.7 W. (that is, about a hundred miles south of Queenstown), steering on an easterly course. She was disguised as a United States cargo

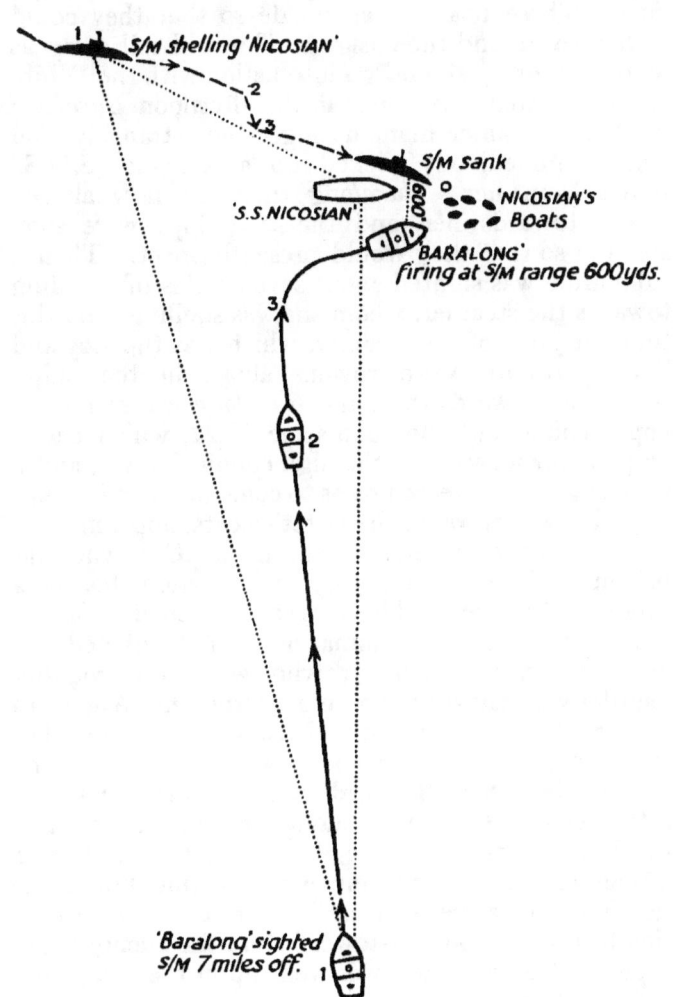

Fig. 1.—Diagram to Illustrate Approximate Movements of 'Baralong' when she sank U 27 on August 19, 1915. The Numerals indicate Simultaneous Positions of Decoy and Submarine.

ship with American colours painted on boards on her sides. These boards were made so that they could be hauled in, and the ensign staff would fall away as soon as the ship should go into action with the White Ensign hoisted. At three in the afternoon *Baralong* sighted a steamer manœuvring rather strangely, and almost immediately picked up a wireless 'S.O.S.' signal from her. *Baralong* therefore now altered course towards her, and the two ships were soon steering so that they would presently meet. Then a submarine was sighted about seven miles off heading towards the steamer, whom she was shelling. By this time the crew of the steamer, which was the Leyland liner *Nicosian*, were rowing about in the ship's boats, and towards these the *Baralong* was seen to be approaching, but the submarine U 27, which had a 22-pounder forward of the high conning-tower, and a similar gun aft, steered so as to come along *Nicosian's* port side and towards the latter's boats, apparently to prevent *Baralong* rescuing the men. One who was present told me the full story, and I made notes and a sketch at the time. This is what happened:

As soon as the submarine was blanketed by *Nicosian*, the *Baralong*, who was now roughly parallel with the other two craft, struck her American colours, hoisted the White Ensign, and trained her guns ready for the moment when the submarine should show herself ahead of *Nicosian's* bows. In a few seconds U 27 came along, and had the greatest of all surprises. The range was only 600 yards, and 12-pounder shells, accompanied by rifle fire, came hurtling along, penetrating the craft on the waterline below the conning-tower before the enemy could reply. The conning-tower went up in the air, panic-stricken Germans jumped into the sea, the submarine

Q-SHIP "BARALONG"

Heroine of two famous victories over submarines. Photograph taken in Malta harbour after the ship had been transferred to the Mediterranean.

Q-SHIP "REDBREAST"

This vessel was commissioned as a Q-ship at the end of March, 1916, but six months later had concluded her service in this capacity.

THE BEGINNING OF SUCCESS 23

heeled over, and in about another minute sank for good and all. The whole incident had happened so quickly that *Nicosian's* people were as surprised as they were amused. The whole of *Baralong's* tactics had been so simple yet so clever and effective; deliverance from the enemy had followed the sudden attack so dramatically, that it was not easy to realize quite all that had happened. *Nicosian* had been holed by the German shells, but *Baralong* took her in tow and headed for Avonmouth. She was down by the head and the tow-rope parted during the night, but she managed to get to port all right.

The sinking of this U 27 was a most useful piece of work, for her captain, Lieut.-Commander Wegener, was one of Germany's best submarine commanders; she had left Germany a fortnight before. This incident, with many of its details, reached Germany via the U.S.A.; for *Nicosian* was carrying a cargo of mules from across the Atlantic to be used by our army, and some of the muleteers were American citizens. On their arrival back home the news came out, and was published in the newspapers, causing considerable sensation. The German nation was furious and made some bitter accusations, forgetting all the time that on this very day they had fired on and killed fourteen of the crew of the British submarine E 13, which had grounded on the Danish island of Saltholm. All the officers, with one exception, and most of the crew of *Baralong* were of the Royal Naval Reserve. A number of decorations was made and the sum of £1,000 was awarded.

This great success in the midst of a terrible tale of shipping losses finally convinced the authorities of the value of the Q-ship. There was a great shortage of tonnage at this time, for ships were being required for carrying mules and munitions from America, munitions to Russia, and every kind of stores across to our armies. However, it was decided to take up some more steamers as decoys and fit them out in a similar manner. Thus the two tramp steamers *Zylpha* (2,917 tons) and the *Lodorer* (3,207 tons) were assigned to Queenstown. The former, after doing excellent work, was sunk on June 15, 1917; the latter, commanded by the officer who eventually became Captain Gordon Campbell, V.C., D.S.O., made history. Under the aliases of *Farnborough* and Q 5 she became the most famous of all the decoy ships. Tramp steamer though she may be, she has a career which, for adventurous fights, honourable wounds, and imperishable glory cannot be approached by any ship in the world, with the solitary exception, perhaps, of the *Vindictive*, for, in spite of everything, *Lodorer* was able at the end of the war to resume her work in the Merchant Service. In another place we shall soon see her exploits as a warship.

In addition to these two a few small coasting steamers were taken up and a couple of transports, and the work of selecting officers of dash and enterprise had to be undertaken with great secrecy and discretion. Unquestionably the most suitable type of Q-ship was the tramp, and the worst was the cross-Channel railway steamer. The first was slow, but could keep at sea a long time without coaling; the latter was fast, but wasteful of coal and had limited bunker space. Of these railway steamers we have already mentioned the G.E.R. Co.'s S.S. *Vienna* (alias *Antwerp*). Another decoy ship was the L. & S.W.R. Co.'s S.S. *Princess Ena*, which was built to run between the Channel Islands and Southampton. She had been commissioned in May, 1915, armed

THE BEGINNING OF SUCCESS

with three 12-pounders, and could steam at 15 knots, but she ceased her decoy work in the following August. The *Lyons*, already referred to, was really a salvage steamer, but much resembled a tug, especially when she hoisted her dummy funnel. She was of 537 tons, could steam at 11 knots, and was armed with four 12-pounders. But it was the 'three-island' tramp type of the *Baralong* breed, which was so ordinary and seen at any time in any sea, that made the ideal Q-ship. She was of 4,192 tons, built in 1901, speed 10 knots, armed with three 12-pounders, and fitted with a single wireless aerial which could excite no suspicion. So skilfully was the armament of these ships concealed that they frequently lay in harbour close to foreign ships without revealing their true nature. I have myself been all over such a ship, commanded by one of the greatest Q-ship officers, and entirely failed to find where he mounted his guns, and yet they were on board ready for immediate use. How much more likely would the German submarine, lying lower down to the water, be deceived! As time went on and these much-feared 'trap-ships' were scrutinized more closely, several minor but fatal characteristics had to be remembered; for instance, the crew sometimes would be too smart or the signalman was too good with his semaphore. But these and similar points were rectified as soon as they were realized.

CHAPTER III

Q-SHIP ENTERPRISE

WITHIN five weeks of her victorious fight *Baralong* had done it again. After the war it was definitely announced in the public Press that U 27 had been sunk by H.M.S. *Wyandra* on August 19. Under this name the ship's crew were awarded the sum of £185 as prize bounty, and in the same court *Wyandra*, her commanding officer this time being Lieut.-Commander A. Wilmot-Smith, R.N., was awarded £170 prize bounty for sinking U 41 on September 24, 1915. It was an open secret that *Baralong* and *Wyandra* were one and the same ship, so we may as well get this matter quite clear. Already we have seen the manner in which this decoy sank U 27, and we shall now be able to note very similar tactics in almost the same locality attaining a like result under her new captain.

U 41 had left Wilhelmshaven on September 12, this being her fourth trip. She was under the command of Lieut.-Commander Hansen, and on the 23rd had sunk three British steamers, each of about 4,000 tons, in a position roughly eighty miles south-east of the Fastnet. The first of these ships was the *Anglo-Columbian*, which was sunk at 9.45 a.m., followed by the *Chancellor* at 3 p.m., and the *Hesione* about four hours later. The news of the first sinking reached *Baralong* (henceforth officially known as *Wyandra*) in Falmouth, so this decoy put to sea, and after

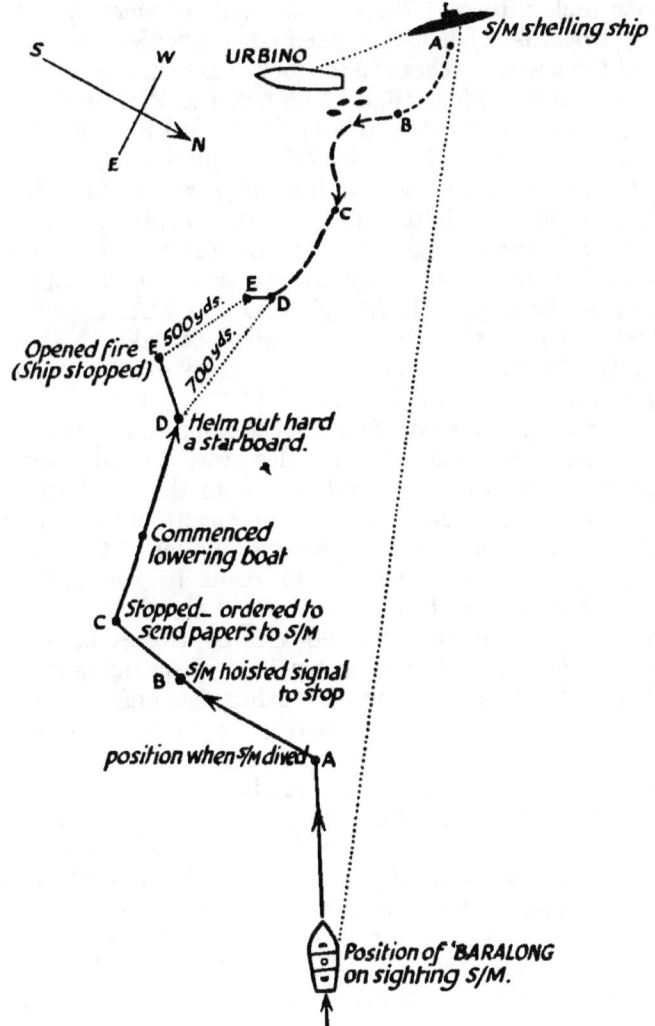

FIG. 2.—DIAGRAM TO ILLUSTRATE APPROXIMATE MOVEMENTS OF 'BARA-LONG' WHEN SHE SANK U 41 ON SEPTEMBER 24, 1915. THE LETTERS INDICATE SIMULTANEOUS POSITIONS OF DECOY AND SUBMARINE.

rounding the Lizard steered a course that would, with luck, intercept the submarine if she were operating towards Ushant, as seemed probable. So the night passed. About 9 o'clock next morning the British S.S. *Urbino* (6,651 tons), of the Wilson Line, was attacked by this U 41 in a position roughly sixty-seven miles S.W. by W. of the Bishop Rock. At 9.45 a.m. up came the *Baralong*, and sighted the *Urbino* about eight miles ahead, on fire, stopped, with a heavy list, and blowing off steam. It was a fine, clear morning; a steady course was maintained, and the Q-ship made ready for action. Already the *Urbino's* crew had been compelled to take to their boats, and the submarine, at a range of 200 yards, had put five shells into her.

Baralong now sighted the submarine's conning-tower, and when about five miles away the submarine dived, so *Baralong* altered course to the southward, so as to compel the enemy, if she meant to attack, to rise to the surface and use her oil-engines. This ruse succeeded, for presently U 41 came to the surface and proceeded at full speed to head the Englishman off. *Baralong* now hoisted United States colours, whereupon the German hoisted 'Stop instantly!' The former obeyed, but by using the engines now and again cleverly manœuvred so as to close the range. The next order from the enemy was for the Englishman to send his papers aboard the submarine, the two craft being now about two and a half miles apart. *Baralong* answered the signal, steamed slowly ahead, altering very gradually towards the enemy, and pretended to be hoisting out a boat on the side visible to the submarine. On board the latter the forward gun was already manned, Ober-Leutnant Crompton being on deck in charge of the

Q-SHIP "BARALONG"
Showing gun on port side of the poop and disguised crew.

Q-SHIP "BARALONG"
Showing disguised marines and method of concealing the gun.

firing. But Hansen had already been outmanœuvred by Wilmot-Smith, just as in the olden days the sailing man-of-war sought to win the weather-gage. For, having got the submarine 2 points on the starboard bow, *Baralong* so steered as to keep her in that position, and the two approached until the range was down to 700 yards.

All this time, though every man in *Baralong* was at his station, there was not a movement that in any way caused the enemy to suspect. The latter was concerned rather with the details of making quite sure she was a neutral. It was then that *Baralong* starboarded her helm so that it might appear as if she were just swinging in order to give the ship's boat a lee while being lowered, a perfectly natural and seamanlike piece of tactics. But when she had swung sufficiently for the starboard and stern guns to bear, down came the disguise, up went the fluttering White Ensign, and a heavy fire at only 500 yards came pouring forth, accompanied by rifle fire from the marines in the well-deck aft. The enemy was taken so completely by surprise that he got off only one round, and this was a long way out. So smartly had *Baralong's* men begun the attack that the second round scored a direct hit at the base of the conning-tower, and several other shells got home with deadly precision. The Germans on deck became panic-stricken, left their guns, and made for the conning-tower hatch, but whilst they were doing this another direct hit struck the conning-tower, blowing Hansen and six men to pieces. After several more hits, U 41 listed to port with a heavy inclination and dived. This submersion was useless, as she was leaking very badly, and the main bilge-pump ceased to function. Down she dropped to a terrible depth, the diving tanks were blown by the compressed air, and with a great sense of relief the Germans who were still alive found their craft coming to the surface. First came the bows, and then the top of the conning-tower showed above water, a large volume of smoke and steam escaping, and then she disappeared for the last time very rapidly, stern first, Ober-Leutnant Crompton and the helmsman escaping through an open hatchway.

After she had sunk finally a large burst of air and oil-fuel rose to the surface, the submarine's bulkheads having apparently burst owing to the pressure due to the deep water, which here was 75 fathoms. Only Crompton and the helmsman were saved, the former having been badly wounded whilst entering the conning-tower. All the others, consisting of five officers and twenty-five men, were lost. In the meantime *Urbino* had sunk, too, from her shell-holes, and *Baralong* picked the whole crew up from their boats to the number of forty-two officers and men, her master, Captain Allanson Hick, stating that his ship was on her way from New York to Hull. *Baralong*, conscious of having obtained another brilliant and brave victory, now proceeded with her survivors to Falmouth, where she arrived in the early hours of the following morning. Lieut.-Commander Wilmot-Smith was awarded the D.S.O., and Temporary Engineer J. M. Dowie, R.N.R., received a D.S.C., a well-deserved decoration; for much depended on the engineers in these ships, and they had much to suffer. Two of the crew received a D.S.M. each, and the sum of £1,000 was also awarded, this being additional to the bounty subsequently awarded in the Prize Court.

At this stage in the world's history there is no intention of exulting in the discomfiture and pain of the enemy. Day after day during this period the writer used to see the sad sight of our survivors without ship or belongings other than the clothes on their backs. It is difficult altogether to forget these incidents or the unchivalrous behaviour of the enemy. Without wishing to be vindictive, it is well to place on record that the nineteen German sailors on the deck of U 41 all jeered at Captain Hick in his distress, and yet although a callous enemy had been sunk in a fair fight, this second *Baralong* incident aroused in Germany a wave of horrified indignation akin to the decoy's former exploit. The German Press referred to the sinking of U 41 as a murderous act, but if this were so there were to be plenty more to follow. Happily, at last, we had found a real, effective means of grappling with the submarine problem. Against us were contending the finest brains of the German Navy, and these determined officers were not over anxious to save life, as we knew from their behaviour at the sinking of *Falaba* and *Lusitania*. Such craft as U 41, over 200 feet long, with a maximum surface speed of 14 knots, but an endurance of 5,500 miles at 10 knots, armed with a couple of guns and eight torpedoes, were formidable foes, and any clever stratagem that could be used against them, without infringing International Law, was surely entirely justified. Thus, very wisely, four colliers were fitted out that same autumn as Q-ships, these being the *Thornhill* (alias *Werribee*, *Wellholme*, and *Wonganella*); the *Remembrance* (alias *Lammeroo*); *Bradford City* (alias *Saros*); and the *Penhallow* (alias *Century*). These, together with *Baralong*, were sent to operate in the Mediterranean, for here the submarine campaign became very serious just at the time when it temporarily died down in North European waters. Diplomatic relations between Germany and the United States, consequent on the sinking of the *Lusitania* and then *Arabic*, were becoming strained, so that Germany had to accept the American demands for the limitation of submarine activity. The result was that from September 24, 1915, up to December 20, 1915, no ships were sunk by German submarines in North European waters, though the Mediterranean had a different story to tell. At the end of December a short, sharp submarine campaign was carried out off Ireland by U-boats, and then there was quiet again until Germany began her extended submarine campaign on March 1, 1916. This in turn lasted only to May 8, and was not resumed until July 5, 1916.

It is as well to bear these periods in mind, for otherwise we cannot appreciate the dull, monotonous weeks and months of cruising spent by the Q-ships when they saw no submarine, received nothing but vague, inaccurate reports, and had to keep their crews from getting disappointed or eventually wondering whether they were really doing any good in this particular service. But as the winter passed and the U-boats displayed their usual spring activity, the Q-ships had their opportunities again. Before we come to see these, let us take a glance at the work which they were performing during the winter in the Mediterranean, where the enemy sought to cut our lines of communication to the Dardanelles.

In December, 1915, the steamship *Margit* had been fitted out as a decoy, and on January 17, 1916, in Lat. 35.34 N., Long. 17.38 E., she was steering west for Malta, when she received S.O.S. signals on her wireless. The time was 9.30 a.m., and presently shots were seen falling close to the S.S. *Baron Napier*, who was about five miles to the southward. The captain of the *Margit* was Lieut.-Commander G. L. Hodson, R.N., who then hoisted the Dutch ensign and altered course towards the *Baron Napier*. The latter kept making signals that she was being shelled and that the submarine was approaching; but when *Margit* got within a couple of miles the submarine transferred the shelling to her. *Margit's* captain conned his ship, lying prone on the bridge and peering through the chinks in the bridge screen. In order to lure the enemy on he pretended to abandon ship, hoisted the international signal 'I am stopped,' and sent away the ship's lifeboat with Sub-Lieutenant McClure, R.N.R., in charge. The ship now had every appearance of having been abandoned, but in addition to the captain lying unseen on the bridge, the guns' crews, under Lieutenant Tweedie, R.N.R., and a sub-lieutenant, were remaining hidden at their stations. Riflemen were similarly placed on the foredeck and aft.

After the 'panic party' had been sent away in the boat the enemy seemed fairly satisfied, ceased shelling, dived, and then reappeared a quarter of an hour later 800 yards away, with a couple of feet of his periscope showing. He was now going to make quite sure this was no trap, so, still submerged, he came within 50 yards of *Margit's* port side and then right round the ship, scrutinizing her carefully. At length, being apparently quite convinced that all was well, he steered for *Margit's* boat about a thousand yards away and came to the surface. Three men then appeared on the submarine's deck, the German ensign was hoisted, and one of them waved *Margit's* boat to come alongside. This was as far as

Lieut.-Commander Hodson deemed it advisable to let matters go. Giving the orders to down screens, open fire, and hoist the White Ensign, the enemy now came under attack. One shot seemed to hit abaft the conning-tower, and the submarine submerged, so fire was ceased and *Margit* proceeded to pick up her boat. The davit-falls had only just been hooked on when the submarine showed her conning-tower 70 yards off, apparently in difficulties. The Q-ship therefore opened fire once more, but

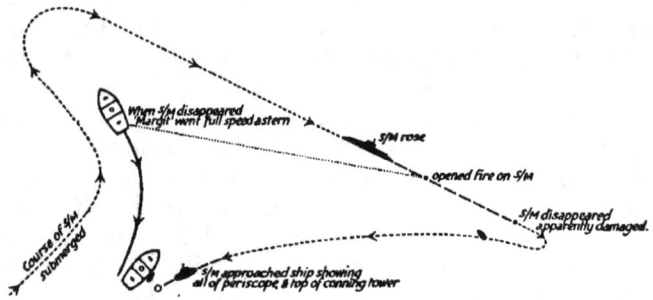

Fig. 3.—Diagram to Illustrate Approximate Movements of 'Margit' in her Engagement with Submarine on January 17, 1916.

the enemy again submerged. Unfortunately the submarine had not been sunk, although no effort had been neglected. From 9.30 a.m. to about midday officers and crew had been compelled to keep in cramped tiring attitudes, with very little knowledge of what was going on; and after he had finally disappeared *Margit* had remained for about three hours in the hope that he might return. By a curious coincidence, at the time when *Baron Napier* was being attacked, another steamer, the *Baron Ardrossan*, belonging to the same owners, happened to be passing

Q-SHIP ENTERPRISE

and saw the shells dropping around, but as she could steam nothing better than 3 knots slower than *Baron Napier* she could not go to her assistance. However, if the submarine had not been destroyed, *Margit* had saved the *Baron Napier* and caused the enemy to break off the engagement.

Mention was made just now of the *Werribee* (alias *Wonganella*, etc.). On February 3, 1916, this ship, which had been fitted out at Gibraltar, under the command of Lieut.-Commander B. J. D. Guy, R.N., left Port Said to cruise on the Malta to Egypt trade route. She was a steamer of 3,848 tons, and had taken in 2,600 tons of sand as ballast. About 9 o'clock on the morning of February 9, *Werribee* was steaming along when she picked up a signal on her wireless to the effect that the S.S. *Springwell*, of 5,593 tons, was torpedoed and sinking by the head. The vessel was soon sighted, and the last boats could be seen already leaving the ship, the position being about sixty miles from Crete. The weather was perfect, with a flat, calm sea and extreme visibility—an ideal day, in fact, for good gunnery.

But it was to be a most difficult experience, and the incident well illustrates the problems which had to be dealt with. About 10.15 a.m., as no submarine could be seen, *Werribee* turned towards the four boats already in the water, and hailed them for information, then examined the condition of *Springwell*, and presently turned again. All of a sudden, a great submarine, painted like the Mediterranean pirate-ships of ancient times, a brownish green, emerged from the sea about 5,000 yards away on *Werribee's* starboard bow, and came close up to *Springwell*, possibly to prevent *Werribee* from salving her. Alarm stations were sounded in the Q-ship, but the submarine's men were already running to their two guns, and opened fire. *Werribee* then decided to haul round and pretend to run away. The third shot from the enemy hit, and it was at first feared that the explosion had disabled one gun's crew, but fortunately the hit was a little further aft. It was immediately evident to *Werribee's* captain that to-day the enemy was not going to allow him to play the abandon-ship game, but was intending to sink him straight away. The submarine's accurate and rapid fire was clearly aimed at *Werribee's* boats, and two of them were soon riddled. It was for Lieut.-Commander Guy to make up his mind quickly what tactics now to pursue, and he decided to reveal the ship's true character and open fire. This was done, and within ten seconds his 4-inch quick-firer was in action, range 4,000 yards. After six rounds from the Q-ship the enemy ceased firing, and the eighth seemed to hit abaft the conning-tower. Then she submerged in a cloud of smoke, about 11.10 a.m., this smoke screen being a favourite ruse for escaping, and she was never seen again that day. *Werribee* now turned her attention to the torpedoed ship, but the latter was too far gone, and foundered at 5.45 that afternoon. The men in *Springwell's* boats were then picked up, and about 6 o'clock the ship made for Malta. It was again sheer bad luck; a combination of difficult circumstances, and the tactics of an astute German captain, had now prevented success coming to the decoy. There was no question about her disguise, and the captain of a merchantman who witnessed the fight accurately spoke of *Werribee* as 'an old tramp with a few patches of paint, firing at the submarine.' Before the war we should have thought no ship in His Majesty's Service could possibly merit such a description as this, but strange

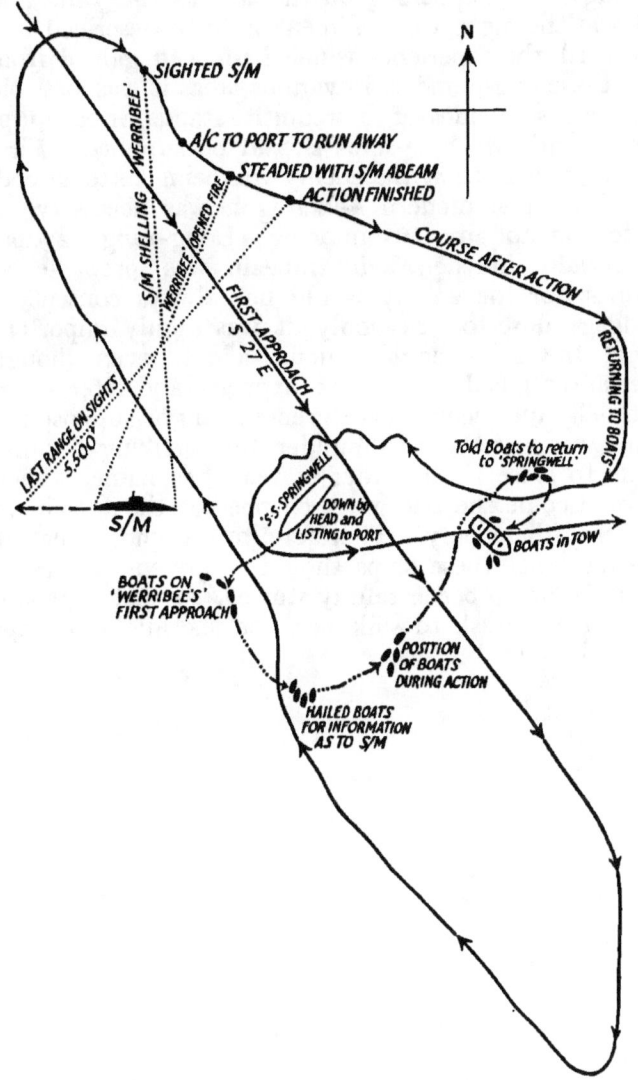

Fig. 4.—Diagram to Illustrate Approximate Movements of 'Werribee' in Action with Submarine on February 9, 1916.

things were happening on the seas at this time, and it was the highest compliment so to be described.

With the experience which had been gained from all these engagements in various areas it was possible to form some idea of the requisite standardized equipment with which Q-ships should be supplied. First of all, inasmuch as the enemy was being better armed, at least one modern 4-inch gun was necessary, in addition to any 12-pounder. Long-range action, especially in the Mediterranean, was probable at times, for the enemy would not always consent to engage close to. Secondly, it was highly important that the ship should remain afloat, even though seriously holed. It might happen—and later on it actually did occur—that the enemy might suppose the ship was just about to founder, thus making it quite safe to close her in order to read her name. Then would come the one great chance for the Q-ship to destroy the enemy. Therefore, to this end, it became certain that these ships should be given cargoes of barrels, or timber, carefully stowed, so that it would be no easy task to sink her, and she might perhaps even be salved.

CHAPTER IV

THE STORY OF THE 'FARNBOROUGH'

Two days before the end of February, 1916, I happened to be returning from leave in England to my ship, which was in Queenstown for boiler-cleaning. In the Holyhead-Kingstown steamer I found myself in conversation with a junior lieutenant-commander, R.N., who also was returning to his ship at Queenstown. We talked of many things all the way down across Ireland, but this quiet, taciturn officer impressed me less by what he said than by what he left unsaid, and it took me a long time to guess the name of his ship. I thought I knew most of the commanding officers of sloops and trawlers and drifters, and so on, at work off the south and south-west coasts of Ireland, but I had neither seen this officer nor heard his name before. At the beginning of the war he was unknown to the public; in fact, not until three weeks after the end of this February did he win distinction, but to-day his name is known and respected in every navy of the world, and his career as a naval officer is different from anything ever recorded in the pages of history.

This was Lieut.-Commander Gordon Campbell, who just before the war was a lieutenant in command of an old-fashioned destroyer based on Devonport. On October 21, 1915—the date is particularly fortunate as having been the 110th anniversary of the Battle of Trafalgar—Lieutenant

40 Q-SHIPS AND THEIR STORY

Campbell commissioned the tramp steamer *Lodorer* at Devonport as a Q-ship, but on passage thence to Queenstown changed her name to *Farnborough*, as it had become gossip that she had been armed for special service. Through that trying winter the little *Farnborough* endured gale after gale, and her young captain, attired in the rig of a typical tramp skipper, with his smart crew trained now to look slovenly yet be mentally alert all the time, never for a moment wavered in the belief that one day would come his opportunity. He had organized his ship to a pitch of perfection, and nothing was lacking except the appearance of a U-boat.

On March 1, 1916, the enemy renewed its submarine campaign after lying dormant since the day when *Baralong* had sunk her U 41, except for the Christmastime temporary outburst. During the first three weeks of March one, or more, submarine had sunk shipping off the Irish coast to the extent of three steamers and one sailing craft. On the morning of March 22, *Farnborough*, who had come from Queenstown, was now cruising up the west coast of Ireland, the exact position being Lat. 51.54 N., Long. 10.53 W., and the time 6.40 a.m. Steaming along at 8 knots, a submarine awash was suddenly sighted by one of the crew named Kaye, an A.B. of the Royal Naval Reserve, about five miles away on the port bow. After a few minutes it dived, and *Farnborough* coolly took no notice but kept jogging along the same course. The submarine had evidently determined to sink the old tramp, for twenty minutes later she fired a torpedo which passed so close ahead of *Farnborough* that bubbles were seen under the forecastle. Still she pretended to take no notice, and a few minutes later the submarine broke surface about

1,000 yards astern, passing from starboard to port, then, having got on the Q-ship's port quarter, fired a shell across the latter's bows and partly submerged.

Farnborough now stopped her engines, blew off steam, and the panic party, consisting of stokers and spare men, were ordered to abandon ship; so away they rowed under Temporary Engineer Sub-Lieutenant J. S. Smith, R.N.R. The enemy then came closer until he was but 800 yards off. Not a human being was visible aboard the 'abandoned' ship, but everyone was lying concealed in expectant readiness, yet Lieut.-Commander Campbell was quietly watching every move of the enemy. A few minutes later the latter, intending to sink the deserted ship, fired a shell, but this fell 50 yards short. Here was *Farnborough's* big opportunity that had been awaited and longed for ever since last Trafalgar Day; now was the time—or never. Thus the collier tramp declared herself a man-of-war, armed as she was with five 12-pounders, two 6-pounders, and one Maxim gun. One of the two ships must certainly go to her doom, and her fate would be settled in a few terrible moments: there would be no drawn-out engagement, but just a violent blow, and then finish. Lieut.-Commander Campbell, in his place of concealment, knew that his men could be trusted to do the right thing, knew that they were waiting only for the word from him. True, the guns' crews were not the kind of expert men you find in battleship or cruiser. They had joined the Service after the declaration of war, but had been trained up splendidly by one of the ship's officers, Lieutenant W. Beswick, R.N.R. On them much depended. If they fired too soon, became excited, made a movement, or bungled their work, they would give the whole show away, and the sinking ship would not be the submarine.

'Open fire!' came the order as the White Ensign was hoisted, and then from the three 12-pounders which could bear came a hail of shells, whilst Maxim and rifle fire also rained down. The light this morning was bad, but the shooting from these newly trained men was so good that the submarine was badly holed by the rapid fire; thus, slowly the enemy began to sink. Observing this, Campbell then endeavoured to give her the knock-out blow, so steamed full speed over the spot and dropped a depth charge. This fairly shook the submarine, who next appeared about ten yards away in an almost perpendicular position, that portion of the craft from the bows to the conning-tower being out of the water. A large rent was discerned in her bow; she was certainly doomed, and one periscope had been hit. Wasting none of the golden opportunity, *Farnborough* reopened fire with her after gun, which put five rounds into the base of the conning-tower at point-blank range, so that the German sank for the last time. Again *Farnborough* steamed over the spot, and let go two more depth charges, and presently up came a large quantity of oil and bits of wood which covered the sea for some distance around. So quickly perished U 68, one of the latest submarines—a 17-knot boat, armed with one 4·1-inch, one 22-pounder, a machine gun, eleven torpedoes, and with a cruising radius of 11,000 miles.

This brilliant success had a most cheering effect on all the patrol vessels working off the Irish coast. With careful reserve the story was breathed in wardrooms, and it percolated through to other stations,

OFFICERS OF Q-SHIP "FARNBOROUGH"
Captain Campbell with his officers, disguised as a mercantile captain.

Q-SHIP HEROES
Captain Gordon Campbell, V.C., D.S.O., R.N., and Lieutenant C. G. Bonner, V.C., D.S.C., of Q-ship "Dunraven," each wearing the Victoria Cross, at the King's Garden Party for V.C.'s. (see Chapter XIV.).

To face p. 42

inspiring even the most bored officer to go forth and do likewise. This victory had a most important bearing on the future of the Q-ship service, and officers and men were eager to take on a job which afforded them so much sport. It meant something more, too. For, junior though he was, Lieutenant-Commander became Commander Gordon Campbell, D.S.O.; Lieutenant W. Beswick, R.N.R., who had trained the guns' crew so well, and the Engineer-Lieutenant Loveless received each a D.S.C., and three of the crew the coveted D.S.M. There followed also the usual £1,000 in addition to prize bounty. Of the ship's complement seven of the officers belonged to the Royal Naval Reserve, and many of the ratings were either of that service or the Royal Naval Volunteer Reserve.

Adventures are to the adventurous. In less than a month from this event *Farnborough* was again engaged with a submarine, under circumstances more difficult than the last. One who was present at the engagement described it to me, and though the submarine managed afterwards to reach Germany, she was wounded, and only just escaped total destruction. However, this in no way detracts from the merits of the story, which is as follows: The scene was similar to that of the previous incident, the exact position being Lat. 51.57 N., Long. 11.2 W. —that is to say, off the west coast of Ireland. The time was 6.30 in the afternoon of April 15, 1916, and *Farnborough* was proceeding northward, doing 5 knots, for Commander Campbell was hoping to intercept a German submarine which had been reported off the Orkneys on the 13th, and was probably coming down the west Irish coast.

At the time mentioned the sea was calm and it

was misty, but about two miles off on the starboard quarter could be seen a steamer. Suddenly, without warning, between the two ships a submarine broke surface, but Commander Campbell pretended to ignore her until she hoisted the international signal TAF ('Bring your papers on board'). Owing to the mist it was impossible to distinguish the flags clearly enough to read them. However, Commander Campbell stopped his ship like a terrified tramp, blew off steam, but quietly kept her jogging ahead so as to edge towards the enemy and avoid falling into the trough of the heavy Atlantic swell. There was the submarine lying full length on the surface, about 300 feet long, with a very large conning-tower amidships, one gun forward, one aft, and most of the hull painted a light grey. In reply to the German's signal *Farnborough* now kept her answering pennant at the dip and hoisted 'Cannot understand your signal.' All this delay was valuable to the Q-ship, for it allowed her to close the range stealthily; and now the submarine also came closer, with her foremost gun already manned. In the meantime, the 'tramp' did what she was expected to do—hoisted the signal 'I am sending boat with ship's papers,' and at the same time the bridge boat was turned out (again in command of Sub-Lieutenant J. S. Smith, R.N.R.), and Commander Campbell was seen to hand his papers to this officer to take over to the submarine. It was now 6.40 p.m., and the German fired a shot which passed over the ship, doing no direct harm, but incidentally spoiling the whole affair. The best laid schemes of Q-ship captains, and the most efficient crews, occasionally go astray. One of *Farnborough's* people, hearing this gun, thought that *Farnborough* had opened fire, so accordingly fired also. It was

STORY OF THE 'FARNBOROUGH' 45

unfortunate, but there it was. This mistake forced Commander Campbell's hand; he at once hoisted the White Ensign and gave the general order to fire. The range was now about 1,000 yards, and he proceeded at full speed so as to bring his after gun to bear, the ships becoming about in this position:

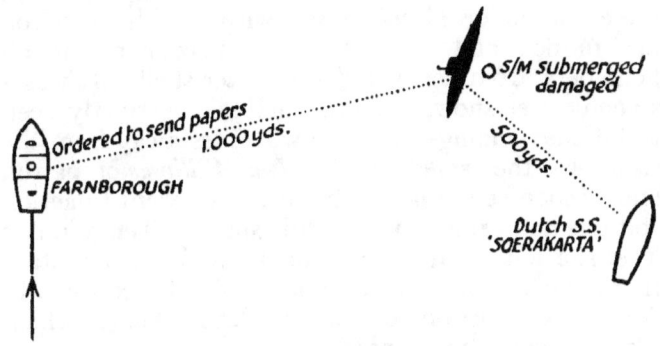

Fig. 5.—Diagram to Illustrate Approximate Positions of 'Farnborough' and Submarine in the Action of April 15, 1916.

The enemy had been about a point before the *Farnborough's* starboard beam, but when the action commenced the former had been brought successfully on the beam. The Q-ship's 12-pounders quickly got off a score of rounds, accompanied by the 6-pounder and the Maxim and rifles. Quite early the enemy became damaged, and eventually she submerged under the screen of smoke, a remarkably near escape which must have made a great impression on her crew. After dropping depth charges, *Farnborough* closed the strange steamer which had been stopped about 500 yards off, and found her to be the Dutch S.S. *Soerakarta*. With true seamanlike chivalry the Dutch captain, pitying the shabby-looking tramp steamship, actually offered Commander Campbell assistance. This neutral was bound from the Dutch East Indies to Rotterdam, via Falmouth and Kirkwall, and on sighting him the submarine had hoisted the usual 'Bring your papers on board.' The Dutchman had just lowered his boat, and was about to row off to the German, when up came the unkempt collier *Farnborough* with a white band on her funnel, and then, to the amazement of all beholders, from her blazed shell after shell. It was a splendid free show, and one shell was distinctly seen to hit the conning-tower. Two miles away from the scene was the armed trawler *Ina Williams* on patrol, and as soon as she heard the firing she went to action stations and came along at full speed. Ten minutes later she felt a couple of shocks, so that her captain thought she had struck something. These were, in fact, the concussions of the two depth charges which *Farnborough* had dropped.

If the submarine had escaped, at least he would be able to warn his superiors at home that they could never tell the difference between a 'trap-ship' and a genuine merchantman, and it would be safer not to attack steamers unless they were perfectly sure. During the rest of that year Commander Campbell continued to cruise in *Farnborough*, but the summer and autumn passed and no further luck offered itself.

Winter followed and was almost merging into spring, and then again this ship made history. In another chapter this thrilling episode will be told. In the meantime much else had happened.

One of the greatest enthusiasts of the Q-ship idea was Vice-Admiral Sir Lewis Bayly, who was in command of the Irish coast. No Q-ship officer serving under this admiral could ever complain that anything was left undone by assistance that could have been performed by the sagacity or advice of this Commander-in-Chief. It was he who made repeated visits to the Q-ships as they lay in Haulbowline Dockyard, in order to see that not the smallest important detail for efficiency was lacking. The positions of the guns, the collapsing of the screens, the erection of the dummy deckhouses concealing the guns, the comfort of the personnel—nothing was too trivial for his attention provided it aimed at the one end of sinking the enemy. As with ships, so with officers. With his vast knowledge of human nature, and his glance which penetrated into a man's very soul, he could size up the right type of volunteer for decoy work; then, having once selected him and sent him to sea, he assisted him all the time whenever wireless was advisable, and on their return to port encouraged, advised, and rested the captains, while the Haulbowline Dockyard paid every attention to improving the Q-ship's fighting power. No keen, capable officer on this station who did his job ever failed to get his reward; and the result of all this, and the certain knowledge that if *in extremis* a Queenstown naval ship would at once be sent to his rescue, created such a fine spirit that an officer would almost sooner die than return to port after making a blunder of an engagement. By reason of this, the Queenstown Q-ships became famous for their high standard and achievements. In the spring of 1916 the four experienced decoys *Farnborough*, *Zylpha*, *Vala*, and *Penshurst*, were operating from that port. They cruised off the south and south-west Irish coasts; between Milford Haven and the Scillies; off the western approach to the English Channel; up the

Irish Sea as far as the north of Ireland. In a few weeks four more decoys were added to that station, so that there were eight of them by July. They cruised along the merchant ship courses as far out into the Atlantic as 17° W., as far south as the middle of the Bay of Biscay, as far east as the Isle of Wight, and as far north as the Hebrides—in other words, just where U-boats were likely to attack. One of these eight was the S.S. *Carrigan Head*, which was commanded by Lieut.-Commander Godfrey Herbert, D.S.O., R.N., late in command of the *Antwerp*. *Carrigan Head* was a fine ship of 4,201 tons, and, in order to make her practically unsinkable, she was sent to Portsmouth, where she was filled with empty casks and timber. As may be expected from her commander, this was a very efficient ship. Below, the timber had been stowed in the holds with great cleverness so that it would have been a considerable time before she could ever founder. I well remember on one occasion wandering all over the decks of this ship, but it was quite impossible to see where her big 4-inch and two 12-pounders were located.

That being so, it was not surprising that a submarine never suspected on September 9, 1916, that this was another 'trap-ship.' It was just before 6.30 in the evening that this steamer was sixty miles south-west of the Lizard, when a submarine was sighted about 2,000 yards off on the starboard bow. The enemy had hoisted some flag signals, but they were too small to be read. It was presumed that it was the usual order to stop, so the steamer hove-to and the captain called up the stokers who were off watch to stand by the lifeboats, for all this time the submarine, who had two guns, was firing at the ship.

STORY OF THE 'FARNBOROUGH' 49

Having lowered the starboard lifeboat halfway down to the water, the Q-ship pretended to try and escape, so went full speed ahead, turned to port, and brought the enemy right astern. The German maintained a rapid fire, many shots coming unpleasantly across the bridge, one entering the forecastle and wounding two men, of whom one afterwards died. Another shell entered the engineers' messroom and slightly injured Temporary Engineer Sub-Lieutenant James Purdy, R.N.R. This same shell also cut the leads to the wireless room just above.

As several shells fell within a few feet of the ship, Commander Herbert decided to feign surrender, hoisted the International Code pennant close up, turned eight points to port, but with the real intention of firing on the submarine, which had now risen to the surface with complete buoyancy and presented a good target. But in turning to port, *Carrigan Head* was thus brought broadside on to the swell, so that the ship began to roll heavily and helm had to be altered to get her head on to the sea. At 6.50 p.m. the enemy was about 1,500 yards away, and while both lifeboats were being lowered the submarine kept up an intermittent fire. Three minutes later Commander Herbert decided to reveal the character of his ship and attack; therefore, going full speed ahead, he fired seven rounds, one of which seemed to hit. The submarine was considerably surprised and at once dived, so having arrived near the spot *Carrigan Head* dropped depth charges. The enemy was not sunk, but she did not reappear, such was her fright, until an hour and a half later when she sank the Norwegian S.S. *Lodsen* off the Scillies. The enemy's behaviour was typical: as soon as he was attacked he broke off the engagement and took to flight by submerging, and it was only on the rarest occasions that he was willing to fight, as were the Q-ships, to a finish.

By reason of their service, Q-ship officers became a race apart. Their arrival and departure were kept a profound secret, night-time or early morning being usually selected. The ships were worked as separate units, not as squadrons, and their cruising ground was always being changed. They went to sea in strange garments, and when they came ashore they usually wore 'plain clothes,' the naval equivalent for the soldiers' expression 'mufti.' At a time when all the nation was in arms and for a healthy man to be seen out of uniform was to excite derisive anger, some of the Q-ship officers had amusing and awkward experiences. Arrived in port at the end of a trying cruise, and rather looking forward to a pleasant respite for a few days, they would run against some old friend in a public place, and be greeted by some such remark as, 'Why aren't you in uniform?' or 'What ship are you serving in? I didn't know *you* were on this station; come and have a drink.' It was difficult to preserve secrecy when such questions were asked direct by old shipmates. Who knew but that the man two paces away was a spy, who would endanger the lives of the Q-ship and crew the next time they put to sea? Surely, if there be occasions when it is legitimate to tell a lie, this was a justifiable one. Thus the life in this special service was one that called for all the ability which is usually latent in any one man. I do not ever remember a Q-ship officer who was not something more than able. Some were killed, some were taken prisoners by submarines, some broke down in health; but in no case did you ever find one who failed to realize the intense seriousness of his job or neglected any means of keeping himself in perfect physical health and the highest possible condition of mental alertness. Not once could he be caught off his guard; the habit was ingrained in him.

CHAPTER V

THE 'MYSTERY' SAILING SHIPS

Most people would have thought that the sail-driven decoys would have had a very short life, and that they would speedily have succumbed. On the contrary, though their work was more trying and demanded a different kind of seamanship, these 'mystery' ships went on bravely tackling the enemy.

The Lowestoft armed smacks, for instance, during 1916 had some pretty stiff tussles, and we know now that they thoroughly infuriated the Germans, who threatened to have their revenge. Looked at from the enemy's aspect, it certainly was annoying to see a number of sailing smacks spread off the coast, each obviously trawling, but not to know which of them would in a moment cut her gear and sink the submarine with her gun. It was just that element of suspense which made a cautious German officer very chary of going near these craft, whereas he might have sunk the whole fishing fleet if he dared. It was not merely annoying; it was humiliating that a small sailing craft should have the impertinence to contend with the super-modern ship of a German naval officer. That, of course, was not the way to look at the matter; for it was a contest, as we have seen, in which brains and bravery were factors more decisive than anything else. The average British fisherman is ignorant of many things which are learnt only in nautical academies, but the last

THE 'MYSTERY' SAILING SHIPS 53

you could accuse him of being is a fool or a funk. His navigation in these sailing smacks is quaint and primitive, but he relies in thick weather chiefly on the nature of the sea-bed. He can almost smell his way, and a cast of the lead confirms his surmise; he finds he is just where he expected to be. So with his character. Hardened by years of fishing in all weathers, and angered to extreme indignation during the war by the loss of good ships and lives of his relatives and friends, this type of man, so long as his decoy smack had any sort of gun, was the keenest of the keen.

One of these smacks was the *Telesia*, armed only with a 3-pounder, and commanded by Skipper W. S. Wharton, who did extraordinarily well in this dangerous service. On March 23, 1916, he was trawling roughly thirty-five miles S.E. of Lowestoft, when about midday he sighted a submarine three miles off, steering to the north-east. At 1.30 p.m. the German, who was evidently one of the cautious type, and having a careful scrutiny before attacking, approached within 50 yards of the *Telesia's* starboard bow, and submerged with her periscope just showing. She came back an hour later to have another look, and again disappeared until 4.30 p.m., when she approached from the north-east. Having got about 300 yards away she attacked, but she had not the courage to fight on the surface a little sailing craft built of wood. Instead, she remained submerged and fired a torpedo. Had that hit, *Telesia* and her men would have been blown to pieces; but it just missed the smack's bows by four feet. Skipper Wharton at once brought his gun into action, and fired fifteen rounds at the periscope, which was the only part of her that could be seen, and an almost impossible target. The enemy disappeared, but arrived back in half an hour, and this time the periscope showed on the starboard quarter, coming straight for the smack, and rising out of the water at the same time. Again she fired a torpedo, and it seemed certain to hit, but happily it passed 40 feet astern. At a range of only 75 yards the smack now fired a couple of shots as the enemy showed her deck. The first shot seemed to hit the conning-tower, and then the fore part of the hull was observed coming out of the water. The second shot struck between the conning-tower and the hatch, whereupon the enemy went down by the bows, showing her propeller. She was a big craft, judging by the size of her conning-tower, and certainly larger than those which had recently been sinking Lowestoft smacks. Skipper Wharton, whilst fishing, had himself been chased, so he was fairly familiar with their appearance. Whether the enemy was actually sunk is a matter of doubt. Perhaps she was not destroyed, although UB 13 was lost this month; how and where are unknown. One thing is certain, however, that the little *Telesia* caused her to break off the engagement and disappear. The smack could do no more, for the wind had now died right away, and this fact demonstrated the importance of these decoy smacks being fitted with motors, so that the craft would be able to manœuvre in the absence of wind; and this improved equipment was now in certain cases adopted. Skipper Wharton well deserved his D.S.C. for this incident, and two of the ship's company also received the D.S.M. The whole crew numbered eight, consisting of Skipper Wharton, a naval chief petty officer, a leading seaman, a marine an A.B., and three fishermen.

THE 'MYSTERY' SAILING SHIPS

On the following April 23 *Telesia*—this time under the name of *Hobbyhawk* and under the command of Lieutenant H. W. Harvey, R.N.V.R.—together with a similar smack named the *Cheero*, commanded by Lieutenant W. F. Scott, R.N.R., put to sea from Lowestoft. They had recently been fitted with specially designed nets, to which were attached mines. It had been found that with 600 yards of these nets towing astern the smack could still sail ahead at a speed of 3 knots. A bridle made out of a trawler's warp was stopped down the towing wire and from forward of the smack, so that she would look exactly like a genuine smack when fishing with the ordinary trawl. All that was required was that the submarine should foul these nets astern, when, if everything worked as it should, destruction to the enemy would follow.

At 5.45 that afternoon, when 10 miles N.E. of the Smith's Knoll Pillar Buoy, the nets were shot and the batteries connected up to the net-mines. The wind was light, so *Cheero*, towing away to the south-east, was going ahead very slowly. Each of these two smacks was fitted with a hydrophone by means of which the beat of a vessel's engines could be heard, the noise of a submarine's being very different from that of reciprocating engines in a steamer. About 7 p.m. *Cheero* distinctly heard on her instrument the steady, quick, buzzing, unmistakable noise of a submarine, and the noise gradually increased. About three-quarters of an hour later the wire leading to the nets suddenly became tight and stretched along the smack's rail. The strain eased up a little, became tight again, then an explosion followed in the nets, and the sounds of the submarine's engines were never heard again. The sea was blown by the explosion 20 feet high, and as the water was settling down another upheaval took place, followed by oil. The crew remained at their stations for a few minutes awaiting further developments, and then were ordered to haul the nets, but a great strain was now felt, so that instead of two men it required six. As the second net was coming in, the whole fleet of nets took a sharp angle down, and a small piece of steel was brought on board. Other pieces of steel came adrift and fell into the sea. As the third net was being hauled in, the whole of the nets suddenly became free and were got in quite easily, whilst the crew remarked on the strong smell of oil. It was found that one mine had exploded, and when the nets were eventually further examined ashore in Lowestoft there could be no doubt but that a submarine had been blown up, and more pieces of steel, some of considerable size, dropped out. Thus UC 3, with all hands, was destroyed. She was one of the small mine-layers which used to come across from Zeebrugge fouling the shipping tracks along the East Anglian coast with her deadly cargoes, and causing the destruction of merchant shipping, Allied and neutral alike. On May 18 of the same year *Hobbyhawk* (*Telesia*) and a similar smack, the *Revenge* (alias *Fame*), had a stiff encounter with a submarine in about the same place, but there is reason to suppose that in this case the enemy was not sunk.

This idea of commissioning sailing smacks as Q-ships now began to be adopted in other areas. Obviously only that kind of fishing craft could be employed which ordinarily were wont to fish those particular waters; otherwise the submarine would at once have become suspicious. Thus, at the end of May, a couple of Brixham smacks, which usually fished out

THE 'MYSTERY' SAILING SHIPS 57

of Milford, were fitted out at Falmouth, armed each with a 12-pounder, and then sent round to operate in the Milford district. These were the *Kermes* and *Strumbles* respectively. They were manned by a specially selected crew, and the two commanding officers were Lieutenant E. L. Hughes, R.N.R., and Sub-Lieutenant J. Hayes, R.N.R. But although they were given a good trial, these craft were not suitable as soon as the autumn bad weather came on. Their freeboard was too low, they heeled over too much in the strong prevailing winds, so that it was difficult to get the gun to bear either to windward or leeward; and, except when on the top of a sea, their range of vision was limited, so before November was out these ships ceased to be men-of-war and were returned to their owners.

Along the Yorkshire coast is found a type of open boat which is never seen farther north than Northumberland and never farther south than Lincolnshire. This is the cobble, a peculiar and rather tricky kind of craft used by the fishermen of Whitby, Scarborough, Bridlington, Filey, and elsewhere. They carry one lug-sail and can be rowed, a single thole-pin taking the place of a rowlock. The smaller type of cobble measures 28 feet long by $2\frac{1}{4}$ feet deep, but the larger type, capable of carrying nine tons, is just under 34 feet long by $4\frac{3}{4}$ feet deep. Here, then, was a boat which, with her shallow draught, could with safety sail about in the numerous minefields off the Yorkshire coast. No submarine would ever suspect these as being anything but fishermen trying to snatch a living. In the early summer of 1916 two of these boats, the *Thalia* and *Blessing*, were commissioned. They were sailing cobbles fitted with auxiliary motors, and were sent to work south-east of the Humber in the Silver Pit area. Here they pretended to fish, towing 300 yards of mine-nets, 30 feet deep, in the hope that, as had happened off Lowestoft, the submarine would come along and be blown up. However, they had no luck, and after a few months' service these boats also were returned to their owners. But in spite of this, Q-sailing-ships were still being taken up, the difficulty being to select the right type. Even in the Mediterranean the idea was employed. Enemy submarines had been destroying a number of sailing vessels, so the Admiralty purchased one local craft, gave her a small auxiliary motor, and towed her to Mudros, where she could be armed and equipped in secrecy. One day she set forth from Malta in company with a British submarine, and two days later was off the coast of Sicily. Here the sailing craft attracted a large enemy submarine, the British submarine of course watching, but submerged. Unfortunately, just when the enemy might have been torpedoed, the heavy swell caused the British submarine to break surface. The enemy was quick to observe this, dived for his life, and disappeared. The rest of the story is rather ludicrous. The British submarine remained submerged in the hope that the enemy would presently come to the surface, while the sailing craft lost touch with her consort and turned towards Malta, using her motor. The next incident was that she sighted 6 miles astern an unmistakable submarine, which was at once taken for the enemy. Being without his own submarine, the somewhat inexperienced R.N.V.R. officer in command made an error of judgment, and, abandoning the ship, destroyed her, being subsequently picked up by a Japanese destroyer. It was afterwards discovered that this was our own submarine who

THE 'MYSTERY' SAILING SHIPS 59

had been working with the sailing craft, and was now on her way back to Malta!

The other day, laid up hidden away at the top of a sheltered creek in Cornwall, I came upon an interesting brigantine. Somehow I felt we had met before, but she was looking a little forlorn; there was no life in the ship, yet she seemed in that curious way, which ships have in common with human beings, to possess a powerful personality. Freights were bad, the miners were on strike, and here was this good little vessel lying idle, and not so much as noticed by those who passed. Then I found out who she was. Here was an historic ship, the famous *Helgoland*, which served right through to the end of the war from the summer of 1916. Now she was back in the Merchant Service, and no one seemed to care; yet hundreds of years hence people will write and talk of her, as they still do of Grenville's *Revenge* or the old clipper-ships *Cutty Sark* and *Thermopylæ*.

Helgoland had been built in 1895 of steel and iron at Martenshoek in Holland, where they specialize in this kind of construction, but she was now British owned and registered at Plymouth. She measured 122 feet 9 inches long, 23 feet 3 inches beam, drew 8 feet aft, and her tonnage was 310 burthen and 182 net. In July, 1916, this shp was lying in Liverpool undergoing an extensive overhaul, and here she was taken over from her owners and sent to Falmouth, where she was fitted out forthwith as a Q-ship. Armed with four 12-pounders and one Maxim, she was known officially in future under the various names of *Helgoland*, *Horley*, *Brig* 10, and *Q* 17. Her crew were carefully chosen from the personnel serving in Auxiliary Patrol vessels at Falmouth, with the exception of the guns' crews; the ship's complement consisting of two R.N.R. officers, one skipper, one second hand, two petty officers, six Royal Navy gunnery ratings, eight deckhands of the Trawler Reserve, one carpenter, one steward, and one cook, the last three being mercantile ratings. Of her two officers one was Temporary Sub-Lieutenant W. E. L. Sanders, R.N.R., who, by reason of his sailing-ship experience, was appointed as mate. This was that gallant New Zealander who had come across the ocean to help the Motherland, performed amazing service in Q-ships, fought like a gentleman, won the Victoria Cross, and eventually, with his ship and all his crew, went to the bottom like the true hero that he was. The story must be told in a subsequent chapter.

When we consider the actions fought by these topsail schooners and brigantines in the Great War we appear almost to be dreaming, to be sent right back to the sixteenth century, and modernity seems to have been swept clean away. While the Grand Fleet was unable, these sailing ships were carrying on the warfare for which they had never been built. In the whole of the Royal Navy there were hardly any suitable officers nowadays who possessed practical experience in handling schooners. This was where the officer from the Mercantile Marine, the amateur yachtsman, the coasting skipper, and the fisherman became so invaluable. In these days of decaying seamanship, when steam and motors are dominant, it is well to set these facts down lest we forget. The last of the naval training brigs has long since gone, and few officers or men, even in the Merchant Service, serve an apprenticeship under sail.

Helgoland left Falmouth after dark, September 6, 1916, on her first cruise as a man-of-war, and she had

THE 'MYSTERY' SAILING SHIPS 61

but a few hours to wait before her first engagement took place. Commanded by Lieutenant A. D. Blair, R.N.R., she was on her way to Milford, and at 1.30 p.m. on the following day was only 10 miles south of the Lizard when she sighted a submarine on the surface 3 points on the starboard quarter. There was an alarm bell fitted up in *Helgoland* which was rung only for action stations, and, as it now sounded, each man crept stealthily to his appointed place. Under the command of Lieutenant W. E. L. Sanders, R.N.R., and following his example of perfect calmness, the guns' crews carried out their work without flurry or excitement.

Within five minutes the enemy, from a distance of 2,000 yards, had begun shelling the brigantine. The first shot fell 10 yards short, but the second and third struck the foretopsail yard—how strange it seems to use the time-honoured phrases of naval warfare for a twentieth-century fight—one shell going right through the yard. It happened that on this fine summer's day there was no wind; so here was the unlucky *Helgoland* becalmed and unable to manœuvre so as to bring her guns to bear as required. It seemed as if the enemy intended to lie off and shell this perfect target with impunity, directing the fire from ahead and astern, which was just the way the brigantine's guns would not bear. However, after the second shot from the submarine, the *Helgoland's* guns would just bear, so Lieutenant Blair dropped his screens and opened fire whilst still there was a chance. The fourth round from the after gun seemed to hit the enemy, and she immediately lurched and dived. Lieutenant Blair then sent two of his hands aloft to look for periscopes, and in a few minutes one was sighted on the starboard quarter 200 yards away and closing. Two rounds from each of the starboard guns were therefore fired, one striking the water very close to the periscope, which again disappeared.

Nothing further happened until half an hour later, when a larger submarine with sail set, about the size of a drifter's mizzen, was sighted right aft. As soon as this U-boat bore 3 points on the port quarter, she also was attacked, and dived under cover of her smoke screen. The afternoon passed, and at dusk (7 p.m.), when there was still no wind, the sound of a submarine's motors was heard as if circling around the brigantine. An hour later *Helgoland* bent her new foretopsail, and just before 9.30 a submarine was seen right ahead, so in the calm the Q-ship could not get her guns to bear. Half an hour later, as there was still no wind, *Helgoland* spoke an armed trawler, who towed her back to Falmouth. Just as the two ships were communicating, the enemy fired a couple of torpedoes which, thanks to *Helgoland's* shallow draught, passed under her amidships. So ended the brigantine's first cruise. It was unfortunate that at long range she had been compelled to open fire and disclose her identity, but that was owing to the calm, and subsequently she was fitted with an auxiliary motor.

Her next fight was in much the same position, about 20 miles S.W. of the Lizard. At 6.20 a.m. on October 24, 1916, *Helgoland*, now commanded by Lieutenant G. G. Westmore, R.N.R., was on an E.S.E. course, the wind being S.W., force 4, and there was a moderate sea. About a mile off on the starboard bow was a large tramp steamer steering a westerly course, and presently was seen a submarine following astern of the tramp. Lieutenant Westmore at once sent his crew to quarters, keeping all of them

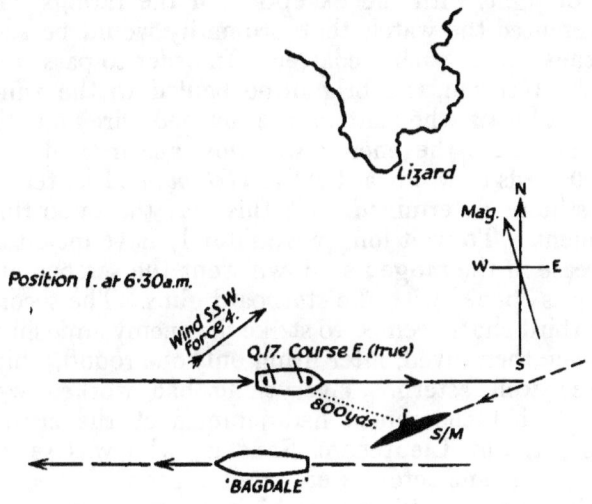
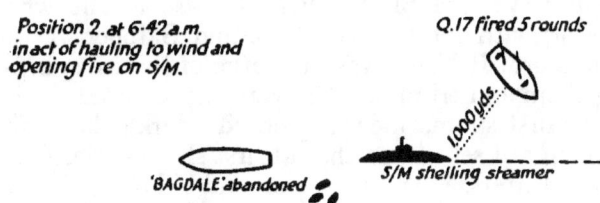
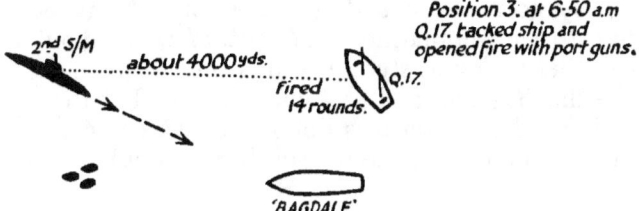

Fig. 6.—Diagram to Illustrate Approximate Movements of 'Helgoland' and Submarine on October 24, 1916.

out of sight, with the exception of the ratings who represented the watch that ordinarily would be seen on the deck of such a coaster. In order to pass close to the German, the brigantine hauled to the wind, and at 6.42 the submarine opened fire on the steamer. As the enemy was now abeam, and only 1,000 yards to windward of the *Helgoland*, Lieutenant Westmore determined that this was the opportune moment. To wait longer would only have meant an increase in the range; so down went the screens and fire was opened with the starboard guns. The second and third shots seemed to strike the enemy amidships, and she then dived, after firing only one round, which passed well astern. Everything had worked well except that the screen had jammed at the critical moment, but Lieutenant Sanders, who was seeing that guns and crew were ready, soon cleared it. While he was looking after his men, and Lieutenant Westmore was generally looking after the ship, Skipper William Smith, R.N.R., was at the wheel steering with marked coolness, and Skipper R. W. Hannaford, R.N.R., was in charge of the sails, handling them and trimming the yards as required.

The first submarine was painted a dark colour, with a brown sail set aft, so that at first she resembled one of our drifters. And now a second U-boat, painted a light colour with no sail, was seen two miles away heading for the tramp steamer. The latter happened to be the Admiralty transport *Bagdale*, whose crew had by now abandoned her, the ship's boats being close to the submarine. *Helgoland* went about on the other tack and stood towards the enemy, so as to save the *Bagdale*, and at 4,000 yards fired at the submarine. The latter was not hit, dived, came to the surface and made off to the south-west, not being seen after this. The brigantine stood by the abandoned *Bagdale*, tacking ship at frequent intervals, so as to prevent the submarine resuming her onslaught. Soon after nine two trawlers were observed, and summoned by gunfire and rockets. They were sent to pick up the crew and to tow the transport into Falmouth. Thus, if no submarine had been sunk, this sailing ship had saved the steamer by frightening away the enemy, and there were more engagements still to follow.

By this—October, 1916—the Q-ship service had increased to such an extent that there were actually forty-seven decoy craft operating. These comprised almost every kind of vessel, from motor drifters to medium-sized steamers. Their success or failure depended partly on captain and crew, but partly on luck. Some Q-ships, as we have seen, never sighted a U-boat; others were in action as soon as they got out of port. The advantage of these Q-sailing-ships was that they could keep the sea independent of the shore for periods much longer than the trawlers or tramps. Owing to their roomy decks, these coasters were well suited for the erection of dummy deckhouses to conceal the armament, and another advantage was that, not utilizing engines or a propeller—except when used occasionally—there was no noise to prevent constant listening on the hydrophones. There was always the chance that during the dark hours, when the enemy on his hydrophones could not hear the sailing ship approaching, the schooner or brigantine might suddenly surprise and sink a submarine lying on the surface charging its batteries. The result was that in the first week of November another sailing craft was requisitioned. This was the three-masted barquentine *Gaelic*, which was then lying at Swansea loaded with 300 tons of coal. *Gaelic*, who was known officially afterwards also under the names of *Gobo*, *Brig* 11, and Q 22, was 126 feet 8 inches long and 24 feet in the beam. She had been built of iron in 1898, was registered at Beaumaris, and remained in service throughout the rest of the war. In August, 1918, she was operating in the Bay of Biscay, and then returned to Gibraltar. At the end of November she left 'the Rock,' reached Falmouth by the middle of December, and then was towed to Milford to be paid off, reconditioned, and returned to commercial work. But before then, as we shall presently see, she was to carry out some first-class work.

There is no person more conservative than the seafaring man; the whole history of the sailing ship shows this clearly enough, and it is curious how one generation is much the same as another. It was Lord Melville who, in the early years of the nineteenth century, stated that it was the duty of the Admiralty to discourage, to the utmost of their ability, the employment of steam vessels, as they considered the introduction of steam was calculated to strike a fatal blow to the naval supremacy of Great Britain. A hundred years later, although the Q-sailing-ship had justified herself, yet there was a sort of conservative prejudice against her development. 'The small sailing vessel,' complained a distinguished admiral, 'will develop into a sailing line-of-battle ship with an electric-light party reefing topsails and a seaplane hidden in the foretopmen's washdeck locker, and everybody seasick.'

Yes: there was much in common between this flag-officer and the noble lord, in spite of the intervening century.

CHAPTER VI

THE 'MARY B. MITCHELL'

It was the activities and successes of the submarines in the western end of the English Channel that had made these small Q-sailing-ships so desirable. The first of these to be used in that area was the *Mary B. Mitchell*. She was a three-masted topsail steel schooner owned by Lord Penrhyn. Built at Carrickfergus in 1892 and registered at Beaumaris, she was 129 feet in length, and of 210 tons gross. In the middle of April, 1916, she happened to be lying in Falmouth with a cargo of china clay, and it was decided to requisition her. The difficulty always was to preserve secrecy during her fitting out, but in this case, luckily, she had recently suffered some damage, and this afforded an excellent excuse for paying off the mercantile crew. A new crew was selected for her and was trained specially for the work while she was being got ready for her special service. She was commissioned on May 5, and left Falmouth for her first cruise on June 26, and then operated for a month on end in the western approaches between Ushant, the Irish coast, and Milford.

Her captain was Lieutenant M. Armstrong, R.N.R., and she was known officially as the *Mitchell* and Q 9. During her cruising she sailed also under three different neutral flags, as convenient. Armed with three guns, her 12-pounder was hidden in a dummy collapsible house on the poop, and under each of the two hatches was a 6-pounder mounted on a swinging pedestal. There were also a couple of Lewis guns, some small arms and Mills hand-grenades. In spite of the thoroughness with which the guns were concealed, the collapsible arrangements had been made so ingeniously that all guns could be brought into action under three seconds. Before leaving Falmouth she was painted black with a yellow streak and bore the name

MARY Y. JOSE

VIGO

on her hull, so as to look like a neutral. But until she had got clear of Falmouth this inscription was covered over with a plate bearing her real name. In order to be able to pick up signals at sea she was fitted with a small wireless receiving set, the wire being easily disguised in the rigging. Rolling about in the swell of the Atlantic or the chops of the English Channel for four weeks at a time is apt to get on the nerves of a crew unable to have a stretch ashore: so in order to keep everyone on board fit and cheery, boxing-gloves and gymnastic apparatus were provided.

No one could deny that she was an efficient ship. During her first cruise she used to carry out gun-trials at night; hatches sliding smoothly off, guns swinging splendidly into position, and a broadside fired as soon as the bell for action sounded. Until that bell was pressed, none of the crew was allowed to be visible on deck other than the normal watch. One of the difficulties in these ships was that the decks might be damaged with the shock of firing, but in the *Mitchell* they had been so strengthened that not a seam was

Q.-SAILING-SHIP "MITCHELL."
Notice the after gun disclosed on the poop.

[*Photo, Opie*

To face p. 68

THE 'MARY B. MITCHELL'   69

sprung nor so much as a glass cracked. You may guess how perfect was her disguise from the following incident. Pretending she was a Spaniard, she was one day boarded at sea and examined by some of the Falmouth patrol trawlers. These were completely deceived, for even though their crews had watched her fitting out, yet she had painted herself a different colour the night before leaving that port. Even in the Bay of Biscay several British transports on sighting the 'Spaniard' altered course and steamed away, evidently suspecting she was co-operating with a submarine.

She was back from her first cruise on July 25 just before midnight and left again at midnight on August 3-4. This time she impersonated the French three-masted schooner *Jeannette*, a vessel of 226 tons, registered at La Houle, for *Mitchell* now made a cruise in the neighbourhood of the Channel Islands and the western channel. During the next few months she continued to sail about the last-mentioned area, in the Bristol Channel near Lundy Island, and in the Bay of Biscay, sometimes as *Jeannette*, sometimes as the *Brine*, of St. Malo, and sometimes as the Russian *Neptun*, of Riga.

It was in January, 1917, that she had an experience which showed the fine seamanship and sound judgment which were essential in the captain of such a secret ship. His name was Lieutenant John Lawrie, R.N.R., a man of strong personality, a real sailor, and possessed of valuable initiative. On the evening of January 7, *Mitchell* was off Berry Head, just east of Dartmouth, when bad weather came on, and this developed into a strong winter's gale. There was every reason why a Q-ship should not run into the nearest port for shelter, as her presence would lead to awkward questions, whereas secrecy was the essence of her existence. The gale blew its fiercest, and by the following night *Mitchell* was having an alarming time. Just after 9.30 p.m the foremast and spars crashed over the side, carrying away her mainmast too. She then lay-to under close-reefed mizzen. A jurymast was rigged on the stump of the foremast, and the wind, having veered from W. through N.W. to N.E., she was able to set a reefed staysail. It was still blowing a strong gale, with what Lieutenant Lawrie described as a 'mountainous sea' running, and she drifted before the gale in a southwest direction towards Ushant.

In this predicament it was time to get assistance if possible, and about 9.15 on the morning of the 9th she signalled a large cargo steamer, who endeavoured to take *Mitchell* in tow, but eventually had to signal that this was impossible, and continued steaming on her way up Channel. The schooner was now about ten miles north of Ushant, an anxious position for any navigator going to leeward, but Lieutenant Lawrie considered she would drift clear. The northeast gale showed no sign of easing up during that evening. Signals of distress were made, a gun being fired every few minutes as well as rocket distress signals, and flares were kept burning; but no answering signal came from the shore. By this time the schooner was getting dangerously near to Ushant, and it could not be long before she and her crew would inevitably perish. However, she never struck, and at 9.30 p.m. the Norwegian S.S. *Sardinia* spoke her and stood by throughout the terrible night until 7 a.m. of the 10th. Then ensued a nice piece of seamanship when the steamer lowered into the sea a buoy with a small line attached. This *Mitchell* managed to pick up, and the tow-line was made fast. *Sardinia* then went ahead and towed her from a position 10 miles west (True) of Creach Point until 11.15 a.m. when near Les Pierres Light. Here a French torpedo-boat came towards them, so Lieutenant Lawrie hoisted the Red Ensign; but having done that he was clever enough also to show the White Ensign over the stern and in such a manner that the Norwegian was unable to see it. The captain of the French torpedo-boat at once understood, signalled to the Norwegian to cast off and that the torpedo-boat would take the schooner in tow. This was done at noon, and the *Sardinia* was informed that the name of the ship was the *Mary B. Mitchell* of Beaumaris, Falmouth to Bristol Channel with general cargo. It was a clever, ready answer on the part of the British captain. The torpedo-boat took the schooner into Brest, and at length, after being remasted and refitted she went back to carry on her work as a Q-ship. I submit that throughout the whole of that gale it was a fine achievement, not merely to have brought her through in safety, but without revealing her identity as a warship.

A different kind of adventure was now awaiting her. During June, 1917, she cruised about first as the French *Marie Thérèse*, of Cette, then as the French *Eider*, of St. Malo, her sphere of operation being, as before, in the western end of the English Channel, the Bay of Biscay, and near the Channel Islands. *Mitchell* was now fitted with a motor, but this was never used during daylight except when absolutely necessary. It was on the twentieth of that month, at 11.30 a.m., that she was in a position Lat. 47.13 N., Long. 7.23 W., when she sighted the conning-tower of a submarine 3 miles away on the port bow. The German began firing, so *Mitchell* was run up into the wind, hove-to, and 'abandoned.' By this time the enemy was on the starboard bow and continued firing for some time after the schooner's boat had left the ship. Unsuspectingly the submarine came closer and closer, and more and more on the beam. Then after a short delay he proceeded parallel with the ship, and, altering course, made as if to go towards the *Mitchell's* boat lying away on the port quarter. Suddenly he began to fire again, and being now not more than 800 yards off and in a suitable position, the schooner also opened fire, the first round from the 12-pounder appearing to hit. Altogether seventeen rounds were fired, seven seeming to be direct hits. The enemy did not reply, and within three minutes of being hit disappeared. Fortunately none of his score of rounds had struck the schooner, though they burst overhead in unpleasant proximity.

A further engagement with what was probably the same enemy occurred later on the same day. It was a favourite tactic for a submarine to follow a ship after disappearing for a while, and then, having got her hours later in a suitable position, to attack her again. I used to hear commanding officers say that they had certainly noticed this in regard to their own ships, and there are not lacking actual records of these methods, especially in the case of the slow-moving sailing Q-ships who could be seen across the sea for a long time; and it was part of these tactics to carry out this second attack just before night came on. Thus at 6.10 p.m., being now in Lat. 47.37 N., Long. 6.38 W., *Mitchell* again sighted a submarine, this time 4 miles away on the port quarter. The schooner kept her course, the submarine overtook her, and at 6.35 again shelled the ship. After the U-boat had fired half a dozen rapid rounds, *Mitchell* was hove-to and 'abandoned,' the enemy taking up a position well out on the port beam and firing until the boat was quite clear of the ship. Then the German stopped, exactly on the beam, 800 yards away, and waited for a long time before making any move. Suddenly he turned end on, came full speed towards the ship, dived, and when 400 yards away showed his periscope on the port side. Having got to within 50 yards he went full speed ahead, starboarded his helm, and began to rise quickly. As soon as the top of the conning-tower appeared and a couple of feet of hull were showing *Mitchell* cleared away and shelled him with the after 6-pounder. This seemed to pierce the conning-tower, a large blue flash and a volume of yellow vapour coming from the hole. Almost simultaneously the 12-pounder hit the enemy in the bows, but after this the enemy was too far forward for the schooner's guns to bear. In a cloud of black smoke, yellow smoke, steam, and spray, she dived and was not seen again until 8.7 p.m. on the surface 5 miles to the westward, just as the 'panic party' were coming back on board the schooner. All speed was made, and the boat towed astern on an easterly course for the French coast. For a time the submarine followed, but then went off to the north-eastward and remained in sight until dark. The reader may wonder how a submarine, having once been holed, could remain afloat: but there are cases of undoubted authenticity where, in spite of being seriously injured, the submarine did get back to Germany. A remarkable instance of one thus damaged by a Q-sailing-ship will be given in a later chapter. But in the present case of the *Mitchell*, even if she had not sunk her submarine, she had fought two plucky engagements, in the opinion of the Admiralty, and the captain, Lieutenant John Lawrie, R.N.R., already the possessor of a D.S.C., was now awarded the D.S.O.—his two officers, Lieutenant John Kerr, R.N.R., and Lieutenant T. Hughes, R.N.R., being given each a D.S.C.

On the following August 3, when 20 miles south of the Start, *Mitchell* had yet another engagement. She had left Falmouth two days before as the *Arius*, of Riga, then as the French *Cancalais*, of La Houle, and cruised between the Lizard and the Owers, to Guernsey, and in the neighbourhood of Ushant. At 1.45 p.m. she was sailing close-hauled on the starboard tack, steering west; there was a fresh breeze, rather a rough sea, and a slight haze. Three miles away on the starboard beam appeared a submarine, who five minutes later began shelling the schooner. Lawrie let his ship fall off the wind, and the shells came bursting around, passing through sails and rigging, so after ten minutes of this the schooner hove-to and 'abandoned' ship. Slowly and cautiously the submarine approached, and when about 3,000 yards off stopped his engines, but continued to fire. Then he came up on the decoy's starboard beam, about 1,000 yards away; but after fifteen minutes of shelling from this position, Lawrie decided that he could tempt the enemy no nearer. It was now 4 p.m., so *Mitchell* started her motor, cleared away all disguises, put the helm hard aport, and so brought the enemy well on the beam, allowing all four guns to bear. Over twenty shells were fired, of which three or four hit the base of the conning-tower; but the submarine, having replied with four shots, dived, and made off. For two hours and a quarter had this engagement been prolonged, and the enemy must have been considerably annoyed to have wasted seventy of his shells in this manner. There was every reason to suppose that he had received injuries, and though there were no fatalities aboard the schooner, yet the latter's windlass, sails, rigging, and deck fittings had been damaged, and two of her men had been wounded. Lieutenant Lawrie received for this gallant fight a bar to his D.S.C., and a similar award was made to Lieutenant T. Hughes.

Such, briefly, was the kind of life that was spent month after month in these mystery sailing ships. It was an extraordinary mixture of monotony and the keenest excitement. From one hour to another no man knew whether he would be alive or dead, and the one essential thing consisted in absolute preparedness and mental alertness. To be surprised by the enemy was almost criminal; to escape narrowly from shipwreck, to remain unmoved under shell-fire, to see the spars crashing down and your shipmates laid out in great pain, to be hit and yet refusing to hit back until the right moment, to keep a clear head and a watchful eye, and all the time handle your ship so that the most was got out of the wind —all this was a part of your duty as a Q-ship man. Officers and men believed that if their Q-ship were torpedoed and any of them were captured, they would be shot as *francs-tireurs*. German prisoners had not hesitated to make this statement, although I do not remember an instance where this was carried out.

There can be no doubt but that these sailing ships had the most strenuous and arduous task of all. They suffered by being so useful, for the Q-steamships, as a rule, did not spend more than eight days at sea out of twelve, and then they had to come in for coal. The schooners, as we have seen, could keep the sea for a month, so long as they had sufficient water and provisions. Several more were added to the list during 1917 and 1918, and there was never any lack of volunteers for them. The only difficulty was, in these days of steam, in choosing those who had had experience in sailing craft. The revival of the sailing man-of-war was certainly one of the many remarkable features in the naval campaign.

CHAPTER VII

MORE SAILING SHIPS

DURING the ensuing months many demands were made on the sailing-ship man-of-war. There were pressed into the service such vessels as the schooner *Result*, the 220-ton lugger *Bayard*, the three-masted schooner *Prize*, the motor drifter *Betsy Jameson*, the ketch *Sarah Colebrooke*, the auxiliary schooner *Glen* (alias *Sidney*), the brigantine *Dargle*, the *Brown Mouse* yacht, built on the lines of a Brixham trawler, and so on. The barquentine *Merops*, otherwise known as *Maracaio* and Q 28, began decoy work in February, 1917. She was fitted out in the Firth of Forth with a couple of 12-pounders and a 4-inch gun. At the end of May she had a severe engagement with a submarine, and was considerably damaged aloft. In March the 158-ton Rye motor ketch *Sarah Colebrooke* was requisitioned, and sent to Portsmouth to be fitted out, appearing in May as the *Bolham*. A month later, 20 miles south of Beachy Head, she fought a submarine, and had quite an unpleasant time. One of the enemy's shells exploded under the port quarter, lifting the ketch's stern high out of the water, another exploded under the port leeboard, sending a column of water on board, and swamping the boat; whilst a third burst on board, doing considerable damage. She fought the submarine until the latter disappeared, but the *Bolham's* motor was by this time so choked with splinters and glass that she could not proceed to the spot where the submarine had last been seen, and of course it so happened that there was no wind.

On June 8 four fishing smacks were captured and sunk off the Start in full view of the Q-smack *Prevalent*, a Brixham trawler armed with a 12-pounder. Again it happened to be a calm, so *Prevalent*, being too far away, was unable to render assistance. After this incident it was decided to fit an auxiliary motor in the trawler-yacht *Brown Mouse*, which was doing similar service and was specially suitable for an engine. On the following day our friend *Helgoland* had another encounter, this time off the north coast of Ireland, the exact spot being 8 miles N. by W. of Tory Island. The fight began at 7.25 a.m., and half an hour later the submarine obtained a direct hit on the after-gun house of the brigantine, killing one man, wounding four ratings, and stunning the whole of the after-guns' crews. But *Helgoland*, with her charmed life, was not sunk, and she shelled the submarine so fiercely that the U-boat had to dive and disappear.

Even a private yacht was taken up for this work in June. This was the 116-ton topsail schooner *Lisette*, which had formerly belonged to the Duke of Sutherland. She had been built as far back as 1873 with a standing bowsprit and jibboom. She was taken from Cowes to Falmouth, where she was commissioned in August, and armed with three 6-pounders. But this old yacht was found to leak so much through her seams, and her construction was so light, that she was never a success, and was paid off in the following spring. In April, 1917, the auxiliary schooner *Sidney* (alias *Glen*) began service

MORE SAILING SHIPS

as a decoy, having been requisitioned from her owners and fitted out at Portsmouth. A crew was selected from the Trawler Reserve, but the guns' crews were naval. Armed with a 12-pounder and a 3-pounder, she was fitted with wireless, and cruised about in the English Channel, her complement consisting of Lieutenant R. J. Turnbull (R.N.R.), in command, one sub-lieutenant (R.N.R.), one skipper (R.N.R.), two R.N.R. seamen, one R.N.R. stoker to run the motor, a signal rating, a wireless operator, four R.N. ratings for the big gun, and three for the smaller one. During the afternoon of July 10, 1917, *Glen* was in combat with a submarine of the UC type, and had lowered her boat in the customary manner. A German officer from the conning-tower hailed the boat, and in good English ordered her to come alongside. This was being obeyed, when something seemed to startle the officer, who suddenly disappeared into the conning-tower, and the submarine began to dive. *Glen* therefore opened fire, and distinctly saw two holes abaft the conning-tower as the UC-boat rolled in the swell. She was not seen again, and the Admiralty rewarded *Glen's* captain and Sub-Lieutenant K. Morris, R.N.R., with a D.S.C. each.

During the month of January, 1917, the naval base at Lowestoft called for volunteers for work described as 'dangerous, at times rather monotonous, and not free from discomfort.' Everyone, of course, knew that this meant life in a Q-ship. The vessel selected was the 122-ton three-masted topsail schooner *Result*, which was owned at Barnstaple, and had in December come round to Lowestoft from the Bristol Channel. Here she was fitted out and commissioned at the beginning of February, being armed with a couple of 12-pounders, but also with torpedo-tubes. As a sailing craft she was slow, unhandy, and practically unmanageable in light winds. At the best she would lie no nearer to the wind than 5½ points, and in bad weather she was like a half-tide rock. True, she had a Bolinders motor, but the best speed they could thus get out of her was 2½ knots. The result was that her officers had great difficulty in keeping her out of the East Coast minefields, and did not always succeed. She took in 100 tons of sand as ballast, and a rough cabin was fashioned out of the hold for the two officers. In command was appointed Lieutenant P. J. Mack, R.N. (retired), a young officer who had seen service at the Dardanelles in the battleship *Lord Nelson* and in the historic *River Clyde*, whence he had been invalided home. As he was not an expert in the art of sailing, there was selected to accompany him as second in command Lieutenant G. H. P. Muhlhauser, R.N.R., who was not a professional seaman, but a keen amateur yachtsman of considerable experience, who had made some excellent cruises in his small yacht across the North Sea and had passed the Board of Trade examination as master of his own yacht. The sailing master who volunteered was an ex-schooner sailor, and her mate also was an old blue-water seaman. The motor man was a motor mechanic out of one of the Lowestoft M.L.'s, and there was a trimmer from the Trawler Reserve. She carried also a wireless operator, a cook, a chief petty officer, deckhands, and some Royal Naval ratings for the armament. All the crew, consisting of twenty-two, had seen considerable service during the war in various craft, and one of the deckhands was in the drifter *Linsdell*, which was blown up on an East Coast minefield at the commencement of the war. He had been then picked up by H.M.S. *Speedy*, who in turn was immediately blown up. This man survived again, and was now a volunteer in a Q-ship. *Result's* crew were trained to go to their 'panic stations' at the given signal, when the bulwarks were let down and the tarpaulins removed from the guns, the engineer on those occasions standing at the hatchway amusingly disguised as a woman passenger, arrayed in a pink blouse and a tasselled cap which had been kindly provided by a lady ashore.

On February 9 *Result* was all ready as a warship, and motored out of Lowestoft. She then disguised herself as a neutral, affixed Dutch colours to her topsides, and proceeded via Yarmouth Roads to the neighbourhood of the North Hinder, the other side of the North Sea, where the enemy was very fond of operating. On the fifteenth of the following month *Result* was cruising off the south-west end of the Dogger Bank when she encountered UC 45 in the morning. Lieutenant Muhlhauser, who was kind enough to give me his account of the incident, has described it with such vividness that I cannot do better than present the version in his own words. It should be added that at the time *Result* was steering E.S.E., and was now in the position Lat. 54.19 N., Long. 1.45 E. The submarine was sighted $2\frac{1}{2}$ miles astern, the wind was northerly, force 5 to 6, the sea being 4 to 5 and rapidly rising. In other words, it was a nasty, cold North Sea day, and one in which it would have been most unpleasant to have been torpedoed. The engagement was a difficult one, as the ship had to be manœuvred so that her guns would bear, and careful seamanship had to be used to prevent her lying in the trough of the sea. As it was, with bulwarks down, the decks and gun-wells were awash and frequently full of water, while the submarine, being only occasionally visible when *Result* was on the top of the sea, made a target that was anything but easy.

'By 7 a.m.,' says Lieutenant Muhlhauser, 'we had got all the topsails off her, and at this moment the C.O. appeared on deck and, looking aft, said, "Why, there is a submarine!" and at the same moment it was reported from aloft. Word was passed to the watches below to stand by. In a few minutes came the report of a gun. I do not know where the shell went. The men ran to their stations, or crawled there according to what their job was, and the ship was brought on the wind. The submarine continued firing at the rate of a shell every minute or thereabouts. The C.O. then ordered the jibs to be run down, and while this was being done a shell stranded the foretopmast forestay, but luckily did not burst. It went off whistling. Some of the shells were fairly well aimed, but the bulk were either 50 or 60 yards short or over, and at times more than that. As the submarine kept about 2,000 yards off, the C.O. ordered the boat away, with the skipper in charge. Four hands went with him. He was reluctant to go, I think, though, as a matter of fact, he ran quite as much risk as did those remaining on board, if not more, as he would have been in an awkward position if by any chance the ship worked away from him and the submarine got him. It would have been a hard job to persuade the submariners that he was anything but British. However, off he went in a nasty sea. In lowering the boat we made efforts to capsize her, but she was difficult to upset, and as the sub. was some way off and unlikely to see the "accident," we

MORE SAILING SHIPS

did not waste much time on it, but let her go down right side up. Away went the skipper and his crew, and he admits feeling lonely with a hostile submarine near by and the ship and her guns working away from him. He says he was struck with the beauty of her lines, and she never appeared more attractive to him. As a matter of fact, his was a rotten position, which was not improved by the sub. firing at him two or three shells, which went over and short. Evidently the submarine, which by the way had closed to 1,000 yards as soon as the boat left the ship, wanted him to pull towards it, instead of which he was digging out after us manfully. Meanwhile the ship appeared quite deserted. Everyone was concealed. The C.O. prowled around the deck on his hands and knees, peering through cracks and rivet holes in the bulwarks to see how the submarine was getting on. All I could see of him was the stern position of his body and the soles of an enormous pair of clogs. I sat on deck at the wheel, trying to get and keep the ship in the wind, so as not to get too far from the boat. All this time the submarine was firing steadily, and one shell went through the mizzen, while others, as the C.O. reported from time to time, burst short, some of them close. Splinters from the latter went through the stay- and fore-sails. At 1,000 yards the ship is a fairly big target, and the shooting of the Huns must be put down as bad.

'It is all very well serving as a target at 1,000 yards, but it is an experience which must not be too long continued in case a lucky shot disables one. In the present case, moreover, the wind and sea were rapidly increasing, and we were leaving the boat in spite of all our efforts to stop. The submarine seemed quite determined not to come any nearer, and the C.O.

decided that the moment had come for our side to begin. Just before this one of the bulwarks, luckily on the side away from the sub., had fallen down, and let a deluge of water on to the decks, but this did not affect things as far as we know.

'At the word, down fell the bulwarks, round came the guns, and up went the White Ensign. Only the after 12-pounder gun would bear. The first shell struck the submarine at the junction of the conning-tower and deck forward. The 6-pounder also fired one shell, and hit the conning-tower. The second shell from the big gun burst short. By the time the smoke had cleared away the submarine had disappeared. Had we sunk her or had she dipped? This is the point which is exercising our minds. The C.O. thinks the evidence of sinking her is not conclusive, but most of us think she has gone down for ever.

'We then made for the boat, which was still labouring after us, and got it hooked on and hoisted. There was quite a decent-sized sea, and the hoisting process was not very pleasant for those left in to hook on, not to mention that they got wet from the exhaust.

'At the time the sub. was firing, one of the officers or crew was standing on the conning-tower rails, probably spotting for the gunners. He was there when the first shell struck, but was not noticed afterwards. Very likely he had fallen into the tower, but he may have fallen into the water.

'We certainly gave them a lesson in gunnery, two hits out of three shots. Compare that with their performance. Moreover, our guns had to be swung into position, while theirs was already pointed.

'Having picked up the boat, we made for the

spot where the sub. had disappeared, but could not be sure that we had reached it. Anyway, we saw no traces of it. We did not spend much time in searching, but put the ship back on her course. The wind and sea were by this time strong and heavy, and after running out for half an hour we turned and headed west, with the idea of being near shelter if a north-east gale, which I had predicted, came along. As a matter of fact it did not, and my reputation as a weather-prophet is tarnished. Our alteration of course was made solely from weather conditions, but it must have seemed very suspicious to a second submarine which now arrived on the scene, and which had probably been chasing us without our knowing it. Instead of it chasing us, it suddenly found us coming to meet it, and must have been puzzled. By way of clearing the air it fired a torpedo from a distance of about 2,000 yards, and missed us by about 200 yards—a bad effort. It then fired three shells at us, which also went wide. There is no doubt that this was another, and smaller, submarine from the first, but we did not grasp this at first, and so without more ado we let drive at it, but unluckily the gun missed fire twice. Fleet then opened the breech, at some risk to himself, and drew out the cartridge and threw it away. But this wasted time, and when he did fire the shell went short. The submarine had taken advantage of the pause to get ready to dive, and did not wait for another shot, but went under as soon as we fired.

'It was no use waiting about, as we should very likely have been torpedoed, so we went on towards the land.

'And so ended what the skipper calls the "Battle of the Silver Pit," from the name of the fishing ground where it took place. As far as it went it was satisfactory, but we should like to be sure that we sank the first. The two engagements took about two hours. Possibly by waiting we might have done better, but, on the other hand, we might have done worse.'

It was eventually known that the first submarine was UC 45, who paid the *Result* the compliment of describing this ship's gunfire as well-controlled. She got back safely to Germany. For the manner in which the fighting had been conducted, Lieutenant Mack and the skipper were both mentioned in despatches.

After the return to Lowestoft, *Result* was altered in appearance and was sent off to the area where this encounter had taken place. This time she used Swedish colours, and called herself the *Dag*. On this voyage, whilst in the vicinity north of the North Hinder Bank, on April 4, about 4 a.m., a submarine was seen on the port bow, but disappeared. It was so big that at first it resembled a steamer or destroyer. Presently a periscope was seen about 4 points on the bow, resembling a topmast, as it had a rake. The lower portion was about 6 inches in diameter, and a narrower stem protruded from this, terminating in a ball, and whilst officers and crew watched it, wondering whether it was the mast of a wreck or not, it slowly dipped and vanished. This was the submarine in the act of taking a photograph. She then retired to a distance convenient for shelling. There was a light westerly breeze, and the enemy now bobbed up at intervals all round the *Dag*, examining her very carefully. Lieutenant Muhlhauser writes of this incident:

'Then followed a pause of nearly half an hour with-

MORE SAILING SHIPS

out our seeing anything of him. The cook was sent to the galley to get on with breakfast and we started the engine. It is hardly necessary to say that as it was particularly wanted it ran very badly, and, indeed, could hardly be kept going at all. Suddenly a shell burst near us, followed by another and another. We could not at first tell the direction from which they came, and thought it was from astern, but found that the submarine had cunningly moved away towards the sun, and had emerged in the mist behind the path of the sun, where he was practically invisible from our ship, while we were lit up and must have offered a splendid target with our white hull and sails. His shooting was very good, and none of the shells missed us by much. He fired rapidly, and was probably using a 4·1-inch semi-automatic gun. The shells all burst on striking the water, and the explosions had a vicious sound. They seemed to come at a terrific speed, suggesting a high-velocity gun. The C.O. calmly walked the deck, the skipper took the wheel, and I sat at the top of the cabin hatchway and noted the times and numbers of shells fired and anything else of interest. The rest of the crew were at their stations, but keeping below the bulwarks, except those who launched the boat and let it tow astern. The eleventh shell struck us just above the water-line, and soused us all with spray which flew up above the peak of the mainsail. It tore a hole in the side and burst in the sand ballast, reducing the skipper's cabin to matchwood, and destroying the wireless instrument. It also knocked down the sides of the magazine and set fire to the wood, starting some of the rockets smouldering. It also smashed up the patent fire extinguishers, and possibly the fumes from these prevented the fire from spreading. Anyway, it was out when we had time to see what was happening.

'In the meantime we could not afford to be hit again, and the C.O. gave the word to open fire. Down went the bulwarks and round swung the guns, but where was the target? Hidden in the mist behind the sun's path it was invisible to the gun-layers looking through telescopes, and they were obliged to fire into the gloom at a venture. The poor little 6-pounder was quite outranged, and it is doubtful if the shells went more than two-thirds of the way. The other guns had sufficient range, but it was impossible to judge the distance or observe the fall of the shots. However, they made a glorious and cheering noise, and Fritz dived as soon as he could. There is not the least reason for thinking that we hit him. The skipper, deceived by the low freeboard revealed when the bulwarks were down, at this stage quickly announced the conviction that she was sinking. Smoke was also pouring out of the hatches, and we had two wounded men to see to: Ryder, who was in the magazine and who was hit in the arm, sustaining a compound fracture, and Morris, also in the magazine, bruised in the back and suffering from shock. We were not, therefore, in a position to continue the battle, and things looked a bit blue. Fritz might be expected to be along in a few minutes submerged, and he would have little difficulty in torpedoing us, as we were very nearly a stationary target. We had no means of warding him off except by a depth charge. That might inconvenience him, but it would hardly delay him long, and he could then either torpedo us or retire out of range of our guns and pound us to pieces, as his gun had a range of about 5,000 yards more than ours. Sure enough he was soon after us, as we crawled along at our 4-knot gait, and raised his periscope right astern about 200 yards off.

' We then slung over a depth charge, and had just got our 10-feet clearance when it went off, and made quite a creditable stir for a little 'un. Fritz promptly disappeared to think things over, and we were relieved of the sight of the sinister-looking periscope. But we had only delayed things a little. He would soon recover and adopt fresh tactics. Still, for ten minutes we should have peace to attend to our wounded and the damage. The C.O. supervised the bandaging of Ryder, who had been lying on deck since he had been drawn out of the magazine. I had passed him—passed over him, in fact—once or twice in going forward, and thought he was dead, as he lay so still. Then the hole in the side wanted attention, and also the fire below. Just then the look-outs reported the *Halcyon** and two P-boats ahead coming our way. We were extremely glad to hear them shout out, as it meant all the difference between being sunk and not being sunk. When the skipper had called out " She is sinking, sir," I thought of the number our little boat would hold, and the number of the crew, and had reflected that my number was up. The arrival of the *Halcyon* and her attendants put a different complexion on things, and while efforts were being made by guns to attract their attention, I set about plugging our hole and trying to find the fire.

' Stringer warned me that he had tried to get below, but had found the fumes too much. By the time I got there they must have cleared, as I did not find them too bad. The place was full of smoke, but

* H.M.S. *Halcyon*, torpedo-gunboat, 1,070 tons.

though I pulled things about blindly, as it was impossible to see anything, I could not see any glow to indicate a fire. Ultimately I did see a light, but on making for it I found it was Dawes and an electric light. He had entered from the mess-deck. There appearing to be no immediate danger from fire, I crawled round to the shot-hole and found water coming in through rivet holes. The main hole had been plugged from the outside by two coal-bags and a shot-hole plug. I got tools and cut up some wood, while Wreford cut up a coal-bag into 6-inch squares. These Dawes and I hammered home, and made her fairly tight.

'Meanwhile great efforts were being made to communicate with the *Halcyon*, to let them know that a submarine was about, and to ask for a doctor. We could not get the *Halcyon*, but one of the P-boats came rushing by at full speed, and asked where we were from! They had not recognized us! We could get nothing out of these ships. They rushed about the horizon at full speed and disappeared into the mist and came out of it again somewhere else, but generally kept away from us, though occasionally a P-boat tore past going "all out."

'While this circus was going on, a number of T.B.D.'s were reported on our starboard quarter, and three light cruisers and then T.B.D.'s swept into sight and seemed to fill the whole horizon. They went on, ignoring our request for a doctor, and disappeared in the mist, but their place was taken by other T.B.D.'s. The place seemed full of them. Where they all came from I do not know, or what they were doing, but everywhere one looked one could see some of these beautiful vessels rushing along. It was a fine, stirring sight. Finally we got one of them to stop and lower a whaler with a doctor. While she was stopped her companion ships steamed round to ward off attack. The doctor came on board, and decided that Ryder ought to go in at once, and the T.B.D. *Torrent* agreed to take him in when asked by signal. So away went poor Ryder in great pain, I fear, in spite of two morphia pills which we gave him. The C.O. was afraid that we had given him too much, but one did not seem to do him much good, so we gave him another one.

'While we were transshipping him, the *Halcyon* came tearing past, and shouted that there was a hostile submarine 3 miles to the southward. This, however, did not worry us with all these T.B.D.'s around. We were in a scene of tremendous, even feverish, activity. There were sweepers, T.B.D.'s, P-boats, and our own submarines all about. At 6 a.m. the world held us and a very nasty, large, hostile submarine, which could both outrange and outmanœuvre us, and the game seemed up. At 6.30 a.m. we were as safe as one could wish to be, with a considerable portion of England's light forces around us. "Some change!"'

CHAPTER VIII

SUBMARINES AND Q-SHIP TACTICS

In order properly to appreciate the difficulties of the Q-ships, it is necessary to understand something of the possibilities and limitations of the U-boats. No one could hope to be successful with his Q-ship unless he realized what the submarine could not do, and how he could attack the U-boat in her weakest feature. If the submarine's greatest capability lay in the power of rendering herself invisible, her greatest weakness consisted in remaining thus submerged for a comparatively short time. On the surface she could do about 16 knots; submerged, her best speed was about 10 knots. As the heart is the vital portion of the human anatomy, so the battery was the vital part of the submarine's invisibility. At the end of a couple of hours, at the most, it was as essential for her to rise to the surface, open her hatches, and charge her batteries as it is for a whale or a porpoise to come up and breathe. It was the aim, then, of all anti-submarine craft to use every endeavour to keep the U-boat submerged as long as possible. Those Q-ships who could steam at 10 knots and over had a good chance then of following the submarine's submerged wake and despatching her with depth charges. If she elected not to dive, there was nothing for it but to tempt her within range and bearing of your guns and then shell her. To ram was an almost

SUBMARINES AND Q-SHIP TACTICS

impossible task, though more than one submarine was in this way destroyed.

The difficulty of anti-submarine warfare was increased when the enemy became so wary that he preferred to remain shelling the ship at long range, and this led to our Q-ships having to be armed with at least one 4-inch against his 4·1-inch gun. The famous Arnauld de la Périère, who, in spite of his semi-French ancestry, was the ablest German submarine captain in the Mediterranean, was especially devoted to this form of tactics. Most of the German submarines were double-hulled, the space between the outer and inner hulls being occupied by water ballast and oil fuel. The conning-tower was literally a superstructure imposed over the hull, and not an essential part of the ship. That is why, as we have already seen, the Q-ship could shell holes into the tower and yet the U-boat was not destroyed. Similarly, a shell would often pierce the outer hull and do no very serious damage other than causing a certain amount of oil to escape. Only those who have been in British and German submarines, and have seen a submarine under construction, realize what a strong craft she actually is.

The ideal submarine would weigh about the same amount as the water surrounding her. That being a practical impossibility, before she submerges she is trimmed down by means of water ballast, but then starts her engines and uses her planes for descent in the same way as an aeroplane. The flooding tanks, as we have seen, are between the two hulls, and the hydroplanes are in pairs both forward and aft. The U-boat has been running on the surface propelled by her internal-combustion motors. Obviously these cannot be used when she is submerged, or the air in the ship would speedily be used up. When about to submerge, the German captain trimmed his ship until just afloat; actually he frequently cruised in this trim when in the presence of shipping, ready to dive if attacked. The alarm was then pressed, the engineer pulled out the clutch, the coxswain controlling the forward hydroplane put his helm down, the captain entered the conning-tower, the hatch was closed, and away the steel fish cruised about beneath the surface.

The U-boat was now running on her electric batteries. By means of two periscopes a view was obtained not merely of the sea above, but also of the sky, so that surface craft and aircraft might be visible. The order would be given to submerge to say 10 metres. Alongside each of the two coxswains was a huge dial marked in metres, and it was the sole duty of these two men to watch the dials, and by operating a big wheel controlling each hydroplane maintain the submarine at such a depth. Horizontal steering was done also by a wheel, and course kept by means of a gyroscope compass, a magnetic compass in this steel ship with so much electricity about being out of the question. The batteries were charged while the submarine was on the surface by turning the oil engines into a dynamo by means of the clutch, the hour before dawn and the hour after sunset being favourable times for so charging.

The reader will have noted the preliminary methods of attack on the part of the submarine and his manner of varying his position. He divided his attack into two. The first was the approach, the second was the attack proper. The former was made at a distance of 12,000 yards, and during this time he was using his high-power, long-range periscope, manœuvring into

SUBMARINES AND Q-SHIP TACTICS 95

position, and ascertaining the course and speed of the on-coming Q-ship. The attack proper was made at 800 or 400 yards, and for this purpose the short-range periscope was used. Now watch the U-boat in his attempt to kill. He is to rely this time not on long-range shelling, but on the knock-out blow by means of his torpedo: he has endeavoured, therefore, to get about four points on the Q-ship's bow, for this is the very best position, and he has dived to about 60 feet. During the approach his torpedo-tubes have been got ready, the safety-pins have been removed, and the bow caps of the tubes opened. The captain has already ascertained the enemy's speed and the deflection or angle at which the torpedo-tube must point ahead of the Q-ship at the moment of firing. When the enemy bears the correct number of degrees of deflection the tube is fired, the periscope lowered, speed increased, and, if the torpedo has hit the Q-ship, the concussion will be felt in the submarine. This depends entirely on whether the Q-ship's speed and course have been accurately ascertained. The torpedo has travelled at a speed of 36 knots, so, knowing the distance to be run, the captain has only to look at his stop-watch and reckon the time when his torpedo should have hit. If the German was successful he usually hoisted his periscope and cruised under the stern of the ship to obtain her name. If he were an experienced officer he never came near her, after torpedoing, unless he was quite certain she was abandoned and that she was not a trap. During 1917 and onwards, having sunk the Q-ship, the submarine would endeavour to take the captain prisoner, and one Q-ship captain, whose ship sank underneath him, found himself swimming about and heard the U-boat's officer shouting to the survivors,

'Vere is der kapitan?' but the men had the good sense to lie and pretend their skipper was dead. After this the submarine shoved off, and my friend took refuge with others in a small raft. But frequently a submarine would wait a considerable time cruising round the sinking ship, scrutinizing her, examining the fittings, and expecting to find badly hinged bulwarks, a carelessly fitted wireless aerial, a suspicious move of a 'deckhouse' or piece of tarpaulin hiding the gun. This was the suspense which tried the nerves of most Q-ship crews, especially when it was followed by shelling.

We have seen that the U-boat sought to disguise herself by putting up a sail when in the vicinity of fishing craft or patrol vessels. The submarine which torpedoed one ship disguised her periscope by a soap box, so that it was not realized till too late that this innocent-looking box was floating *against* the tide. At the best the submarine was an unhandy craft, and it took her from three to six minutes to make a big alteration of course, inasmuch as she had to dive deeper lest she should break surface or disturb the surface of the water. Again, when running submerged, if she wished to turn 16 points—*e.g.*, from north to south—the pressure on her hull made it very difficult.

It may definitely be stated that those who went to their doom in U-boats had no pleasant death. When the Q-ship caused the enemy to be holed so that he could not rise and the water poured in, this water, as it moved forward in the submarine, was all the time compressing the air, and those of the crew who had not already committed suicide suffered agonies. Moreover, even if a little of the sea got into the bilges where the batteries were placed there

SUBMARINES AND Q-SHIP TACTICS

was trouble also. Sea-water in contact with the sulphuric acid generated chlorine, a very deadly gas, which asphyxiated the crew. There is at least one case on record of a U-boat surrendering to a patrol boat in consequence of his crew having become incapacitated by this gas; and on pulling up the floorboards of a British submarine, one has noticed the chlorine smell very distinctly. The dropping by the decoy ship of depth charges sometimes totally destroyed the submarine, but even if this was not accomplished straight away, it had frequently a most salutary effect: for, at the least, it would start some of the U-boat's rivets, smash all the electric bulbs in the ship, and put her in total darkness. The nasty jar which this and the explosion gave to the submarine's crew had a great moral effect. A month's cruise in a submarine in wintry Atlantic weather, hunted and chased most of the way from Heligoland to the Fastnet and back, is calculated to try any human nerves: but to be depth-charged periodically, or surprised and shelled by an innocent-looking tramp or schooner, does not improve the enthusiasm of the men. Frequently it happened that the decoy ship's depth charges merely put the hydroplanes out of gear so that they jammed badly. The U-boat would then make a crash-dive towards the bottom. At 100 feet matters became serious, at 200 feet they became desperate; and presently, owing to pressure, the hull would start buckling and leaking. Then, by sheer physical strength, the hydroplanes had to be coaxed hard over, and then up would come the U-boat to the surface, revealing herself, and an easy prey for the Q-ship's guns, who would finish her off in a few fierce minutes. Life in a U-boat was no picnic, but death was the worst form of torture, and such as could be conveyed to the imagination only by means of a Théâtre Guignol play.

It was the obvious duty of the Q-ships to make the life of a U-boat as nearly as possible unbearable, and thus save the lives of our ships and men of the Mercantile Marine. It was no easy task, and even with perfect organization, well-thought-out tactics, and well-trained crews, it would happen that something would rob the decoy of her victory. On October 20, 1916, for instance, the Q-ship *Salvia*, one of the sloop-class partially reconstructed with a false counter-stern to resemble a 1,000-ton tramp, was off the west coast of Ireland when a submarine appeared astern, immediately opened fire, and began to chase. *Salvia* stopped her engines to allow the enemy to close more rapidly, but the U-boat, observing this, hauled out on to the *Salvia's* starboard quarter, and kept up her firing without shortening the range of 2,000 yards. *Salvia* next endeavoured to close the range by going slow ahead and altering slightly towards the enemy, but the latter's fire was now becoming so accurate that *Salvia* was soon hit on the starboard side by a 4·1-inch high-explosive shell. This burst through in nine places in the engine-room bulkhead, smashing an auxiliary steam-pipe and causing a large escape of steam. The engines were now put full ahead, and course was made for the enemy, who sheered away and shortly afterwards dived.

That being so, *Salvia* deemed it prudent to pretend to run away, but in the middle of the evolution her steering gear unfortunately broke down, and before control was established again with hand-steering gear, the ship had swung 90 degrees past her course, and the submarine reappeared on the port beam about

SUBMARINES AND Q-SHIP TACTICS 99

1,500 yards away, but presently disappeared. The breakdown had been most unfortunate, for otherwise a short, sharp action at about 700 yards would have been possible, followed by an excellent chance of dropping a depth charge very close to the enemy. In that misty weather, with a rough sea and a fairly

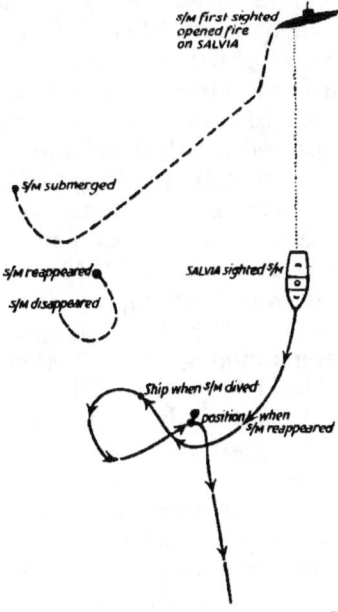

Fig. 7.—Diagram to Illustrate Approximate Movements of 'Salvia' in her Action with Submarine on October 20, 1916.

strong breeze, it had been difficult to see any part of the U-boat's hull, for she had trimmed herself so as to have little buoyancy, and only her conning-tower could be discerned. Below, in the Q-ship, the engine-room staff found themselves up against difficulties; for it was an awkward job repairing the leaking steam-pipe, as the cylinder tops and the engine-room were full of live steam and lyddite fumes. The chief artificer and a leading stoker were overcome by the fumes, but the job was tackled so that steam could be kept up in the boilers.

A few months later *Salvia* (alias Q 15) ended her career. Just before seven o'clock on the morning of June 20, 1917, when in Lat. 52.15 N., Long. 16.13 W.—that is to say, well out in the Atlantic—she was struck on the starboard side abreast the break of the poop by a submarine's torpedo. Troubles did not come singly, for this caused the depth charge aft to explode by concussion, completely wrecking the poop, blowing the 4-inch gun overboard, and putting the engines totally out of action. Here was a nice predicament miles from the Irish coast. At 7.15 a.m., as the after part of the ship was breaking up, her captain sent away in the boats all the ship's company except the crews of the remaining guns and others required in case the ship should be saved. The submarine now began to shell *Salvia* heavily from long range, taking care to keep directly astern. The shells fell close to the boats, so these were rowed farther to the eastward. A shell then struck the wheelhouse and started a fire, which spread rapidly to the upper bridge. It was now time for the remainder of the crew to leave in Carley rafts, and temporarily the submarine ceased fire; but when one boat started to go back to the ship the enemy at once reopened his attack. He then closed the rafts and took prisoner *Salvia's* captain, who arrived safely in Germany, and was released at the end of the war. At 9.15 a.m. the ship sank, and ten minutes later the submarine disappeared. Thus *Salvia's* people were suddenly bereft of ship and skipper, with the broad Atlantic to row about

SUBMARINES AND Q-SHIP TACTICS 101

in, boisterous weather, and a heavy sea. The boat which had endeavoured to return to the ship then proceeded to search for the men in the Carley rafts, but could see nothing of them. After about an hour this boat sighted what looked like a tramp steamer, so hoisted sail and ran down to meet her. At 11.20 a.m. this steamer picked them up: she happened to be another disguised sloop, the Q-ship *Aubrietia*, commanded by Admiral Marx, a gallant admiral who had come back to sea from his retirement, and as Captain, R.N.R., was now taking a hand in the great adventure. Search was then made, and within two hours the men in the rafts were picked up, and a little later the other three boat-loads were located: but five men had been killed, three by the first explosion in *Salvia* and two by shell-fire. It had been a sad, difficult day.

In the Mediterranean the enemy was showing an increased caution against likely decoys, and by the beginning of December, 1916, had already sunk a couple of Q-ships. The Q-ship *Saros* (Lieut.-Commander R. C. C. Smart) was operating in this sea, and had an engagement on October 30, thirteen miles from Cape San Sebastian. The engine-room was ordered to make smoke, as though the stokers were endeavouring to get the utmost speed out of the ship: at the same time the engines were rung down to 'slow.' But the enemy realized the ruse and slowed down, too. Lieut.-Commander Smart endeavoured to make the enemy think a panic had seized the ship. So the firemen off watch were sent below to put on lifebelts and then to man the boats. Stewards ran about, placing stores and blankets in the boats, but the enemy insisted on shelling, so *Saros* had to do the same, whereupon the submarine's guns' crews made a bolt for the inside of the U-boat, and then made off. As soon as she had got out of sight, *Saros* changed her disguise, taking the two white bands off the funnel, hoisting Spanish colours, and altering course for the Spanish coast.

Three days later *Saros* was returning to the Gibraltar-Malta shipping track, heading for the Cani Rocks, after carrying out firing exercises. At half-past four in the afternoon, the officer of the watch heard a shot, and saw a submarine 7,000 yards off on the starboard beam. She was not trimmed for diving, and was apparently trimmed to cruise like this during the night on the surface. She seemed quite careless and slow about her movements, evidently never suspecting *Saros'* true character. *Saros* altered course towards the enemy, who was firing all the time, one round exploding and falling on board and several coming close over the bridge. The U-boat, after going on an opposite course, very slowly turned to starboard to get on a parallel course, and men were seen hoisting up ammunition on deck. The light was bad, and it was becoming late, but *Saros* had manœuvred to get the German in a suitable position as regards the sun, so at 5,500 yards range opened fire with her 4-inch and 12-pounder at 4.44 p.m. This shocked the Teuton, so that the crew which had been sitting around smoking, and apparently criticizing the old 'merchantman,' suddenly became active, lowered the wireless masts and disappeared below. By the tenth round, the enemy, who appeared to have been hit, dived, and at 4.50 p.m. *Saros* ceased fire. Course was then altered to where she had last been seen, and, just before turning, the enemy for a moment showed himself, but as the gun-layer was ready the German disappeared, and then artfully cruised about sub-

SUBMARINES AND Q-SHIP TACTICS 103

merged, so as to get in a good position. She was never seen again, but at 5.15 p.m. a torpedo passed just ahead of the *Saros*, and thereafter the latter zigzagged at her utmost speed. During the night there was a

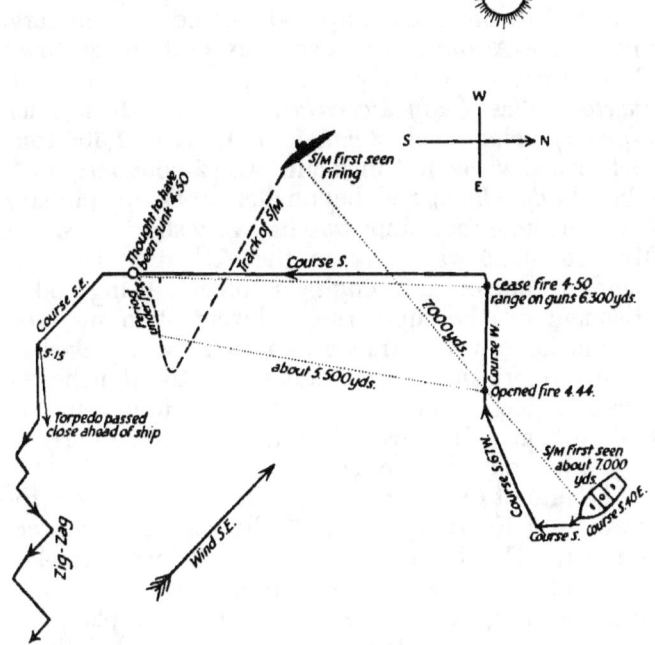

FIG. 8.—DIAGRAM TO ILLUSTRATE APPROXIMATE MOVEMENTS OF 'SAROS' IN HER ACTION WITH SUBMARINE ON NOVEMBER 3, 1916.

moon until midnight, and an anxious time was spent. Owing to the amount of sea, *Saros* was not doing more than $8\frac{1}{2}$ knots, but no further attack took place. It had been one able captain against another, and no actual result had been made. So the warfare went on in the Mediterranean. *Baralong*, now called *Wyandra*, who had been sent to the Mediterranean, had an engagement earlier in the year with a submarine, on the evening of April 13, 1916, and probably hit the enemy.

In the spring of 1917 three more Q-ships, Nos. 24, 25, and 26, had been taken up to be fitted out and serve under Vice-Admiral Sir Lewis Bayly, at Queenstown. These were respectively the *Laggan* (alias *Pladda*), *Paxton* (alias *Lady Patricia*), and the *Mavis* (alias *Nyroca*), being small steamers of 1,200 or 1,300 tons, each armed with one 4-inch and two 12-pounders. Q 18 (alias *Lady Olive*) had begun her work in January. Now, of these four ships two had very short lives. On May 20 Q 25 was sunk in the Atlantic, her commanding officer and engineer officer being taken prisoners by the submarine. Twenty-two survivors were picked up by a trawler, and four were picked up by an American steamer and taken to Manchester. Three officers and eight men were found by the United States destroyer *Wadsworth*, who had arrived only a few days before from America.

The fate of Q 18 was as follows: At 6.35, on the morning of February 19, 1917, she was at the western end of the English Channel, when she was attacked by a submarine who was coming up from 3 miles astern shelling her. After the usual panic party had been sent away and the others had concealed themselves, the submarine came close under the stern, evidently so as to read the ship's name. At 7.10 *Lady Olive* opened fire, the first two shots hitting the base of the conning-tower, the other shot putting the enemy's gun out of action and killing the man at the gun, the range being only 100 yards. Six more effectual shots were fired, the man in the conning-tower being also killed. The submarine then submerged. Lieutenant F. A. Frank, R.N.R., the captain of the Q-ship, now rang down for full speed ahead, with the intention of dropping depth charges. No answer was made to his telegraph, so he waited and rang again. Still no answer. He then left the bridge, went below to the engine-room, and found it full of steam, with the sea rising rapidly. Engine-room, stokehold, and the after 'tween deck were filling up, the dynamo was out of action, it was impossible to use the wireless, and the steam-pipe had burst owing to the enemy having landed two shots into the engine-room.

As the ship was sinking, the only thing to do was to leave her. Boats and rafts were provisioned, the steel chest, containing confidential documents, was thrown overboard, the ship was this time *really* abandoned in earnest, and all took to the three boats and two rafts at 9.30 a.m. Thus they proceeded in single line. Fortunately the weather was fine, and Lieutenant Frank decided to make for the French coast, which was to the southward, and an hour later he despatched an officer and half a dozen hands in the small boat to seek for assistance. So the day went on, but only the slowest progress was made. At 5 p.m. Lieutenant Frank decided to leave the rafts and take the men into the boats, as some were beginning to faint through immersion in the cold February sea, and it was impossible to make headway towing those ungainly floats with the strong tide setting them at this time towards the Atlantic. The accommodation in each boat was for seventeen, but twenty-three had been crowded into each.

With Lieutenant Frank's boat leading, the two little craft pulled towards the southward, and about

9 p.m. a light was sighted, but soon lost through the mist and rain. An hour later another light showed up, and about this time Lieutenant Frank lost sight of his other boat, but at eleven o'clock a bright light was seen, evidently on the mainland, and this was steered for. Mist and rain again obscured everything, but by rowing through the night it was hoped to sight it by daylight. Night, however, was followed by a hopeless dawn, for no land was visible. It was heartbreaking after all these long hours. The men had now become very tired and sleepy, and were feeling downhearted, as well they might, with the cold, wet, and fatigue, and, to make matters no better, the wind freshened from the south-west, and a nasty, curling sea had got up. Lieutenant Frank put the boat's head on to the sea, did all he could to cheer his men up, and insisted that he could see the land. Everyone did a turn at pulling, and the sub-lieutenant, the sergeant-major of marines, the coxswain, and Lieutenant Frank each steered by turns. Happily by noon of the twentieth the wind eased up, the sea moderated, and Lieutenant Frank had a straight talk to his men, telling them their only chance was to make the land, and to put their hearts into getting there, for land in sight there was. Exhorting these worn-out mariners to put their weight on to the oars, he reminded them that everyone would do 'spell about,' for the land must be made that night.

Every man of this forlorn boat-load buckled to and did his best, but, owing to the crowded condition, and the weakness of them all, progress was pathetically slow. Thus passed another morning and another afternoon. But at 5.15 p.m. a steamer was sighted. Alas! she ignored them and turned away to the westward, and apparently was not coming near them. Then

SUBMARINES AND Q-SHIP TACTICS

presently she was seen to alter course to the east, and began to circle towards them. This was the French destroyer, *Dunois*, who had seen a submarine actually following this English rowing boat. The destroyer, which had to be handled smartly, came alongside the boat, and shouted to the men to come aboard quickly, as she feared she might lose the submarine. Here was rest at last; but, just as the boat had got alongside, *Dunois* again caught sight of the Hun, had to leave the boat and begin circling round and firing on the pest. At six o'clock the destroyer once more closed the boat, and got sixteen of the men out, when she suddenly saw the U-boat, fired on her, and went full speed ahead, the port propeller guard crashing against the boat, so that it ripped out the latter's starboard side.

There were still seven men in the boat, and it seemed as if they were destined never to be rescued after their long vigil, and moreover the boat was now nearly full of water. *Dunois* came down again; some of the Q-ship's seven jumped into the water, the destroyer lowering her cutter and picking up the rest. The submarine was not seen again; the destroyer arrived safely in Cherbourg, where the Englishmen were landed, and next morning they met a trawler with the crew of the second cutter on board.

Such, then, were action and counter-action of Q-ship and submarine; such were the hardships and suffering which our men were called upon to endure when by bad luck, error of judgment, or superior cleverness of the enemy, the combat ended unfavourably for the mystery ship. Not all our contests were indecisive or victorious, and some of these subsequent passages in open boats are most harrowing tales of the sea. Men became hysterical, went mad, died, and had to be consigned to the depths, after suffering the terrors of thirst, hunger, fatigue, and prolonged suspense. It was a favourite ruse for the U-boat, having seen the survivors row off, to remain in the vicinity until the rescuing ship should come along, so that, whilst the latter was stopped and getting the wretched victims on board, Fritz could, from the other side, send her to the bottom with an easily-aimed torpedo. There can be no doubt that, but for the smartness of *Dunois'* captain, she, too, would have suffered the fate of the Q-ship, and then neither British nor French would have survived. It is such incidents as these which make it impossible to forget our late enemies, even if some day we forgive.

CHAPTER IX

THE SPLENDID 'PENSHURST'

On November 9, 1915, the Admiralty, who had taken up the steamer *Penshurst* (1,191 gross tons), commissioned her at Longhope as a Q-ship, her aliases being Q 7 and *Manford*. This inconspicuous-looking vessel thus began a life far more adventurous than ever her designers or builders had contemplated. Indeed, if we were to select the three Q-ships which had the longest and most exciting career, we should bracket *Penshurst* with *Farnborough* and *Baralong*.

The following incidents illustrate that no particular rule could be laid down as to when a Q-ship could get in touch with the enemy. We have seen that *Baralong* set forth for a particular locality to look for a definite submarine and found her. Other decoys searched for submarines but never so much as sighted one; others, again, when everything seemed quiet, suddenly found themselves torpedoed and sinking. Others, too, had an engagement to-day, but their next fight did not come until a year later. The case of *Penshurst* is interesting in that on two consecutive days she fought a submarine, but she is further interesting as having been commanded by an officer who, with Captain Gordon Campbell, will always remain the greatest of all Q-ship captains.

Commander F. H. Grenfell, R.N., was a retired officer who, like so many others, had come back

110   Q-SHIPS AND THEIR STORY

to the service after the outbreak of war. After serving for a year in the 10th Cruiser Squadron as second-in-command of *Cedric*, he was appointed to command *Penshurst*, cruised up and down first off the north of Scotland, then off Ireland, and in the English Channel for nearly a year without any luck. On November 29, 1916, a year after her advent

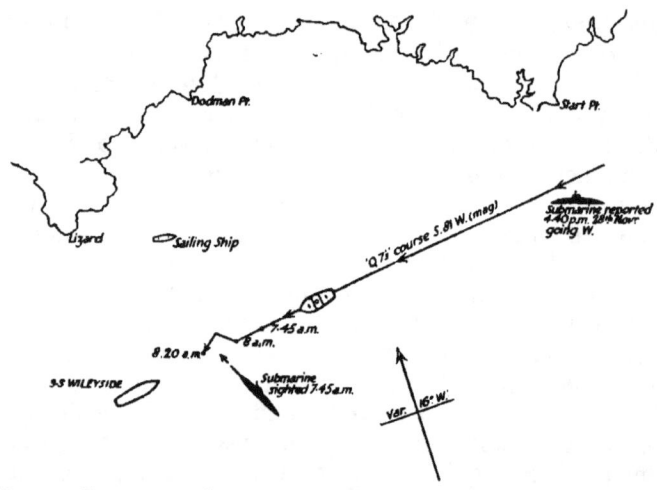

Fig. 9.—Diagram to Illustrate Approximate Movements of 'Penshurst' in her Engagement with Submarine on November 29, 1916.

into this special service, *Penshurst*, who, with her three masts, low freeboard, and funnel aft, resembled an oil-tanker, was steaming down the English Channel at 8 knots. The time was 7.45 a.m., and her course was S. 81 W. (Mag.), her position at this time being Lat. 49.45 N., Long. 4.40 W. She was definitely on the look-out for a certain submarine which had been reported at 4.30 the previous afternoon in Lat. 50.03 N., Long. 3.38 W. As *Penshurst* went jogging

THE SPLENDID 'PENSHURST' 111

along, picture a smooth sea, a light south-west wind, and the sun just rising. Fine on the port bow 7 miles away was the British merchant steamer *Wileyside*, armed, as many ships were at this time, defensively with one gun aft; while hull down on *Penshurst's* starboard bow was a sailing ship of sorts. Then, of a sudden, a small object was sighted on the port beam against the glare of the horizon, so that it was difficult to make out either its nature or its distance. However, at 7.52 a.m. this was settled by the object firing a shot and disclosing herself as a submarine. The shot fell 60 yards short, but a few minutes later came another which passed over the mainmast without hitting. The range was about five miles, but owing to the bad light Captain Grenfell could not see whether the enemy was closing. In order to induce her so to do, at 8 a.m. he altered course to N. 45 W.

This brought the enemy nearly astern, and at the same time *Penshurst* slowed down to half speed. By this time the sun was above the horizon, and the light was worse than before, but the submarine was apparently altering course to cut off the *Wileyside*, and ignoring *Penshurst*. Therefore, at 8.6 a.m. the latter altered course so as again to bring the submarine abeam. This had the desired effect, for at 8.10 a.m. the submarine fired a third shot, which fell about 200 yards short of *Penshurst*, and this proved that Q-ship and submarine were closing. Two minutes later *Penshurst* stopped her engines and the usual 'panic' evolution was carried out, by which time the submarine had closed to within 3,000 yards, and turned on a course parallel with the Q-ship, reducing to slow speed and being just abaft the *Penshurst's* port beam and silhouetted against the glare of the sun, three Germans being seen standing in the conning-tower. In order to spin out the time, the Q-ship's boats were being turned out and lowered as clumsily as possible, and now the U-boat sent along a couple more shots, one of which fell over and the other short.

Thus far it had been a contest of brain, and Captain Grenfell had succeeded in making the enemy conform to the British will. At 8.20 a.m., as there seemed no possibility of inducing the submarine to come any closer, *Penshurst* opened fire, but there was time to fire only a couple of rounds from the 12-pounder and 6-pounder and three rounds from the 3-pounder before the German hurriedly dived, for all three guns had dropped their shots pretty close to the target. The shooting had been done under difficult circumstances, for it was at a black spot against a strong glare. When once the enemy submerged, *Penshurst* went full speed to the spot and dropped a depth charge, but the German had escaped, and she would live to warn her sister submarines about the Q-ship which had surprised her.

For this U-boat had had a careful look at *Penshurst*, and Captain Grenfell could hardly hope to surprise the submarine again and bring her to action, so he altered course to the eastward with the object of intercepting another U-boat, whose presence had been reported at 11.15 that forenoon 5 miles north of Alderney. Very likely the submarine with whom he had just been engaged would send out by her *telefunken* wireless a full description of the Q-ship, so, as she steamed along, *Penshurst* now altered her appearance by painting herself a different colour and by lowering the mizzen-mast during the night. Thus, when the sun rose on November 30, on what was to be *Penshurst's* lucky day, she seemed to be a totally different ship.

THE SPLENDID 'PENSHURST' 113

During the forenoon of November 30 we should have seen this transformed *Penshurst* going down Channel again well south of the Dorset chalk cliffs. At noon she was in the position Lat. 50.11 N., Long. 2.31 W. (see track chart), steering N. 89 W.,

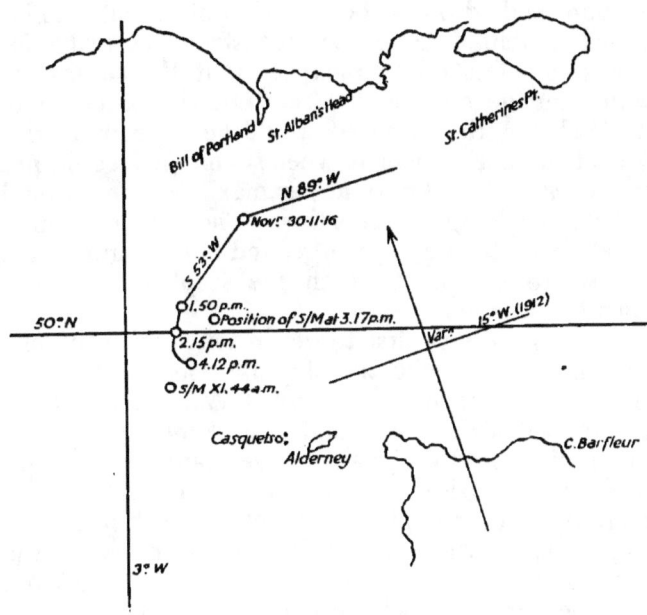

FIG. 10.—DIAGRAM TO ILLUSTRATE APPROXIMATE MOVEMENTS OF 'PENSHURST' IN HER ACTION WITH SUBMARINE ON NOVEMBER 30, 1916.

when she intercepted a wireless signal from the Weymouth-Guernsey S.S. *Ibex* that a submarine had been seen at 11.44 a.m. 20 miles N.W. of the Casquets; so the Q-ship altered course towards this position, and at 1.50 p.m. the conning-tower of a submarine was observed 5 miles to the southward, apparently chasing a steamer to the westward. A few minutes later the German turned eastward and then submerged. It was then that *Penshurst* saw a seaplane, which had come across the Channel from the Portland base, fly over the submarine's position and drop a bomb without effect. This caused Captain Grenfell to reconstruct his plans, for it was hopeless now to expect that the submarine would engage on the surface. On the other hand, the Q-ship with her speed would be superior to this type of submarine, which, when submerged, could not do better than 6 knots at her maximum, but would probably be doing less than this. The weapon should, therefore, be the depth charge, and not the gun. He decided to co-operate with the seaplane, and ran down towards her.

It was necessary first to get in touch with the airman and explain who the ship was, so at 2.22 p.m., being now in Lat. 50 N., Long. 2.48 W., Captain Grenfell stopped his engines, and after some attempts at communication by signal, the seaplane alighted on the water alongside. Captain Grenfell was thus able to arrange with the pilot to direct the Q-ship and fire a signal-light when the ship should be over the submarine; a depth charge could then be let go. But the best-laid schemes of seamen and airmen sometimes went wrong: for, just after the seaplane had risen into the air, she crashed on to the water, broke a wing, knocked off her floats and began to sink. This was annoying at a time when the Q-ship wanted to be thinking of nothing except the enemy; but *Penshurst* lowered her gig and rescued the airmen, then went alongside the injured seaplane, grappled it, and was preparing to hoist it on board

Q SHIP "PENSHURST"
Showing bridge-screen dropped on port side and bridge gun ready for action.

THE SPLENDID 'PENSHURST' 115

when at 3.14 p.m. a shell dropped into the sea 200 yards ahead of the ship. Other shots quickly followed, and then the submarine was sighted about 6,000 yards on the port quarter. How the enemy must have laughed as, through his periscope, he saw the aircraft which so recently had been the aggressor, now a wreck! How certain a victim the innocent-looking steamer seemed to him!

Captain Grenfell, by change of circumstances, had once more to modify his plans, stop all salvage work, cast off the seaplane and swing in his derrick, which was to have hoisted the latter in. The men in the gig could not be left, and he was faced with two alternatives. Either he could hoist the gig on the port quarter in full view of the enemy, or he could tow her alongside to starboard, and risk her being seen. He chose the latter, and at 3.24 p.m. proceeded on a south-westerly course at slow speed. The submarine now came up right astern, so course had to be altered gradually to keep the German on the port quarter and out of sight of the gig.

Slowly the submarine overhauled the Q-ship, firing at intervals, and at 4.12 p.m., when she was within 1,000 yards, *Penshurst* stopped her engines, the panic party 'abandoned' ship, and the two boat-loads pulled away to starboard. The German now sheered out to port, swept round on *Penshurst's* port beam, and passed close under the stern of her with the object of securing the ship's papers from the captain, whom the enemy supposed to be in the boats. A party of Germans would then have boarded the ship and sunk her with bombs. But these intentions were suddenly frustrated at 4.26 p.m., when, the submarine being on *Penshurst's* starboard quarter and all the latter's guns bearing, the British ship opened fire at the delightfully convenient range of only 250 yards. This was the last thing the enemy was expecting. No one was standing by her 8·8-centimetre gun forward of the conning-tower, the attention of all the Germans on deck being directed towards the Q-ship's boats rowing about. Thus completely and utterly surprised, the Germans never made any attempt to return the fire. The second shot, fired from *Penshurst's* starboard 3-pounder, penetrated right through into the engine-room and prevented the submarine from submerging. At this ridiculous range the British guns were able to be worked at their maximum rapidity, so that over eighty rounds were fired and almost every shot took effect. Very soon the submarine's hull was fairly riddled with holes, and large parts of the conning-tower and hull plating were blown away by the shells from the 12-pounder.

After only ten minutes' engagement the submarine foundered, bows first, but not before *Penshurst's* boats had taken off the survivors and also those who had leapt into the sea. These survivors included Ober-Leutnant Erich Noodt, Leutnant Karl Bartel, Ingenieur-Aspirant Eigler, and thirteen of the crew; but seven had been killed. Thus perished UB 19, who had left Zeebrugge on November 22, having come via the Straits of Dover. She was about 118 feet long, painted grey, had the one gun, two periscopes, and had been built the year previous. She was of the smaller class of submarines belonging to the Flanders flotilla which operated for three weeks on end in the waters of the English Channel, carrying only three torpedoes, one of which had already been used to sink a Norwegian ship. It was learned from her crew that her submerged speed was about 4 knots; so Captain Grenfell, but for the accident to the sea-

Q-SHIP "PENSHURST"

This shows a dress rehearsal. The "panic party" are seen rowing away in one of the ship's boats, the White Ensign is being hoisted on the foremast and the guns are about to open fire. In this picture she has her mizzen mast up.

Q-SHIP "PENSHURST" AT SEA

Seen with only two masts, the mizzen having been lowered. The crew's washing is displayed as in a tramp steamer. The funnel has been painted a different colour. But behind the white wind screen on the lower bridge is a 6-pounder gun—one each side—which can fire from ahead to astern. Inside the boat on the main hatch just forward of the funnel is the dummy boat in which a 12-pounder is concealed. Two 3-pounders are in the after deck-house. Depth charges were released through ports in the counter.

To face p 116

THE SPLENDID 'PENSHURST' 117

plane, would have been able to get right over her and destroy her by depth charge.

Thus, at length, after a year of hard work, disappointment, and all kinds of weather, Commander Grenfell, by his doggedness and downright skill, had scored his first success. The King rewarded him with a D.S.O., another officer received the D.S.C., and one of the crew the D.S.M. The ship's complement consisted of Commander Grenfell, three temporary (acting) R.N.R. lieutenants, and one assistant paymaster, who was engaged during the action in taking notes. The crew numbered fifty-six, which included R.N.R. and R.N.V.R. ratings. The sum of £1,000 was awarded to the ship, and, after the war, Lord Sterndale in the Prize Court awarded a further sum as prize bounty.

The gallant *Penshurst* had not long to wait for her next adventure. December passed, and on January 14, 1917, there was another and newer UB boat ready for her. It was ten minutes to four in the afternoon, and the Q-ship was in Lat. 50.9 N., Long. 1.46 W.—that is to say, between the Isle of Wight and Alderney, when she saw a submarine heading towards her. Five minutes later, the German, when 3,000 yards off, fired, but the shot fell short. The Q-ship then stopped her engines, went to 'panic' stations, and sent away her boats with the 'abandon ship' party. *Penshurst* then gradually fell off to port, and lay with her head about W.N.W., bringing the submarine on the starboard bow. Closing rapidly on this bearing, the UB boat kept firing at intervals, and when about 700 yards off turned as though to cross Captain Grenfell's bows. The latter withheld his fire, thinking the enemy was going round to the boats on the port quarter, and he would be able to get her at close range. But the German stopped in this position, exposing her broadside, and quickened her rate of fire, hitting the steamer twice in succession. It was this kind of experience which always tested the discipline and training of the Q-ship, as a well-trained boxer can receive punishment without losing his temper, knowing his chance will come presently.

The first hit broke an awning ridge-pole on *Pens-*

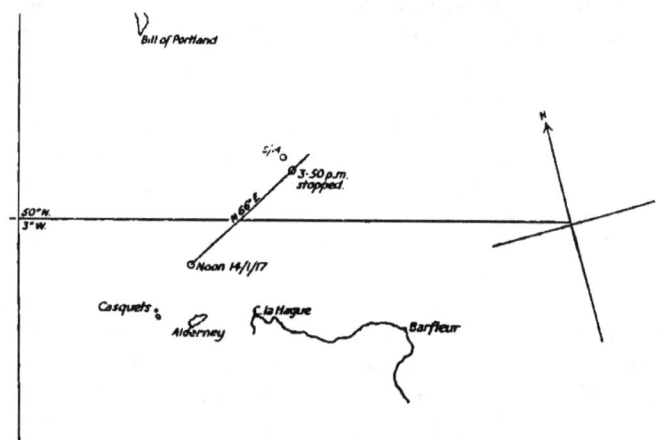

Fig. 11.—Diagram to Illustrate Approximate Movements of 'Penshurst' in her Action with Submarine on January 14, 1917.

hurst's bridge, the second shell struck the angle of the lower bridge, severing the engine-room telegraph connections and the pipe connecting the hydraulic release gear, by means of which the depth charge aft could be let go from the bridge. This shell also killed the gun-layer and loading-number of the 6-pounder, wounding its breech-worker and the signalman who was standing by to hoist the White Ensign. So at 4.24 p.m. *Penshurst* opened fire, her

THE SPLENDID 'PENSHURST' 119

first shot from the 12-pounder hitting the base of the enemy's conning-tower and causing a large explosion, as though the ammunition had been exploded. Large parts of the conning-tower were seen to be blown away, and a big volume of black smoke arose. The second British shot from this gun hit the enemy a little abaft the conning-tower and also visibly damaged the hull. The starboard 3-pounder hit the lower part of the conning-tower at least four times, and then the enemy sank by the stern. *Penshurst* wanted to make sure, so steamed ahead and dropped depth charges over her, then picked up her boats and made for Portland, where she arrived at ten o'clock that evening and sent her wounded to the Naval Hospital. It had been another excellent day's work, for UB 37, one of those modern craft fitted with net-cutters forward for the purpose of cutting a way through the Dover Straits barrage, had been definitely destroyed without a single survivor. More rewards followed, and, later on, more prize bounty.

Penshurst resumed her cruising, and just about a month later she was in the western approach to the English Channel, the exact date being February 20, and the position Lat. 49.21 N., Long. 6.16 W. At 12.36 p.m. a German submarine rose to the surface, and a quarter of an hour later began firing at a range of 3,000 yards. *Penshurst* then 'abandoned' ship, and at 1.4 p.m. opened fire and scored a hit with her 6-pounder. At 100 yards range the other guns came into action, and the enemy was hit above the water-line in the centre of the conning-tower and abaft this superstructure. She then submerged and was depth-charged; yet this submarine, in spite of all this, was not sunk. This again illustrated the statement already made that a submarine could be severely holed and yet be able to get back home. A still more illuminating example is to be found in the following incident.

Only two days had elapsed and *Penshurst* was again busily engaged. It was at 11.34 a.m., February 22, and the ship was off the south coast of Ireland, the exact position being Lat. 51.56 N., Long. 6.46 W. *Penshurst* was steering S. 89 W. when she saw a submarine steering west. The steamship therefore steamed at her utmost speed, but could not get up to her, for we may as well mention that this was U 84, a very up-to-date submarine which had a surface speed of 16 knots and could do her 9 knots submerged for a whole hour. It is not to be wondered, therefore, that she could run away from this slow steamer and at 11.55 a.m. disappear. At this time there was in sight 8 miles away H.M.S. *Alyssum*, one of Admiral Bayly's sloops based on Queenstown, who was escorting the large four-masted S.S. *Canadian*. As *Penshurst* proceeded, she sighted at 12.18 p.m. a boat with men in it, these being from the torpedoed sailing ship *Invercauld*, which had been sunk 22 miles S.E. of Mine Head, Ireland, that same day. A few minutes later and *Penshurst* observed the keel of this ship floating bottom up. At 12.35 the periscopes of U 84 were seen to emerge 400 yards on the port beam, and the track of a torpedo making straight for the midships of *Penshurst*. By at once starboarding the helm, disaster was avoided, but the torpedo passed as close as 15 feet.

The Q-ship then altered course to E. ½ S. as though running away, and reduced to half speed to allow the enemy to come up. Boats were turned out, the panic party stood by with lifebelts on, and just after one o'clock, at 3,500 yards range, the U-boat opened fire,

Q-SHIP "PENSHURST"

In this dummy boat mounted on the main hatch is seen hidden the 12-pounder gun. The sides of the boat were movable. The voice pipe from the bridge to the two after guns was lashed to the derrick and thus hidden from the enemy.

Q-SHIP "PENSHURST"

This shows how the concealed 12-pounder gun could be brought into action by removing the boat's sides. The bow end of the boat has been moved to the far side of the gun, where Captain Grenfell, attired in his "mystery" rig of a master mariner, is seen standing. As will be seen from the other photograph, the sides of the boat when in position were a perfect fit. The coil of rope was intended to hide the gun's pedestal from observation by the enemy.

THE SPLENDID 'PENSHURST'

whereupon the Q-ship 'abandoned' ship. Then the enemy closed to 1,500 yards on the starboard bow, but cautiously submerged, and then, closely and leisurely, inspected the ship from the periscope. Having done that, and apparently been quite satisfied that this was no trap-ship, the submarine emerged on the port quarter, 600 yards away and broadside on. One German officer then came out of the conning-tower and two other men looked out of the hatch. The first then shouted for the captain to come alongside with the ship's papers, but the British petty officer in charge of the boat party, in order to gain valuable time, ingeniously pretended not to understand. The German then repeated his order, so the petty officer replied he would bring the boat round by the stern, the intention, of course, secretly being for the purpose of affording *Penshurst* a clear range.

The petty officer's crew had not rowed more than three strokes when bang went *Penshurst's* guns, at which the German officer leapt through the hatch of his conning-tower, a shot hitting the after part of this superstructure just as the officer disappeared. Two more shells got home in the centre, another hit the hull abaft the conning-tower and burst, one holing the hull below the conning-tower's base. The submarine dived, but after a few minutes her bows came up out of the water at a steep angle. Fire was then reopened at her, and one shot was seen to go through her side, and then once more she submerged. Two depth charges were dropped near the spot and exploded, and then again the bows of the enemy broke surface at a steep angle, but 3,000 yards to the westward. Next the after deck came to the surface, and all the crew came out and lined the deck. *Penshurst* resumed shelling, hit her again, but U 84 now returned the fire. She was a big submarine, 230 feet long, armed with a 4·1-inch and a 22-pounder, and a dozen torpedoes which could be fired from six tubes.

But now approached H.M.S. *Alyssum* from the north and began to shell the enemy, so that the latter made off to the southward. The speed of *Penshurst* was 8 knots—that is to say, about half that of the enemy. Nor could the sloop overtake the latter, who, after being chased for three hours, disappeared at 5.12 p.m. These sloops had been built for minesweeping work, and not as anti-submarine ships, and it was only because of the shortage of destroyers— thanks largely to the demands in this respect by the Grand Fleet—that these single-screwed, comparatively slow vessels were engaged on escort and patrol duties.

In this engagement between the Q-ship and submarine everything had been done that could have been brought about by a most experienced, skilful, and determined British officer. His guns had kept on hitting, and yet the enemy had escaped. Fortunately we now know the story from the enemy's side, as an account of this incident was published in the German Press, and bears out all that has been said above. The German version mentions that U 84 took the British ship for a tank steamer. This is not in the least surprising, for the *Penshurst* was one of those small ships with her engines aft just as you see in an 'oil-tanker,' and such a craft was sure enough bait for any submarine. The Germans say the torpedo was fired at 765 yards range, and missed because the British ship was going 'faster than we supposed.' The Q-ship's disguise was perfect, for it was not until she opened fire that she was suspected

THE SPLENDID 'PENSHURST'   123

of being a 'trap.' As to the latter's shelling, the German account admits that the superstructure abaft the conning-tower was at once penetrated, and that hardly had the hatch been closed than 'there is a sharp report in the conning-tower, a yellow flash, and explosive gases fill the air. A shell has penetrated the side of the conning-tower and exploded inside.' The result was that one man was injured. She then dived, and at 65·6 feet they felt the two depth charges, which made the boat tremble and put out some of the electric lights. The forward hydroplane jammed, and this was the reason she came to the surface at such a steep angle. The gyro compass, the main rudder, the trimming pump, and all the control apparatus also broke down. But what about the leaks made by the shells? These were plugged, the tricolour flag of the French sailing ship *Bayonne*, which they had sunk on February 17 in the English Channel, being also used for that purpose.

The German account goes on to say this submarine was now compelled to proceed on the surface and run away, and the numerous men then seen on her deck were engaged in bringing up ammunition, 'all the men who are not occupied below' being thus employed. The submarine at first took *Alyssum* for a destroyer, and certainly bow on she was not unlike one. It needs little imagination to realize how narrowly the enemy had escaped, and the moral effect which was made on the German crew. We know now that a German petty officer was killed and an officer wounded. It mattered little that the conning-tower was holed, for, as has been already pointed out, this is not an essential part of the submarine's construction. By closing the hatch on deck no water could get down into the hull from here;

and the other holes being also plugged, U 84 could thus get back home by keeping out to sea during daylight hours, avoiding our patrols, and passing headlands under cover of night.

A month later *Penshurst* again fought a sharp action under Commander Grenfell at the eastern end of the English Channel, the position being in Lat. 50.28 N., Long. 0.12 W. In this engagement she did not sink the enemy, but was herself badly damaged and so seriously holed that she had to be towed to Portsmouth the following day. Here she underwent a long refit, and then went forth to fight again and to fight, as ever, splendidly. She had a new commanding officer, Lieutenant Cedric Naylor, R.N.R., who had been second-in-command to Captain Grenfell, now invalided ashore, and this lieutenant well maintained the traditions of the Q-service, and added to the distinctions won by this wonderful ship. Oft in danger, but always emerging from the tightest of corners, leaving the enemy seriously wounded, the gallant *Penshurst* carried on.

On July 2 she was steaming her 8 knots, as usual, and was in the western approaches (Lat. 49.10 N., Long. 8.25 W.), when at 1.30 p.m. a submarine was seen crossing the ship's bows 6,000 yards away. She dived and waited for *Penshurst* to approach in the manner of attack outlined in a previous chapter as being the tactics of a submarine. Then, after a while, the periscope was sighted 500 yards away on the port beam, so *Penshurst*, knowing a torpedo was imminent, waited, and, the torpedo having been sent, altered course to avoid it, just missing by a matter of 10 feet. The ship's company then went to 'panic' stations and the ship was 'abandoned.' At 3.35 p.m. the enemy came to the

THE GALLANT CAPTAIN AND OFFICERS OF Q-SHIP "PENSHURST"

From left to right: Paymaster-Lieut. W. R. Ashton, R.N.R.; Lieut. S. P. R. White, R.N.R.; Sub-Lieut. J. R. Stenhouse, R.N.R. (in command of the "Aurora" in Sir E. Shackleton's Antarctic Expedition, 1914-15); Captain F. H. Grenfell, R.N.; Lieut. C. Naylor, R.N.R. (First Lieut.); and Lieut. W. S. Harrison, R.N.R. (Navigating Officer).

MEN OF THE Q-SHIP "PENSHURST"

The ship's gunlayers and carpenter. The man in the centre wearing service uniform was the gunlayer of the bridge 6-pounder who was killed in the action of January 14, 1917. The others are wearing their Q-ship "rig."

surface 5,000 yards away on the starboard quarter, at 3.39 p.m. opened fire and continued until 4.13 p.m., when ⁻enshurst herself started firing at 4,500 yards, ⁻eding in hitting the enemy sixteen times, and undoubtedly seriously damaging him. The submarine managed to pass out of range and was not sunk. Three destroyers now came on the scene and gave chase, but the German got away. For this engagement Lieutenant Naylor received the D.S.O.

In accordance with *Penshurst's* previous experience, not many weeks elapsed before she was again in combat. It was the following August 19, and she was cruising again in the western approaches. That morning a steamship had sighted a submarine, and *Penshurst*, who was now in Lat. 47.45 N., Long. 8.35 W., was steering S. 50 W., doing 8 knots, when she saw the enemy 6 miles ahead steering across the bows, evidently making the 'approach' in his tactics. There was little north-west wind, a moderate westerly swell, and the sky was clear, but there was a strong glare from the sun. At 5.8 p.m. the enemy dived, and Lieutenant Naylor estimated that she would probably attack with torpedo about 5.45 p.m. Exactly at 5.44 a torpedo was observed to break water 1,000 yards from the ship, 3 points on the starboard bow, just forward of the sun's rays. *Penshurst* put her helm hard aport, and at 5.45 the torpedo struck her—but fortunately it was only a glancing blow immediately below the bridge. The smart handling of the ship had thus saved her from being struck further aft, where the consequences would have been even more serious. As it was, the explosion caused a high volume of water to rise in such quantities that upper and lower bridges and after deck were flooded, overwhelming the gun's crew concealed there, and filling the starboard boat hanging in the davits over 70 feet away from the point of impact. Furthermore, it caused the ship to take a heavy list to starboard so that the sea poured in over the bulwarks, and she afterwards rolled to port, the water then pouring in on this side also.

Some of the crew were hurled with force against the ceiling of the cabins, but perfect discipline still continued, as might well be expected with such a well-tried crew. She had been torpedoed in No. 2 hold, the starboard side of the lower bridge had been stripped, and unfortunately the 12-pounder there kept screened was thus exposed. Unfortunately, too, the sides of the dummy boat amidships, which hid another 12-pounder, were thrown down by the explosion, thus exposing this gun, flooding the magazine, putting out of action all controls from the bridge as well as the ship's compasses and so on. What was to be done now? Lieutenant Naylor wisely decided not to 'abandon' ship since the guns had been disclosed; the ship could not be manœuvred so as to hide this side, and the enemy would probably make another attack. She was therefore kept under way, the steering gear was connected up with the main steering engines, the wireless repaired, and at 5.58 a general signal was sent out to H.M. ships requesting assistance.

At five minutes past six the submarine showed herself on the port quarter 6,000 yards away. This made things better, for if the enemy had not already observed the exposed guns she could still be kept in ignorance, as the sides of the false boat had in the meantime been replaced in position. Therefore the 3-pounder on the top of the gunhouse aft opened fire at 5,000 yards. This was quite a normal happening,

FIG. 12.—THE HUMOROUS SIDE OF Q-SHIP WARFARE.

This amusing sketch of *Penshurst*, by one of her officers, shows her being shelled by a submarine and the panic party in two boats rowing off. In the bows of each boat one of the crew is semaphoring. BILL (*in boat No. 1*): ''ARRY!' 'ARRY (*in boat No. 2*): 'What?' BILL (*anxiously*): 'Did yer make the tea afore we left 'er?' 'ARRY: 'Nar!' BILL (*much relieved*): 'Good!'

for many a small mercantile steamer was thus armed defensively. The enemy replied, and at 6.21, as the latter showed no intention of decreasing the range, *Penshurst* opened fire with all guns on the port side, and appeared to hit, so that at 6.24 the enemy submerged. Meanwhile the *Penshurst* was not under control and steamed round in circles, but help was approaching, for at 6.50 p.m. H.M.S. *Leonidas* wirelessed saying she would reach *Penshurst* at 7.30 p.m. At 7.5 the submarine was 7 miles astern, waiting stationary to see what would happen, but at 7.26 she dived on observing the approaching destroyer. Nightfall came, and as the water was still gaining in the Q-ship, all the men who could be spared were transferred to the *Leonidas*. *Penshurst* then shaped a course E.N.E. for Plymouth, and next day at 1.30 p.m. was taken in tow by a tug which had been sent out with two armed trawlers from the Scillies Naval Base. Thus, wounded yet not beaten, she passed through Plymouth Sound, and on August 21 made fast to a Devonport jetty, happily having suffered no casualties to any of her personnel. Lieutenant Naylor received a bar to his D.S.O., the ship had a thorough refit, and in place of a 12-pounder she was now given a 4-inch gun, which would enable her to fight the 4·1-inch U-boat gun on more equal terms.

Then, still commanded by Lieutenant Naylor, she went forth again. We can pass over the intervening weeks and come to Christmas Eve, 1917. At a time when most non-combatants ashore were about to take part in the great festival, this most gallant ship, heroine of so many fights, was in the direst straits. At midday she was approaching the southern end of the Irish Sea, shaping a course to intercept a sub-

THE SPLENDID 'PENSHURST' 129

marine operating off the Smalls, when ten minutes later she sighted a U-boat two points on the port bow, in Lat. 51.31 N., Long. 5.33 W., about 5 miles ahead, steering at right angles to *Penshurst* and beginning the 'approach' of her attacking tactics. *Penshurst* was making her usual 8 knots, and at 12.12 p.m. the enemy, as was expected, submerged. Although the Q-ship zigzagged and tried to make the enemy break surface astern and attack by gunfire, the German was too good at his own job, and at 1.31 p.m. came the torpedo, fired from 300 yards away, half a point forward of the port beam. Only the track of the torpedo was seen, the ship's helm was put hard aport, but the torpedo could not be avoided and struck the ship between the boilers and engine-room.

Violent was the explosion, great was the damage, so that the ship stopped dead and began to settle by the stern. The sides of the dummy boat amidships had fallen down, thus exposing the midships 4-inch gun, and the after gunhouse had also collapsed, revealing the guns here placed, though the 12-pounder guns on the bridge remained intact and concealed, with the guns' crews close up and out of sight. The ship was now 'abandoned,' and panic parties were sent away in the one remaining boat and two rafts. The enemy, still submerged, proceeded to circle the ship, inspect her closely, approach the boat and rafts, and then at 2.40 p.m. rose to the surface on the port bow 250 yards off and began shelling *Penshurst* with her after gun. The Q-ship was about to open fire, but, owing to having settled down so much by the stern, the gun there could not be sufficiently depressed to bear. It was only when the ship rolled or pitched enough that advantage was taken of such movement and the enemy fired at. Six rounds were fired, the second hitting the submarine on the starboard side of the deck forward, the fourth hitting abaft the conning-tower. The enemy dived, and at 3.47 p.m. reappeared on the starboard beam 5 miles away. But now one of H.M. P-boats, those low-lying, specially constructed anti-submarine craft, rather like a torpedo-boat, arrived on the scene, so that the submarine was frightened away and not sighted again on that day, though she was probably the one sunk by a P-boat on Christmas Day.

As for *Penshurst*, help had come too late. The crew were saved, but the ship herself sank at 8.5 p.m. on December 24, 1917. Lieutenant Cedric Naylor, who already possessed the decorations of D.S.O. and bar and D.S.C., and had for his gallantry been transferred from R.N.R. to the Royal Navy, now received a second bar to his D.S.O., and Lieutenant E. Hutchison, R.N.R., received a D.S.O. Thus after two years of the most strenuous service, full of honours, this *Penshurst* ended her glorious life as a man-of-war. Wounded, scar-stained, repaired and refitted, her gallant crew, so splendidly trained by Captain Grenfell, had kept taking her to sea along the lanes of enemy activity. Insignificant to look at, when you passed her on patrol you would never have guessed the amount of romance and history contained in her hull. Naval history has no use for hysteria and for the sensational exaggeration of 'stunt' journalism, but it is difficult to write calmly of the great deeds performed in these most unheroic-looking ships. To-day some Q-ship officers and men are walking about, looking for jobs, and there are not ships in commission to employ them. But yesterday they were breaking the spirit of the U-boat personnel, risking their lives to the uttermost limits in the endeavour to render ineffectual the submarine blockade and the starvation of the nation.

Bravery such as we have seen in this and other chapters was greater than even appears: for, having once revealed the identity of your ship as a man-of-war, the wounded submarine would remember you, however much you might disguise yourself; and the next time he returned, as he usually did, to the same station, he would do his best to get you, even if he spent hours and days over the effort. That officers and men willingly, eagerly, went to sea in the same Q-ships, time after time, when they might have obtained, and would certainly have deserved, a less trying appointment afloat or ashore, is surely a positive proof that we rightly pride ourselves on our British seamanhood. Through the centuries we have bred and fostered and even discouraged this spirit. In half-decked boats, in carracks, galleons, wooden walls, fishing boats, lifeboats, pleasure craft; in steam, and steel-hulled motor, cargo ships, in liner and tramp and small coaster, this seamanlike character has been trained, developed, and kept alive, and now in the Q-ship service it reaches its apotheosis. For all that is courageous, enduring, and inspiring among the stories of the sea in any period, can you beat it? Can you even equal it?

CHAPTER X

FURTHER DEVELOPMENTS

ONE of the great lessons of the Great War was the inter-relation of international politics and warfare. It was an old lesson indeed, but modern conditions emphasized it once more. We have already seen that the torpedoing in 1915 of the Atlantic liners *Lusitania* and *Arabic* caused pressure to be put on the German Government by the United States of America. In the spring of 1916 the submarine campaign, for the Germans, was proceeding very satisfactorily. In February they had sunk 24,059 tons of British merchant shipping, in March they sank 83,492 tons, in April 126,540 tons; but in May this dropped suddenly to 42,165 tons. What was the reason for this sudden fall?

The answer is as follows: On March 24, 1916, the cross-Channel S.S. *Sussex* was torpedoed by a German submarine, and it happened that many citizens of the U.S.A. were on board at the time and several were killed. This again raised the question of relations between the U.S.A. and Germany, the *New York World* going so far as to ask, 'Whether anything is to be gained by maintaining any longer the ghastly pretence of friendly diplomatic correspondence with a Power notoriously lacking in truth and honour.' On April 20, therefore, the U.S.A. presented a very sharp note to the German Government, protesting against the wrongfulness of the submarine campaign waged versus commerce, and threatened to break off diplomatic relations. The result of this was that Germany had to give way, and sent orders to her naval staff to the effect that submarine warfare henceforth was to be carried on in accordance with Prize Law: that is to say, the U-boats—so Admiral Scheer interpreted it—were ' to rise to the surface and stop ships, examine papers, and all passengers and crew to leave the ship before sinking her.'

Now this did not appeal to the German mind at all. 'As war waged according to Prize Law by U-boats,' wrote Admiral Scheer,* 'in the waters around England could not possibly have any success, but, on the contrary, must expose the boats to the greatest dangers, I recalled all the U-boats by wireless, and announced that the U-boat campaign against British commerce had ceased.' Thus we find that after April 26 the sinkings of British merchant ships became low until they began to increase in September, 1916, and then rapidly mounted up until in April, 1917, they had reached their maximum for the whole war with 516,394 tons. It is to be noted that after May 8, until July 5, 1916, no sinkings by U-boats occurred in home waters, although the sinkings went on in the Mediterranean, where risk of collision with American interests was less likely to occur.

Having regard to the increasing utility and efficiency of the Q-ships, we can well understand Admiral Scheer's objection to U-boats rising to the surface, examining the ship's papers, and allowing everyone to leave the ship before sinking her. This was the

* 'Germany's High Sea Fleet in the World War,' p. 242.

recognized law, and entirely within its rights the Q-ship made full use of this until she hoisted the White Ensign and became suddenly a warship. It shows the curious mental temper of the German that he would gamble only when he had the dice loaded in his favour. He had his Q-ships, which, under other names, endeavoured and indeed were able to pass through our blockade, and go raiding round the world; but until his submarines could go at it ruthlessly, he had not the same keenness. It was on February 1, 1917, that his Unrestricted Submarine Campaign began, and this was a convenient date, seeing that Germany had by this time 109 submarines. We know these facts beyond dispute, for a year after the signing of Armistice Germany held a 'General National Assembly Committee of Inquiry' into the war, and long accounts were published in the Press. One of the most interesting witnesses was Admiral von Capelle, who, in March, 1916, had succeeded von Tirpitz as Minister of Marine; and from the former's lips it was learned that one of the main reasons why Germany in 1916 built so few submarines was the Battle of Jutland; for the damage inflicted on the High Sea Fleet necessitated taking workmen away from submarine construction to do repairs on the big ships. The number and intensity of the minefields laid by the British in German waters in that year caused Germany to build many minesweepers to keep clear the harbour exits. This also, he says, took men away from submarine building. It needed a couple of years to build the larger U-boats and a year to build the smaller ones; and though at the beginning of the Unrestricted Campaign in February, 1917, there were on paper 109 German submarines, and before the end of the war, in spite of sinkings by Allied forces, the number even averaged 127, yet there were never more than 76 actually in service at one time, and frequently the number was half this amount. For the Germans divided the seas up into so many stations, and for each station five submarines were required, thus: one actually at work in the area, one just relieved on her way home for rest and refit, a third on her way out from refit to relieve number one, while two others were being overhauled by dockyard hands. Geographically Germany was unfortunately situated for attacking the shipping reaching the British Isles from the Atlantic and Bay of Biscay. Before the submarines could get into the Atlantic they had either to negotiate the Dover Straits or go round the North of Scotland. The first was risky, especially for the bigger and more valuable submarines, and during 1918 became even highly dangerous; but the second, especially during the boisterous winter months, knocked the submarines about to such an extent that they kept the dockyards busier than otherwise.

All this variation of U-boat activity reacted on the rise, development, and wane of the Q-ship. In the early part of 1917, when the submarine campaign was at its height, the Q-ships were at the top of their utility. It was no longer any hole-and-corner service, relying on a few keen, ingenious brains at one or two naval bases, but became a special department in the Admiralty, who selected the ships, arranged for the requisite disguises, and chose the personnel. The menace to the country's food had by this time become so serious—a matter of a very few weeks, as we have since learned, separated us from starvation—that every anti-submarine method had to be carried out with vigour, and at that time no method promised greater success than these mystery ships. Altogether about 180 vessels of various sorts were taken up and commissioned as Q-ships. Apart from the usual tramp steamers and colliers and disguised trawlers, thirty-four sloops and sixteen converted P-boats, named now 'PQ's,' were equipped. The P-boat, as mentioned on a previous page, was a low-lying craft rather like a torpedo-boat; but her great feature was her underwater design. She was so handy and had a special forefoot that if once she got near to a submarine the latter would certainly be rammed; in one case the P-boat went clean through the submarine's hull. The next stage, then, was to build a suitable superstructure on this handy hull, so that the ship had all the appearance of a small merchant ship. Because of her shallow, deceptive draught she was not likely to be torpedoed, whereas her extreme mobility was very valuable.

In every port all over the country numerous passenger and tramp steamers and sailing ships were inspected and found unsuitable owing to their peculiar structure or the impossibility of effective disguise combined with a sufficient bearing of the disguised guns. All this meant a great deal of thought and inventive genius, the tonnage as a rule ranging from 200 to 4,000, and the ships being sent to work from Queenstown, Longhope, Peterhead, Granton, Lowestoft, Portsmouth, Plymouth, Falmouth, Milford, Malta, and Gibraltar. And when you ask what was the net result of these Q-ships, the whole answer cannot be given in mere figures. Generally they greatly assisted the merchantman, for it made the U-boat captain very cautious, and there are instances where he desisted from attacking a real merchant ship for the reason that something about her suggested a Q-ship. In over eighty cases Q-ships damaged German submarines and thus sent them home licking their wounds, anxious only to be left alone for a while. This accounts for some of those instances when a merchant ship, on seeing a submarine proceeding on the surface, was surprised to find that the German did not attack. Thus the Q-ship had temporarily put a stop to sinkings by that submarine. But apart from these indirect, yet no less valuable, results, no fewer than eleven submarines were directly sent to their doom of all the 203 German U-craft sunk during the war from various causes, including mines and accidents.

But as time went on it became inevitable that the more a Q-ship operated the more likely would she be recognized and the less useful would be her work. By August, 1917, Q-ships were having a most difficult time, and during that month alone six Q-ships were lost. By September their success, broadly speaking, was on the wane. This, however, does not mean that their service had ceased to be productive or that they were no longer deemed worth while. On the contrary, as we shall see presently, they were to perform more wonderful work, and the number of Q-ships was actually increased, especially in respect of sailing ships in home waters; but those which happened to make an unsuccessful attack were at once ordered to return to their base and alter both rig and disguise. Similarly, in the Mediterranean, where the submarines were doing us so much harm, the number of Q-ships was increased, and one was cleverly included in the outward-bound convoys, to drop astern as soon as in the danger zone, after the manner of many a lame-duck merchantman whose engines had caused him to straggle. Then would come the Q-ship's chance, when she revealed herself as a warship and fooled the submarine from attacking the convoy, which had just disappeared over the horizon in safety.

The converted 'flower' class sloops, originally built as minesweepers, but by the able work of the naval dockyard staff now made to resemble little merchantmen, were having a busy time. *Tulip* (Q 12), for instance, which had begun her Q-ship service at the end of August, 1916, was sunk eight months later by a submarine in the Atlantic and her captain taken prisoner, though eighty survivors were picked up by the British destroyer *Mary Rose* and landed in Queenstown.* The sloop *Viola* began this special work towards the end of September, 1916, and a month later was shelled by a submarine, who suddenly gave up the attack and made off to the northward, having evidently realized the sloop's disguise, which none but an expert seafarer could have penetrated. Now, in each submarine there was usually carried as warrant navigating officer a man who had served in German liners and freighters and would be familiar with the shipping normally to be found in the area to which each U-boat was assigned. In this particular incident his practised eye had evidently been struck by the position of the above-water discharge being vertically under the imitation cargo hatch and derrick forward of the mainmast. These were important details which had to be watched if the disguise was to be successful.

* *Tulip* was sunk by U 62, whose captain reported that she was a very well-disguised trap, having the appearance of a medium-sized cargo steamer. Suspicion was aroused by the way the merchant flag was hoisted, and the fact that she appeared to have no defensive gun.

Q-SHIP "TULIP"
This vessel was originally built as a sloop, but was given a false stern and generally altered to resemble a merchantman.

Q-SHIP "TAMARISK"
Like the "Tulip," this vessel was originally built as a warship. She was cleverly altered so that both in hull and upperworks she resembled a merchant steamer.

FURTHER DEVELOPMENTS 139

Another converted sloop was *Tamarisk,* who began that rôle at the end of July, 1916, and was commanded by Lieutenant John W. Williams, R.N.R. Towards the end of November she was shelled by a submarine at long range, so that the Q-ship had to declare herself and reply, whereupon the enemy beat a retreat and dived. Hitherto the excellent Q-ship gunnery had depended on the fact that first-class men had been selected who would be able at short range to score hits with the first or second rounds. But this incident of the *Tamarisk,* involving at least 6,000 yards range, showed that a small range-finder would be very useful, and this was accordingly supplied. Other sloops thus converted to resemble merchantmen were the *Begonia, Aubrietia, Salvia, Heather,* and so on.

The Q-ships operated not merely in the North Atlantic, English Channel, North Sea, and Mediterranean, but in such areas as off Lapland and the other side of the North and South Atlantic. For instance, the S.S. *Intaba* (Q 2), under Commander Frank Powell, on December 8, 1916, was in action with a submarine not far from the Kola Inlet, and had been sent to these northern latitudes inasmuch as German submarines for some time had been sinking our merchant ships off that coast. Another Q-ship operated with a British E-class submarine near Madeira and the Canaries; and another Q-ship was in the South Atlantic looking for a German raider. At other times there were the ocean-going submarines *Deutschland* and *Bremen* to be looked out for. There was thus plenty of work to be carried out by these decoy vessels in almost every sea.

But it was especially those Q-ships based on Queenstown who had to bear the brunt of the submarine warfare. Strategically, Queenstown was an outpost of the British Isles, and there was scarcely a day in the week when one Q-ship was not leaving or entering Queenstown, or in the Haulbowline Dockyard being got ready for her next 'hush' cruise. Bearing in mind that this base was in a country whose inhabitants were largely anti-British, that there had been a great rising in Dublin at Eastertide, 1916, and that the German disguised S.S. *Aud* had made an ineffectual attempt to land a cargo of arms, and that Sir Roger Casement had arrived, it may well be realized how great was the responsible task of enshrouding these decoys in secrecy. Perhaps for weeks a recently requisitioned ship would be alongside the dockyard quay having her necessary disguises made, and yet the enemy knew nothing about it until he found himself surprised, and forced to keep at long range or hide himself in the depths of the sea. Sound organization, constant personal attention on the part of the Commander-in-Chief, and loyal, enthusiastic co-operation on the part of the officers and men, achieved the successes which came to this difficult work of Q-ships. It was all such a distinctly novel kind of sea service, which was of too personal and particular a kind to allow it to be run by mere routine. During the whole of its history it was experimental, and each cruise, each engagement, almost each captain added to the general body of knowledge which was being rapidly accumulated. It seemed for the professional naval officer as if the whole of his previous life and training had been capsized. Instead of his smart, fast twin-screw destroyer, he found himself in command of an awkward, single-screw, disreputable-looking tramp, too slow almost to get out of her own way. On the other hand, officers of

FURTHER DEVELOPMENTS 141

the Mercantile Marine, fresh from handling freighters or liners, in whom throughout all their lives had been instilled the maxim 'Safety first,' now found they had to court risks, look for trouble, and pretend they were not men-of-war. Q-ship work was, in fact, typical of the great upheaval which had affected the whole world.

In some cases the transition was gradual. Some officers, having come from other ships to command sloops, found their aspirations satisfied not even in these ships, whose work went on unceasingly—escorting all but the fastest Atlantic liners, patrolling, minesweeping, picking up survivors or salvaging stricken ships, or whatever duty came along. Transferring as volunteers from sloops to sloops rebuilt as Q-ships, they had to forget a great deal and acquire much more. One of such officers was Lieut.-Commander W. W. Hallwright, R.N., who, after doing very fine work as captain of one of H.M. sloops based on Queenstown, took over command of the disguised sloop *Heather* (Q 16). One April day in 1917, while cruising in the Atlantic about breakfast time, *Heather* was suddenly attacked by a submarine, whose sixth shot killed this keen officer, a piece of shell passing through his head whilst he was watching the movements of the German through a peep-hole on the starboard side of the bridge. Lieutenant W. McLeod, R.N.R., then took command, opened fire, but the submarine dived and made off as usual.

Other Q-ship captains perished, and that is all we know. On a certain date the ship left harbour; perhaps a couple of days later she had reported a certain incident in a certain position. After that, silence! Neither the ship nor any officers or crew ever returned to port, and one could but assume that the enemy had sent them to the bottom. In spite of all this, the number of volunteers exceeded the demand. From retired admirals downwards they competed with each other to get to sea in Q-ships. Bored young officers from the Grand Fleet yearning for something exciting; ex-mercantile officers, yachtsmen, and trawler men, they used every possible means to become acceptable, and great was their disappointment if they were not chosen.

CHAPTER XI

THE GOOD SHIP 'PRIZE'

IN the summer of 1914 I happened to be on a yachting cruise in the English Channel. In July we had seen the Grand Fleet, led by *Iron Duke*, clear out from Weymouth Bay for Spithead. In single line ahead the battle squadrons weighed and proceeded, then came the light cruisers, and before the last of these had washed the last ounce of dirt off her cable and steamed into position, the *Iron Duke* and *Marlborough* were hull down over the horizon: it was the most wonderful sight I had ever witnessed at sea. A week or two later I had arrived in Falmouth, the war had begun, and yachting came to a sudden stop. One morning we found a new neighbour had arrived, a typical, foreign-built, three-masted schooner, who had just been brought in and anchored. She was destined to be an historic ship in more ways than one. Actually, she was the first prize to be captured from Germany, and it was a unique sight then to see the White Ensign flying over German colours. Within four or five hours of declaration of war this craft had been captured at the western entrance of the English Channel, and she never became German again.

But she was to be historic in quite another way. Of all the splendid little Q-ships during the war, not excepting even the *Mitchell* mentioned in another chapter, no sailing craft attained such distinction, and her captain will be remembered as long as British naval history has any fascination. This German schooner was named the *Else*, and had been built of steel and iron in 1901 at Westerbrock, by the firm of Smit and Zoon, but registered at Leer, Germany. She was 112 feet 6 inches long, her net tonnage being 199. I can still see her disconsolate German skipper standing aft, and it must have grieved him that his ship was about to be taken from him for ever. For she was afterwards put up for auction and sold to the Marine Navigation Company, who, because of her experience already mentioned, changed her name from *Else* to *First Prize*. In November, 1916, she was lying in Swansea, and as the Admiralty was looking out for a suitable vessel to carry out decoy work after the manner of *Mitchell* and *Helgoland*, she was surveyed, found suitable, and requisitioned. A few weeks later the Managing Director of the Company patriotically decided to waive all payment for hire, and lent her to the Admiralty without remuneration.

By February, 1917, this auxiliary topsail schooner was ready for sea as a disguised man-of-war, with a couple of 12-pounders cleverly concealed on her deck. She had changed her name from *First Prize* to *Prize*, alias Q 21, and in command of her went Lieutenant W. E. Sanders, R.N.R., whom we saw behaving with distinction when serving in the Q-sailing-ship *Helgoland*. No better man could have been found than this plucky New Zealander, and he had already shown that he had a genius for this extra special type of Q-ship work. *Prize* had been sent to work in the western waters, and on April 26, 1917, she left Milford Haven for a cruise off the west coast of Ireland, this

THE GOOD SHIP 'PRIZE'

being the month when, of all months in the war, German submarines were the most successful. At 8.35 on the evening of April 30, *Prize* was in Lat. 49.44 N., Long. 11.42 W. It was fine, clear, spring-like weather, with a light N.N.E. wind, calm sea, and good visibility. *Prize* was under all sail, steering on a north-west course, and making about 2 knots. Two miles away on her port beam, and steering a parallel course, was sighted a big submarine. This was U 93, a most modern craft, commanded by one of Germany's ablest submarine officers, Lieut.-Commander Freiherr von Spiegel. She was a powerful vessel, who had relieved U 43 on this station, and was over 200 feet long, armed with two 10·5-centimetre guns, 500 rounds of ammunition, and 18 torpedoes, her complement consisting of 37 officers and men. This latest submarine was on her maiden trip in the Atlantic, having left Emden on Friday, April 13. For those who are superstitious the day and the date will be interesting. She had had a most successful cruise, having sunk eleven merchantmen, and was now on her way back to Germany. Von Spiegel was anxious to be back home as soon as possible, for, be it said, he was certainly a sportsman, and he happened to have a couple of horses running in the Berlin races in the second week of May.

The sighting of this little topsail schooner made him avaricious. He had sunk eleven: why not make the number a round dozen? So, at 8.45 p.m., he altered course towards the *Prize*, and ordering on deck to see the fun all his men who could be spared, he opened fire with both guns. Lieutenant Sanders therefore brought *Prize* into the wind, and sent his panic party to row about. This party consisted of six men in charge of Skipper Brewer, of the Trawle

Reserve, who had been intentionally visible on deck, and now launched their small boat. In the meantime, at the sounding of the alarm, Lieutenant Sanders and Skipper Meade (also of the Trawler Reserve) had concealed themselves inside the steel companion-cover amidships, and the rest of the crew were hiding under the protection of the bulwarks or crawling to their respective stations. *Prize's* two guns were placed one forward, concealed by a collapsible deckhouse, and one aft, on an ingenious disappearing mounting under the hatchway covers of the after hold, and she carried also a couple of Lewis guns. Lieutenant W. D. Beaton, R.N.R., who was second in command of the ship, was in charge of the gunnery forward, and lay at the foot of the foremast with his ear to a voice-pipe which led back to where Lieutenant Sanders was conning the ship.

The contest could not fail to be interesting, for it resolved itself into a duel between one 'star-turn' artist and another. Neither was a novice, both were resourceful, plucky men, and the incident is one of the most picturesque engagements of all the Q-ship warfare. Taking it for granted that this little trader out in the Atlantic was what she appeared to be, von Spiegel closed. *Prize's* head had now fallen off to the eastward, so the submarine followed her round, still punishing her with his shells, to make sure the abandon-ship evolution had been genuine. Two of these shells hit *Prize* on her waterline—you will remember she was built of iron and steel—penetrating and bursting inside the hull. One of them put the auxiliary motor out of action and wounded the motor mechanic: the other destroyed the wireless room and wounded the operator. That was serious enough, but cabins and mess-room were wrecked, the mainmast

THE GOOD SHIP 'PRIZE'

shot through in a couple of places, and the ship now leaking. Such was the training, such was the discipline of these men under their gallant New Zealand captain, that, in spite of this nerve-wracking experience, they still continued to remain on deck, immobile, unseen, until Lieutenant Sanders should give the longed-for word. They could see nothing, they could not ease the mental strain by watching the enemy's manœuvres or inferring from what direction the next shot—perhaps the last—would come. This knowledge was shared only by Lieutenant Sanders and Skipper Meade as they peeped through the slits of their lair. Several times Sanders crept from this place on hands and knees along the deck, encouraging his men and impressing on them the necessity of concealment.

Meanwhile, closer and closer drew the submarine, but the latter elected to remain dead astern, and this was unfortunate, for not one of *Prize's* guns would thus bear. Then there was a strange sound aft. Everyone knows that the inboard end of a patent log fits into a small slide, which is screwed down on to the taffrail of a ship. Suddenly this slide was wrenched and splintered, for the enemy had got so close astern that she had fouled and carried away the log-line in her endeavour to make quite sure of her scrutiny. U 93 then, apparently convinced that all was correct, sheered out a little and came up on the schooner's port quarter only 70 yards away, being about to send her quickly to the bottom.

Thus had passed twenty long, terrible minutes of suspense on board the Q-ship, and it was five minutes past nine. But patience, that great virtue of the really brave, had at length been rewarded. Through his steel slit Sanders could see that his guns would bear, so 'Down screens!' 'Open fire!' and up went the White Ensign. Covers and false deckhouses were suddenly collapsed, and the *Prize's* guns now returned the fire, as the pent-up feelings of the crew were able to find their outlet in fierce activity. But even as the White Ensign was being hoisted, the submarine fired a couple more shots, and the schooner was twice hit, wounding one of the crew who had rushed below to fetch from the bottom of the ladder a Lewis gun. Von Spiegel was now evidently very angered, for putting his helm hard aport he went full speed ahead to ram the schooner, and with that fine bow he might have made a nasty hole at the waterline, through which the sea would have poured like a waterfall. But he realized that he was outside his turning circle, so put his helm the other way and tried to make off. It was then that a shell from the *Prize's* after gun struck the forward gun of the submarine, blowing it to pieces, as well as the gun's crew. The second shot from the same British gun destroyed the conning-tower, and a Lewis gun raked the rest of the men on the deck. The third shot from *Prize's* after gun also hit so that she stopped, and as she sank shell after shell hit, and the glare was seen as of a fire inside the hull. At 9.9 p.m., after the *Prize* had fired thirty-six rounds, the enemy disappeared stern first. Lieutenant Sanders could not use his engines as they were already out of action, and there was practically no wind, so he could not go to the spot where she had last been seen.

The darkness was fast falling, and the panic party in the boat rowed over the scene to search for any survivors, and picked up three. These were Von Spiegel, the submarine's captain, the navigating warrant officer, and a stoker petty officer. Covered by Skipper Brewer's pistol, these were now taken on board the schooner. But *Prize* herself was in a bad way. Water was pouring through the shell-holes, and, in spite of efforts to stop it, the sea was gaining all the time. Had it not been calm, the vessel would certainly have gone to the bottom. Von Spiegel, on coming aboard, offered his word of honour to make no attempt to escape, and undertook that he and his men would render all assistance. His parole being accepted, captors and captives set to work to save the ship. There was a possibility that another submarine known to be in the area would come along and finish off the sinking *Prize*, so all had more than an interest in the proceedings.

As the ship was leaking so badly, the only thing to do was to list her. This was done by swinging out the small boat on the davits filled with water; by passing up from below both cables on deck and ranging them on the starboard side; by shifting coal from port to starboard and by emptying the port fresh-water tanks. By this means the shot-holes were almost clear of the water, though the crew had to continue baling night and day. Troubles never come singly. Here was this gallant little ship lying out in the Atlantic night, crippled and becalmed. An attempt was made to start the engines, but owing to sparks from the motor igniting the oil which had escaped from a damaged tank, a fire broke out in the engine-room. This was prevented from reaching the living quarters and magazine, and was eventually put out. Meanwhile, the German navigating warrant officer had dressed the wounds of *Prize's* wounded crew, and now, at 11.45 p.m., *Prize's* wounded stoker petty officer, assisted by the second motor-man and the German stoker petty officer, succeeded in starting one engine, and course was shaped for the Irish coast all sail being set; but the nearest land was 120 miles to the north-east.

That night passed, and the next day, and the forenoon of the day following; but on the afternoon of May 2 the Irish coast was sighted, and *Prize* was picked up 5 miles west of the Old Head of Kinsale by H.M.M.L. 161 (Lieutenant Hannah, R.N.V.R.), who towed her into Kinsale, where the wounded were disembarked. On May 4—that notable sunny day when the first United States destroyers reached Queenstown from America—*Prize*, still with her three German prisoners on board, left Kinsale Harbour, towed by H.M. Drifter *Rival II.*, who took her to Milford. But on the way *Prize* sighted a German mine-laying submarine on the surface 2 miles away to the southward. The crew therefore went to action stations, and for an hour the enemy steered on a parallel course, but finally the latter drew ahead and disappeared. Arrived in Milford the prisoners were taken ashore, and the *Prize* at length came to rest.

It has been told me by one who ought to know, that when Von Spiegel came aboard *Prize*, after being picked up out of the water, he remarked to Sanders: 'The discipline in the German Navy is wonderful, but that your men could have quietly endured our shelling without reply is beyond all belief.' Before leaving the *Prize* he said good-bye to Sanders and extended an invitation to stay with him on his Schleswig-Holstein estate after the war. No one will deny the extraordinary gallantry of *Prize's* crew and the heroic patience in withholding their fire until the psychological moment, though the temptation was very trying. To Lieutenant W. E. Sanders was

THE GOOD SHIP 'PRIZE'

awarded the Victoria Cross, and he was promoted to the rank of Temporary Lieut.-Commander, R.N.R. To Lieutenant W. D. Beaton, R.N.R., was awarded a D.S.O.; the two skippers each received a D.S.C., and the rest of the brave ship's company the D.S.M.

But the ending of this story is yet to be told. U 93 was not sunk, but got safely back to Germany! Von Spiegel had thought she was sunk, and the crew of *Prize* were not less certain. She had been holed in her starboard ballast tank, in her starboard fuel tank, and her conning-tower, and she was assuredly in a very bad way. If it had been daylight she would most certainly have been finally destroyed; as it was she was unable to dive, and escaped in the darkness deprived of her wireless. Sub-Lieutenant Ziegler took over the command, with one of his crew killed, three wounded, and three already taken prisoners. With the utmost difficulty, and compelled to navigate all the time on the surface, he managed to get his craft home. It was certainly a fine achievement; the Kaiser was much impressed, and promoted him to lieutenant. But, at the time, we in this country had never supposed that any submarine could stand so much battering. It is interesting to bear this incident in mind when reading other accounts in this book, where it seemed so sure that the submarine must have been sunk: yet the greatest care has been taken to verify every enemy submarine sunk, and in each case the number has been given. But U 93 was doomed, and had not much longer to live after her refit. Early in the following January, one fine clear morning at a quarter past four, the time when human nature is at its weakest and most collisions occur at sea, this submarine was rammed by a steamer and sunk for the last time.

After her very necessary refit, Lieut.-Commander Sanders still remained in the *Prize*. Admiral Jellicoe, First Sea Lord, had sent for him and offered him command of another ship: he could have had a destroyer, a P-boat, or any ship within reason, but his undaunted spirit, to which Lord Jellicoe on arriving in New Zealand after the war paid such high tribute, refused a safer appointment, and preferred to carry on. I have been told by an officer who enjoyed Sanders' friendship and confidence at this time, that he went out to sea again with the consciousness that before long he would have played the live-bait game too far, and that the fish would get away with the bait. If that is true, then we must admire Sanders still more for his heroism in his devotion to duty. It is surely of this stuff that the great martyrs of Christendom have been made.

On June 12, 1917—that is, six weeks after the previous incident, just time enough to give leave to all the crew, get the ship refitted and sailed to her new area—*Prize* left Killybegs (Ireland) to cruise to the westward of the Irish coast. At 11 a.m. on this day she was under all sail on a N.N.W. course, doing not more than a knot through the water, when she sighted a submarine 1½ miles to the E.S.E. proceeding slowly on the same course as *Prize*. The movements of this submarine thereafter are worth noting. It is only reasonable to suppose that on his return to Germany in U 93 Ziegler would give a full description of the trap-ship which had so nearly destroyed him. This information would, of course, be passed on to the other submarine captains who frequented this Irish area, and we may be quite certain that they would be on the look-out for her, anxious to revenge their service. Now, in these modern times, and in any twenty-four hours, you will see far more steamers of all sorts than 200-ton sailing craft: it certainly was so during the war off the west and south-west coast of Ireland. During the years I was on patrol there, with the exception of quite small local fishing craft and an occasional full-rigged ship making the land after her voyage across the Atlantic, one scarcely ever sighted a sailing vessel of any kind. Ziegler would have reported in effect: 'Look out for a three-masted topsail schooner of about 200 tons. She has a bow like this . . ., her stern is like this . . ., and her sheer is so . . . You will probably find she has a dummy deckhouse placed here . . .;' and a rough sketch would afford his comrades a pretty accurate idea. You cannot ever disguise the appearance of such a sailing ship altogether, no matter what name you give her, nor what colour you paint her hull. A three-masted topsail schooner is that and nothing else, and would henceforth be regarded with the utmost suspicion. Then, on comparing her with the sketch and examining her with the eye of seamanlike experience, no astute submarine officer could have had much doubt in his mind. A British officer who knew this ship well has told me that in his opinion there was one small detail, in respect of the wireless, which, to a careful observer, would always give her character away. This may be so: at any rate, the following incidents seem to indicate that the enemy were on the look-out for her during the rest of her career, and persistently attacked her.

On the occasion of June 12, as soon as the submarine came to the surface and opened fire, *Prize* as usual, after the necessary intentional bungling, sent away her boat, which took up a position half a mile away on the starboard bow. The enemy kept on firing, and at 11.30 the schooner was hit twice, so three minutes later, as the enemy was turning away to increase the range, Sanders ordered the screens to be lowered, and opened fire from both starboard guns at 1,800 yards. One shell seemed to hit, and the enemy immediately dived. But two hours later a submarine was seen on the surface 4 miles away on the starboard quarter, and remained in sight for a quarter of an hour. Then next morning at 6.30 a submarine was sighted stopped, $1\frac{1}{2}$ miles ahead on the surface. Five minutes later he dived, but came up after four minutes 1,500 yards off on the starboard bow. At 6.43 he again dived, and was not seen again. Probably each of these three appearances was the same submarine. On the first he was repulsed, on the second he would have a perfect opportunity of making a detailed sketch, on the third he may have been intending to attack by torpedo, but the westerly swell from the Atlantic possibly interfered with accurate firing. But, apart from all surmise, it is absolutely evident that the enemy was able to obtain a picture of the schooner, which beyond all doubt would establish her identity on a future occasion. The importance of this will presently be seen.

For this action of June 12 Lieut.-Commander Sanders was given a D.S.O. to wear with his V.C. He had had a very trying time. When, at 11.30, the German shells had hit, the falls of the port davit had been shot away, and another shot had struck the ship on the starboard side amidships just on the top of the sheer strake plate. This shell had exploded and caused the ship to leak. Lieut.-Commander Sanders, who was lying concealed between the mast and the hatch, put up his arms to shield his face from the burst fragments and so received a piece of shell

THE GOOD SHIP 'PRIZE'

in his right arm above the wrist. In addition, the force of the explosion knocked him over and hurled him to the other side of the deck, where he was picked up by Skipper Mead. In spite of the pain and the shock, Sanders was just sufficiently conscious to give the order 'Action' at 11.33, when screens were downed, White Ensign run up, and fire was returned. The schooner came back to her base, her gallant captain recovered from his wound, and two months later we find her operating in the Atlantic again to the north-west of the N.W. Irish coast. On this occasion she was cruising with one of our D-class submarines, the idea being that when the enemy came along *Prize* would be attacked and heave-to in the customary manner, while the British submarine would stealthily make for the enemy and torpedo him whilst, so to speak, he was not looking.

On the forenoon of August 13, imagine this schooner with her newly-painted black topsides and red boot-topping, flying the Swedish flag and heading east. Suddenly UB 48 was sighted to the north, so Sanders hove-to and signalled the British submarine that there was a German submarine to port. Shells began to be fired from the enemy, who closed. The British submarine saw the shots falling but could not see the enemy until 4.10 p.m., when the German was descried to starboard of the *Prize*. There was a considerable lop on at the time, and *Prize* was seen with White Ensign flying at the peak, and her guns manned. Five hours later the British submarine came to the surface and spoke *Prize*, who stated that she had opened fire on the enemy at 200 yards, and had hit him. This we now know from another source was perfectly true, but the hits were not in a vital part of the German. During the dark hours UB 48 bided his time, and at midnight fired two torpedoes, the second of which hit, causing a terrific explosion, so that nothing more was seen, and the good ship *Prize*, with her gallant captain and all his brave men, ended her career after one of the most brilliant periods that can be found in the records of sea achievement. UB 48 was on her maiden voyage from Germany via the north of Scotland and N.W. of Ireland to Cattaro in the Adriatic, where she arrived on September 2, sinking merchantmen on the way. This modern type of submarine, with her 4·1-inch gun and her ten torpedoes, was a difficult craft to sink. Her second officer had been taken from the German Mercantile Marine, so we can assume that his critical eye would scrutinize the schooner and detect something which convinced his captain that this was really a trap-ship. That the submarine should have been content, whilst on a long passage, to waste so many hours over a mere sailing craft of quite small tonnage would have been doubtful; but the *Prize* having once shown her White Ensign and used her guns to effect decided the German that she must be settled with after dark, when she would be a good target in that August night. It was a fair fight, but the chances were all in favour of the German, since it is practically impossible to see a periscope at night, whereas the Q-ship's sails would loom up and show in which direction the target was heading; and, further, the submarine had the advantage of mobility all the time.

The facts which have just been stated are authentic, and it is as well that they should now be made known. Ignorance always breeds falsehood, and after the loss of *Prize* there were all sorts of wild stories going about both in the Service and in the Mercantile

THE GOOD SHIP 'PRIZE'

Marine. Some of them are too ghastly to be related, but a favourite version was that the brave Sanders had been taken prisoner and lashed to the submarine's periscope, which then submerged and so drowned him. Another story, which was very prevalent, was that he had been cruelly murdered. There is not a word of truth in these suggestions. Lieut.-Commander Sanders died as he would have wished, aboard his ship with his men. His body rests in the Atlantic where the remains of his glorious *Prize* sank: but his memorial, unveiled by Lord Jellicoe as Governor of New Zealand, will inspire generations who come after.

For dogged devotion to dangerous duty, for coolness in peril, for real leadership of men, for tenacity in 'sticking it,' this hero among those great and gallant gentlemen of the Q-ship service will remain as a model of what a true British sailor should be. Had he lived, his influence would have been tremendous, but by his refusing a safe billet when he was fully entitled to it, and preferring deliberately to court death because that way duty and honour pointed, his example should be a great source of strength to every young apprentice beginning his life in the Merchant Service, every midshipman of His Majesty's Navy, and every young man content to learn the lessons which are taught only by the sea. On land, for their historic exploits at the Dardanelles and in France we gratefully remember the Australians and New Zealanders. It is fitting that one of the latter should have bequeathed to us such distinction on the sea: it is characteristic of the great co-operation when the children of the Empire flocked to help their mother in her throes of the World War.

CHAPTER XII

SHIPS AND ADVENTURES

INDEPENDENCE of character is a great asset in any leader of men, but it is an essential, basic virtue when a man finds himself in command of a ship: without such an attribute he is dominated either by his officers, his own emotions, or the vagaries of chance. In the case of a Q-ship captain, this aloofness was raised to a greater degree of importance by reason of the special nature of the work. Can you think of any situation more solitary and lonely than this? There are, of course, all kinds and conditions of loneliness. There is the loneliness of the airman gliding through celestial heights; there is the loneliness of the man in the crowd; there is the loneliness of the sentry, of the hermit, of the administrator in the desert. But I can conceive of nothing so solitary as the Q-ship captain lying alone on the planking of his bridge, patiently waiting and watching through a slit in the canvas the manœuvres of an artful U-boat.

Such a figure is morally and physically alone. He is the great brain of the ship; at his word she is transformed from a tramp to a warship. It is he who has to take the fateful, and perhaps fatal, decision; and to none other can he depute this responsibility as long as life lasts. Only a big character, strong and independent, can tackle such a proposition. Alone, too, he is physically. Most of his men have left the ship and are over there in the boats, sometimes visible on the top of the wave, sometimes obliterated in the trough. The rest of his crew are somewhere below the bridge, under the bulwarks, at their guns, crouching out of sight. His officers are at their respective stations, forward, aft, and amidships, connected to him by speaking-tubes, but otherwise apart. He himself, arbiter of his own fate, his men, and his ship, has to fight against a dozen contending impulses, and refuse to be panic-stricken, hasty, or impetuous. This much is expected of him; his crew are relying on him blindly, absolutely. However, by long years of experience and moulding of character he has learnt the power of concentration and of omitting from his imagination the awful possibilities of failure. Before putting to sea, and whilst on patrol, he has envisaged every conceivable circumstance and condition likely to occur. He has mentally allowed for every move of the submarine, for the wounding of his own ship: and he has had the ship's action stations thus worked out. Accidents will, of course, occur to spoil any routine, though some of these, such as the breakdown of the wireless and the bursting of a gun, or the jamming of a screen, may be foreseen and allowed for.

But after all that could be prepared for has been done, there always remains some awkward possibility which the wit of man can never foresee. Take the incident of the Q-ship *Ravenstone*, which was commissioned as a Q-ship on June 26, 1917, under the name of *Donlevon*. A month later she was torpedoed one afternoon in the Atlantic, 40 miles south of the Fastnet. Fortunately there were no casualties, and fortunately, too, the ship did not straight away founder. There was a heavy sea running, and she was soon down by the head; but she was also prevented from using her engines, for the torpedo had struck her in No. 2 hold, and the force of the explosion had lifted and thrown overboard from the fore well-deck a 7-inch hemp hawser. This had fallen into the sea, floated aft, and there fouled the propeller so effectually that the ship could go neither ahead nor astern. It was a most annoying predicament, but who could have foreseen it? The submarine apparently 'hopped it,' for she made no further attack, and one of Admiral Bayly's sloops, H.M.S. *Camelia*, stood by *Donlevon*, and from Berehaven arrived the tug *Flying Spray*, who got her in tow. Another sloop, the *Myosotis*, had her in tow for thirty-one hours, handling her so well in the heavy sea that, in spite of *Donlevon* being down by the head and steering like a mad thing, she safely arrived in Queenstown, and was afterwards paid out of the Service. Ten thousand pounds' worth of damage had been done.

In the early summer of 1917, at a time when the United States Navy had just begun to help us with their destroyers and the enemy was hoping very shortly to bring us 'to our knees,' we had thirteen different Q-ships based on Queenstown. There was the converted sloop *Aubrietia*, commanded by Admiral Marx, M.V.O., D.S.O., who, in spite of his years, had come back to the Service and accepted a commission as captain R.N.R. For a time he was in command of H.M. armed yacht *Beryl*, owned by Lord Inverclyde. From this command he transferred to the more exciting work of decoying submarines, and it is amusing when one thinks of an admiral pretending to be the skipper of a little tramp. Of this thirteen there was Captain Grenfell's

SHIPS AND ADVENTURES 161

Penshurst, about which the reader has already been informed. Captain Gordon Campbell was in *Pargust*, and Commander Leopold A. Bernays, C.M.G., was in *Vala*. The latter was one of the most unusual personalities in a unique service. Before the war he had left the Navy and gone to Canada, where he had some pretty tough adventures. On the outbreak of war he joined up, and crossed to England as a soldier, but managed to get transferred quite early to a minesweeping trawler, where he did magnificent work month after month; first in sweeping up the minefield laid off Scarborough at the time of the German raid, December, 1914, and afterwards in clearing up the difficult Tory Island minefield, which had been laid by *Berlin* in October, 1914, but was not rendered safe for many months afterwards. When in the summer of 1915 a British minesweeping force was required for Northern Russia, Bernays was sent out with his trawlers. Here, with his usual thoroughness and enthusiasm, he set to work, and again performed most valuable service, and buoyed a safe channel for the ships carrying munitions from England to voyage in safety.

But Bernays was no respecter of persons, especially of those who were not keen on their job. With Russian dilatoriness and inefficiency, and in particular with the Russian admiral, he soon found himself exasperated beyond measure. His own trawlers were working in the most strenuous fashion, whereas the Russians seemed only to be thwarting instead of helping, and at any rate were not putting their full weight into the contest. I do not know whether the yarn about Bernays in exasperation pulling the beard of the overbearing Russian admiral is true, but there was a big row, and Bernays came back to England, though for his good work he received the coveted British order C.M.G. After further minesweeping off the Scotch coast, where once more he distinguished himself, he came to Queenstown to serve in his Q-ship. Here he went about his job in his usual fearless manner, and on one occasion had played a submarine as he used to play a fish. He had slowed down, and the U-boat was coming nicely within range, when just as everything was ready for the bait to be swallowed, up came a United States destroyer at high speed to 'rescue' this 'tramp.' The submarine was frightened away, and *Vala* lost her fish. Then one day Bernays took *Vala* on another cruise. What happened exactly we do not know, but evidently a submarine got her, and sank her without a trace, for neither ship nor crew was ever heard of again.

Bernays was just the man for Q-ship work. He was one whom you would describe as a 'rough customer,' who might have stepped out of a Wild West cinema. A hard swearer in an acquired American accent, in port also a hard drinker; but on going to sea he kept everything locked up, and not even his officers were allowed to touch a drop till they got back to harbour. The first time I met him was at 3 o'clock one bitterly cold winter's morning in Grimsby. It was blowing a gale of wind and it was snowing. Some of his minesweepers had broken adrift and come down on to the top of my craft, and were doing her no good. There was nothing for it but to rouse Bernays. His way of handling men, and these rough North Sea fishermen, was a revelation. It was a mixture of hard Navy, Prussianism, and Canadian 'get-to-hell-out-of-this-darned-hole.' There was no coaxing in his voice;

every syllable was a challenge to a fight. On the forebridge of his trawler he used to keep a bucket containing lumps of coal, and in giving an order would at times accentuate his forcible and coloured words by heaving a lump at any of his slow-thinking crew.

Having said all this, you may wonder there was never a mutiny; but such a state of affairs was the last thing that could ever happen in any of Bernays' ships. From a weak man the crew would not have stood this treatment a day, but they understood him, they respected him, they loved him, and in his command of the English tongue they realized that he was like unto themselves, but more adept. Follow him? They followed him everywhere—through the North Sea, through Russian and Irish minefields, and relied on him implicitly. And this regard was mutual, for in spite of his rugged manner Bernays had a heart, and he thought the world of his crew. I remember how pleased he was the day he was ordered to go to the dangerous Tory Island minefield. 'But I'm not going without my old crew; they're the very best in the world.' Bernays, as an American officer once remarked, 'certainly was some tough proposition,' but he knew no cowardice; he did his brave duty, and he rests in a sailor's grave.

Another of these thirteen was the converted sloop *Begonia*, commanded by Lieut.-Commander Basil S. Noake, R.N., an officer of altogether different temperament. Keen and able, yet courteous and gentle of manner, tall, thin, and suffering somewhat from deafness, this gallant officer, too, paid the great penalty. For *Begonia* was destined to have no ordinary career. Built as a minesweeping sloop, she carried out escort and patrol work until one day she was holed, but managed to get into Queenstown. Here she was repaired and transformed into a decoy, with a counter added instead of her cruiser stern, and with the addition of derricks and so on she was a very clever deception. During one cruise she was evidently a victim to the enemy, for she disappeared, too.

The remaining ships of this thirteen were the *Acton* (Lieut.-Commander C. N. Rolfe, R.N.), *Zylpha* (Lieut.-Commander John K. McLeod, R.N.), *Cullist* (Lieut.-Commander S. H. Simpson, D.S.O., R.N.), *Tamarisk* (Lieut.-Commander John W. Williams, D.S.O., R.N.R.), *Viola* (Lieut.-Commander F. A. Frank, D.S.O., R.N.R.), *Salvia* (Lieut.-Commander W. Olphert, D.S.O., D.S.C., R.N.R.), *Laggan* (Lieutenant C. J. Alexander, R.N.R.), and *Heather* (Lieutenant Harold Auten, R.N.R.). In this list there is scarcely a name that did not receive before the end of the war at least one D.S.O., while two of them received the Victoria Cross.

Acton had an indecisive duel with a submarine on August 20, 1917. It was a fine day with a calm sea when the enemy was sighted, and on being attacked *Acton* abandoned ship. In order to make this doubly real, fire-boxes were started in the well-deck, and steam leakage turned on, which made the ship look as if she were on fire. The enemy inspected the ship closely, so closely in fact that he actually collided with *Acton*, shaking the latter fore and aft. But after he had come to the surface and *Acton* opened fire, hitting, loud shouts came from the conning-tower, and he submerged, thus escaping. *Acton* went on with her work until the end of hostilities.

Zylpha and *Cullist* both had tragic ends to their careers. *Zylpha* was a 2,917-ton steamer, built at

Sunderland in 1894, and had been commissioned as a Q-ship as far back as October, 1915. Early in June, 1917, she steamed along the south Irish coast and then out into the Atlantic, as if bound for New York. On June 11, at 9.45 a.m., when about 200 miles from the Irish coast, she was torpedoed by a submarine that was never seen again, and totally disabled. Her engines had stopped for the last time, and the sea had poured in, though her closely-packed cargo of wood was at present keeping her afloat. Having 'bleated' with her wireless, one of the United States destroyers, based on Queenstown, proceeded to her assistance. This was the *Warrington*, and she stood by the ship for a whole twenty-four hours—from 2 p.m. of the eleventh until 2.30 p.m. of the twelfth. By the time *Warrington* had arrived *Zylpha's* engine-room and boiler-rooms were already awash, Nos. 2 and 3 holds flooded, the wireless out of action, and one man killed. The *Warrington* kept patrolling round her, requested a tug by wireless, and went on zigzagging through the long hours. By the evening *Zylpha* was in a bad way, and the Atlantic swell was seriously shaking the bulkheads, but she was still afloat next morning. By this time the *Warrington*, who had been some time on patrol, was running short of oil, so, at 2.30 p.m., regretfully had to return to harbour for fuel.

This was a sad blow to the *Zylpha* people, but whilst waiting for the arrival of the U.S. destroyer *Drayton* and two Queenstown tugs which were being sent to her, *Zylpha* actually made sail with what little canvas she had, and made good at $1\frac{1}{2}$ knots. At noon of the fourteenth she was picked up by H.M. sloop *Daffodil*, and was then taken in tow. Next day, at 1 p.m., tugs reached her, but she could not last out the night, and, after having been towed for most of 200 miles, she gradually sank when quite near to the west coast, finally disappearing at 11.20 p.m. near the Great Skelligs. So ended *Zylpha*.

Cullist was commanded by an officer who had served a long time off this coast in a sloop. Her real name was the *Westphalia*, but she was also known as the *Jurassic*, *Hayling*, and *Prim*. She was of 1,030 gross tons, and in the spring of 1917 was lying at Calais, when she was requisitioned and sent to Pembroke Naval Dockyard to be fitted out. She was commissioned on May 12 by Lieut.-Commander Simpson, and Admiral Bayly then sent her to cruise along certain trade routes. She was capable of steaming about 10 knots, and was armed with a 4-inch and two 12-pounder guns, as well as a couple of torpedo-tubes, and all these had been well concealed. A few weeks later, on July 13, *Cullist* was between the Irish and French coasts, and it was just after 1 p.m. when a submarine appeared on the horizon.

About two minutes later the enemy from very long range opened fire, but as his shots were falling about 3,000 yards short, he increased speed towards the *Cullist*. By 1.30 a large merchant ship was seen coming up from the south, so *Cullist* hoisted the signal ' You are standing into danger,' whereupon the big steamer altered course away. *Cullist* then zig-zagged, keeping always between sun and enemy, and by dropping eight smoke-boxes at various intervals succeeded in enticing the submarine down to a range of 5,000 yards, a distance which was maintained for the rest of the action. From 1.45 the enemy continually straddled *Cullist* so that the decks were wet with the splashes, and shell splinters were rattling on masts and deck. By 2.7 the enemy had fired sixty-eight rounds, but had not hit once. *Cullist* now decided to engage, and her third round was seen to hit just below the submarine's gun, the remainder hitting regularly along the deck and on the conning-tower, causing bright red flames which rose higher than the conning-tower. Three minutes after *Cullist* had opened fire the enemy sank by the bows in flames, and then the ship steamed to the spot and dropped a depth charge. Three of *Cullist's* crew saw a corpse dressed in blue dungarees, floating face upwards, but the submarine was never seen again. By 3.30 H.M.S. *Christopher* arrived on the scene and both ships searched for the enemy. He was evidently seriously damaged, but he had made his escape. Lieut.-Commander Simpson, for this engagement, was awarded a D.S.O.; Lieutenant G. Spencer, R.N.R., a D.S.C.; Sub-Lieutenant G. H. D. Doubleday, R.N.R., also a D.S.C.; while two other officers were 'mentioned.'

Cullist's next adventure was on August 20 in the English Channel, when she was shelled for most of two and a half hours at long range, during which the submarine expended over eighty rounds with only one hit. This, however, had penetrated the waterline of the stokehold, injuring both firemen who happened to be on watch, and causing a large rush of water into the stokehold. By plugging the hole and shoring it up this defect was for the present made good. At 7.25 p.m., inasmuch as the light was fading and the enemy declined to come nearer than 4,000 yards, *Cullist* started shelling and seemed to make two direct hits on the base of the conning-tower. This was enough for the German, who then dived very rapidly and made off. *Cullist* was practically uninjured, for the only other hits on her had been that the port depth charge had been struck with shell splinters and the patent log-line had been shot away.

But on the eleventh of the following February a much more serious attack was made, and this illustrates the statement that suddenly without the slightest warning a Q-ship might find herself in the twinkling of an eye changed from an efficient man-of-war into a mere wreck. *Cullist* at the time was steaming on a southerly course down the Irish Sea, Kingstown Harbour being to the westward. The officer of the watch and the look-out men were at their posts, and Lieut.-Commander Simpson was walking up and down the deck. Suddenly, from nowhere, the track of a torpedo was seen approaching, and this struck the ship between the engine-room and No. 3 hold. Lieut.-Commander Simpson was hurled into the air and came down on to the edge of the deck with a very painful arm. Realizing the condition of the *Cullist*, he ordered his men to abandon ship, but such was the zeal of the crew in remaining at action stations until the last moment that many of them were drowned: for in less than two minutes *Cullist* had gone to the bottom. This part of the Irish Sea then consisted of a number of Englishmen swimming about or keeping alive on one of the large improvised wooden rafts which had been kept specially rigged and provisioned ready for the inevitable day that was expected sooner or later. The submarine when half a mile astern of where *Cullist* sank, came to the surface and rapidly approached. Then she stopped, picked up two men, inquired for the captain, examined survivors through glasses, and having abused them by words and gestures, made off to the southward. After swimming about for some time, Lieut.-Commander Simpson was then pulled on to one of these rafts—the only one that got clear of the ship. It was a bleak February afternoon, and here were a few men able to keep from death by joining hands on this crowded raft. As the hours went on, the usual trying thirst assailed them and the fatal temptation to drink the sea-water, but the captain wisely and sternly prevented this. How long they would be left crowded in this ridiculous raft, cold and miserable, no one knew: it was obvious that human strength could not last out indefinitely.

But just as it was getting dusk, about 6 p.m., a trawler was seen. Relief at last! Someone held up an oar in the raft to make it more easy for the trawler to recognize them. It was a patrol trawler, for the gun was visible; in a few moments they would be rescued. But just then these sopping-wet survivors were horrified to see the trawler manning her gun and laying it on to the raft. What hideous mistake was this? 'Sing at the top of your voices.' So they sang 'Tipperary' with all the strength they had left. Then a slight pause was followed by the trawler dismissing the gun's crew and coming towards them as quickly as her engines would go round. The survivors were picked up and taken into Kingstown, where they landed about 10 p.m., and none too soon for some of them. By the time they were in hospital they were almost done. But what was the trawler's explanation? She had sighted something in the half-light which resembled a submarine, and on examining it again it still more resembled such a craft. It was only when the unmistakable sound of British voices chanting 'Tipperary' reached their ears that they looked again and found that the 'periscope' was the oar, and the 'conning-tower' was the men linked together on the raft.

But it had been a near thing, for owing to the approaching darkness, the visibility was limited!

Even more varied was the career of the *Privet* (alias *Island Queen*, Q 19, *Swisher*, and *Alcala*). This was a small steamer of 803 tons, which had begun her service in December, 1916, her captain being Lieut.-Commander C. G. Matheson, R.N.R. On the following twelfth of March she was on passage from Land's End to Alderney, and was steaming at 9 knots, when just before three in the afternoon a torpedo was seen to pass under the ship at the engine-room. *Privet* was presently shelled by the submarine, who rose to the surface on the starboard side aft, the first nine rounds hitting *Privet* five times. One of these rounds burst among the 'abandon ship' party, causing many casualties and destroying the falls of both boats. *Privet's* hull had been badly holed, and she was compelled to send out a wireless S.O.S. signal, stating that her engines were disabled, but two minutes later she opened fire with her port battery—she was armed with four 12-pounders—and during the first seven rounds the enemy received punishment, being hit abreast the fore part of the conning-tower, and twice well abaft the conning-tower. The German now tried to escape by submerging, but evidently he found his hull leaking so badly that he was seen trying to reach the surface again by using his engines and hydroplanes. Thus *Privet* managed to get in a couple more hits and then the U-boat disappeared stern first at an angle of forty-five degrees. *Privet* in this manner had definitely sunk U 85, belonging to the biggest U-class submarines, 230 feet long, armed with two guns and twelve torpedoes. The whole incident, from the moment the torpedo was fired to the destruction of the attacker, had covered forty minutes; but now, ten minutes later, *Privet's* engine-room was reported to be filling up with water owing to one of the enemy's shells getting home. Twenty minutes later the chief engineer reported that the water was now over the plates and rising. Efforts were made to plug the hole with hammocks and timber, but this was found impossible, and this small ship, in spite of her victory, was in great peril. After another few minutes the men and wounded were ordered into the lifeboat and skiff, for the engine-room was full of water and the after bulkhead might give way suddenly any minute. Half an hour later this actually happened, but by this time the two British destroyers *Christopher* and *Orestes* had arrived on the scene.

Privet was in a pitiable condition, and, after throwing overboard confidential books and rendering the depth charges safe, she was finally abandoned, though she did not at once sink. In fact, an hour and a half later she was still afloat; so Lieut.-Commander Matheson, his officers, a seaman, and a working party from *Orestes* went back on board her, and within an hour *Orestes* had begun to tow her under great difficulties. However, everything went fairly well until they were approaching Plymouth Sound, when *Privet's* last bulkheads collapsed, and she started now to settle down quickly. This was rather hard luck, having regard to what she had gone through, but there was no mistake about it, she was sinking fast. Those in charge of her are to be congratulated, for they were able just in time to get her into shoal water, and she sank in only $4\frac{1}{2}$ fathoms opposite the Picklecomb Fort, and that closed chapter one in her not uninteresting career.

From this position she was very soon raised, taken into Devonport, and recommissioned at the end of April. Thus, having sunk a submarine and herself being sunk, she returned to the same kind of work, and actually succeeded in sinking another submarine on the night of November 8-9, 1918, this being the last to be destroyed before Armistice. The incident occurred in the Mediterranean and the submarine was U 34. Truly a remarkable career for such a small steamer, but a great tribute to all those brains and hands who in the first instance fitted her out, fought in her, got her into Plymouth Sound, salved her, fitted her out again, took her to sea, and undauntedly vanquished the enemy once more! In the whole realm of naval history there are not many ships that can claim such a record against an enemy.

Another trying incident was that which occurred to the 1,295-ton steamer *Mavis* (alias Q 26 and *Nyroca*), armed with a 4-inch and two 12-pounders. This vessel had been fitted out at Devonport, her Merchant Service cranes being landed and replaced by dummy derricks. The hatches to her holds were plated over, access to the same being provided by manholes. In order to give her the maximum chance should she ever be torpedoed, she was ballasted with closely packed firewood; and only those who have seen torpedoed ships carrying a cargo of timber can realize for what a long time such an apparently sinking ship will keep afloat, though necessarily deep in the water. I remember, during the war, the case of a steamer torpedoed off Brow Head (south-west Ireland) after she had just arrived from across the Atlantic. She was deserted by her crew, the sea was over the floors of her upper-deck cabins, and she was obviously a brute to steer in such an unseaworthy condition, but with great difficulty and some patience we managed to tow her into port, where, owing to her sinking condition, she drew so much water that she touched the ground every low tide. But she was salved and eventually patched up. It was her timber cargo which had kept her afloat just long enough, and inasmuch as ship and freight were worth no less than £250,000, this was more than worth while. So it was with *Mavis*.

On the last day of May, 1917, under command of Commander Adrian Keyes, R.N., this Q-ship had left Devonport to cruise in the Atlantic. At 6.45 a.m. on June 2 she sighted a ship's lifeboat coming along under sail and found it contained three men who were in a very exhausted condition. These were the survivors from the Greek S.S. *N. Hadziaka*, which had been torpedoed and sunk a little further to the westward. This torpedoing had occurred in a heavy sea, and in lowering away the boats, one of them had been smashed and the other swamped. The captain and twenty-two men had clung to the wreckage when the German submarine broke surface, approached, but made no attempt at rescue, and then went away. For forty-eight hours these wretched men kept more or less alive in the water and then gradually dropped off one by one until only three remained. These then managed to patch one boat, upright her, bale her out, and make sail. They had been sailing for ten hours during the night when they had the good luck to be picked up by *Mavis*, having been fifty-eight hours without food or water.

Having rescued them, *Mavis* continued on her western course, but after dark turned east, setting a course to pass 10 miles south of the Lizard. During the following day she passed through considerable wreckage. At 9.45 p.m. she was 20 miles south of the Wolf Rock when a torpedo was seen to break surface 40 yards from the ship on the starboard beam. It struck *Mavis* abreast of the engine-room and penetrated the side, so that the ship stopped at once, and both engine-room and boiler-room were flooded. It was impossible to send out a wireless call, as the emergency apparatus had been wrecked too, but three rockets were fired and eventually the destroyer *Christopher* came up, followed later by the trawler *Whitefriars* and several tugs. Then began the difficult and slow process of towing, and they got her just inside Plymouth Sound, but by this time she was in such a crank condition that it was feared she might capsize, so they managed to beach her in Cawsand Bay on the west side of the Sound. It was her ballast of firewood that had saved her from total loss, and for this both British and Greeks must have felt more than thankful.

Another incident, which well illustrates the risks run by these Q-ships, is now to be related. Among those officers who had retired from the Service and come back after the outbreak of war was Commander W. O'G. Cochrane, R.N., who for part of the war was captain of one of the sloops off the south of Ireland. In the spring of 1917 I well remember the very excellent sport we had in company, but in separate ships, exploring and destroying the minefields laid by the enemy submarines right along the whole south coast from Cape Clear to the Old Head of Kinsale. At the beginning of the following November, Commander Cochrane left Devonport in command of the Q-ship *Candytuft*, together with a convoy of merchant ships bound for Gibraltar. *Candytuft* was disguised to represent a tramp steamer,

Q-SHIP "CANDYTUFT"

This Q-ship had the misfortune to be attacked by a submarine who used torpedoes to blow both the bow and stern off the Q-ship. The "Candytuft" was afterwards beached on the North African coast.

and on the eighth, when in the vicinity of Cape St. Vincent, had an encounter with a submarine, in which the usual tactics were employed. One of the enemy's shells struck the Q-ship's bridge, exploding under the bunk in Captain Cochrane's cabin, wrecking the wireless and steering-gear. *Candytuft* was able to fire three shots, but the enemy disappeared, made off, and was never seen by the Q-ship again.

After having been repaired at Gibraltar, *Candytuft* left in company with the merchant ship *Tremayne* for Malta. This was on November 16. Two days later they were off Cap Sigli, when a torpedo crossed *Tremayne's* bows, but struck *Candytuft* on the starboard quarter, entirely blowing off the ship's stern and killing all the officers excepting Captain Cochrane and Lieutenant Phillips, R.N.R., who was on the bridge, but very badly wounding Lieutenant Errington, R.N.R.

With sound judgment and true unselfishness Captain Cochrane now ordered *Tremayne* to make for Bougie as fast as she could, and in the meantime the Q-ship hoisted her foresail to assist the ship to drift inshore. Most of the ship's company were sent away in boats, only sufficient being kept aboard to man the two 4-inch guns, and everyone kept out of sight. Within half an hour a periscope was seen by Captain Cochrane, concealed behind the bridge screens. A periscope is a poor target, but it was fired at, though ineffectually. On came the torpedo, striking *Candytuft* just forward of the bridge, completely wrecking the fore part of the ship. This explosion wounded several men in a boat, covered the bridge with coal barrows and other miscellaneous wreckage, blew a leading-seaman overboard—happily he was picked up unhurt—blew Captain Cochrane up also, but some of the falling wreckage struck him on the head, knocked him back inboard, and left him staggering off the bridge.

Presently the ship gave a sudden jerk, and rid herself of her bow, which now floated away and sank. *Candytuft* drifted towards the African shore, and after the captain and one of his crew had gallantly closed the watertight door at the foreward end of the mess-deck, up to their middles in water and working in almost complete darkness, with tables and other articles washing about, it became time for these last two to leave the ship. They were taken off by a French armed trawler and landed at Bougie. *Candytuft*, minus bow and stern, drifted ashore on to a sandy beach, and eventually the two 4-inch guns were salved. Lieutenant Errington had died before reaching land, and the wounded had to be left in hospital. But afterwards some of *Candytuft's* crew went to sea in another Q-ship, and so the whole gallant story went on. Ships may be torpedoed, but, like the soldiers, sailors never die. They keep on 'keeping on' all the time, as a young seaman once was heard to remark.

Q-SHIP "CANDYTUFT"

This shows some of the damage done by the enemy submarine's torpedo. She is lying beached and one of the guns is being salved and lowered down the side.

CHAPTER XIII

MORE SAILING-SHIP FIGHTS

IF, in accordance with the delightful legend, Drake during the recent war had heard the beating of his drum and had 'quit the port o' Heaven,' come back to life again in the service of his Sovereign and country, he would assuredly have gone to sea in command of a Q-sailing-ship. His would have been the Victoria Cross and D.S.O. with bars, and we can see him bringing his much battered ship into Plymouth Sound as did his spiritual descendants in the Great War. And yet, with all the halo of his name, it is impossible to imagine that, great seaman as he was, his deeds would be more valiant than those we are now recording.

If we had, so to speak, put the clock back by the re-introduction of the fighting sailing ship, it was an anachronism that was well justified by results. More of these craft and various rigs were still being taken up. In the spring of 1917 the topsail schooner *Dargle* was requisitioned, fitted out at Granton with a 4-inch and two 12-pounders, and then sent to Lerwick, whence she operated. Similarly the ketch *George L. Muir* (alias *G. L. Munro*, *G.L.M.*, and *Padre*), which was accustomed to trade between Kirkwall and the Firth of Forth, was chartered and armed with a 12-pounder.

On April 22, 1917, the 174-ton auxiliary barquentine

Gaelic (otherwise known as *Brig* 11, *Gobo*, and Q 22), which had been taken up at the end of 1916, and was armed with a couple of 12-pounders, had a very plucky fight. She had left Falmouth on the nineteenth under the command of Lieutenant G. Irvine, R.N.R., and at 6.30 p.m. was now 48 miles south of the Old Head of Kinsale, steering S.E. under all fore-and-aft sail. It was a fine, clear day, the sea was calm, there was little wind, but the ship was making about 2 knots under sail and starboard motor. It was a quiet Sunday evening: one of those gentle spring days which came gladly to the Irish coast after the long nights and continuous gales of the dark winter. The watch, consisting of four men, were all aloft getting in the square sails, when one of them hailed the deck that he could see a submarine about four points on the starboard bow. She was distant about 5,000 yards to the southward and steering to the N.W. at slow speed.

Hands were called down from aloft immediately, and action stations sounded on the alarm gong. The enemy began the tactics of keeping well away from the ship and firing shell after shell, of which six hit the *Gaelic*, killing two of the deckhands and wounding four, besides putting the port motor out of action and seriously damaging the rigging. For a time both vessels maintained their respective courses, and when the enemy was bearing a couple of points abaft *Gaelic's* starboard beam, the sailing ship unmasked her guns and opened fire. It was now 6.50; the enemy had already fired twenty rounds, but as soon as the attack was returned he altered course and despatched a torpedo at 4,000 yards. This luckily *Gaelic* was able to avoid in time by starboarding her helm so that the torpedo missed by about 150 yards, passing parallel along the starboard side. *Gaelic's* forward gun had now fired three shots, but her fourth hit the submarine. By a piece of bad luck, soon after this, the firing pin of the port forward gun broke and the gun was temporarily out of action, so *Gaelic* had to be brought round until the starboard guns would bear. Thus the fight went on until 7.20 p.m., when the enemy came round under port helm and started to move slowly away to the S.W., still firing. Another trouble now occurred in the barquentine. One of the shells had caused the fresh-water tank on deck to leak. This water then came through a hole in the deck on to the starboard engine, putting it out of action, and so with both engines useless and no wind the unfortunate *Gaelic* could not be manœuvred, though the guns continued to bear. Firing was maintained and two more hits were scored on the German target. About eight o'clock the submarine ceased fire, ported his helm, headed towards the barquentine, and ten minutes later, the range being still 4,000 yards, *Gaelic* hit him again. This was the end of the action, each craft having fired about 110 rounds. It seems pretty certain that though the submarine was not sunk she was badly knocked about, for she broke off the engagement and dived. A hand was sent aloft who reported that he could distinctly see the submarine below making to the south-east. *Gaelic* did her best to follow, but by this time darkness was rapidly setting in, so with both motors useless, sails and rigging also in a dreadful condition, she set a course for the Old Head of Kinsale, and at daybreak, when 10 miles short of that landfall, was picked up by H.M. sloop *Bluebell* and towed into Queenstown. She was then refitted and eventually went out to the Mediterranean, being based on Gibraltar.

Allusion has been made in another chapter to the auxiliary schooner *Glen* (alias *Sidney* and *Athos*), which began her special service on April 5, 1917, under Lieutenant R. J. Turnbull, R.N.R. On May 17 she had a most successful duel, in which she managed to sink the small UB 39, one of those submarines about 121 feet long, and possessing extreme surface speed of 8½ knots, which, armed with one gun and four torpedoes, used to come out from Zeebrugge, negotiate the Dover Straits—for which she was fitted with a net-cutter at the bows—and then operate in the English Channel. The enemy's gun was a 22-pounder; *Glen* carried a 12-pounder and a 3-pounder. It was six o'clock in the evening, and *Glen* was about 35 miles south of the Needles, steering north-east, close hauled on the starboard tack, the wind being E. by S., force 4. There was a moderate sea on, and the ship was bowling along under all sail. Suddenly out of nowhere a shot was heard, and five minutes later could be seen the flash of a second, and UB 39 was sighted to the southward, 2½ miles away. *Glen* therefore backed her fore-yard, and eased away all sheets, so as to check her way. The submarine then ceased firing, but her captain must have been one of those less experienced men, who were characteristic of the later stages of the war, and did foolish things; for he was indiscreet enough in this case to close schooner, who then 'abandoned ship.' On came the German and submerged when 800 yards off until only her periscope and part of her bridge dodger were showing. Still she approached until now she was only 200 yards distant, steering a course parallel with the schooner on the latter's starboard side. All this happened so quickly that the 'panic party' were just leaving the ship, when UB 39 rose to the surface just abaft the schooner's beam, and now only 80 yards off. For such temerity the German, who must have been amazingly credulous, paid with his life. Lieutenant Turnbull gave the order for 'action,' and within five seconds the first shot from the 12-pounder was fired, which fell over the submarine abaft the conning-tower. The enemy was evidently quite surprised, for the hatch in the conning-tower was now opened, and there appeared the head and shoulders of a man who seemed dazed, and as the second 12-pounder shell came bursting on the hull under the conning-tower this man apparently fell back down the hatch.

The submarine now commenced to dive, and as the stern rose out of the water the third and fourth shots from the same gun burst on the after part of the hull in the middle line, the holes made by these three shots being plainly visible to those in the schooner. The 3-pounder had also come into action, and out of six rounds the second shot had hit the hull on the water-line forward of the conning-tower, the third had hit her on the water-line under the gun, the fourth and fifth bursting on the after part of the hull just as she was sinking, and the sixth bursting on the water as her stern disappeared. Badly holed, leaking from all these holes, UB 39 listed over to port towards the schooner, vanished from sight for evermore, and then a large quantity of oil and bubbles came to the surface. There were no survivors.

Having definitely disposed of the enemy, it would be reasonable for the crew of the *Glen* to feel elated; but just as UB 39 was finally disappearing, another submarine was seen approaching about 4,000 yards off on the starboard bow. *Glen* opened fire and the enemy submerged, only to reappear about 600 yards away on the port bow. *Glen* fired once more, and next time the submarine appeared a few minutes later on the port quarter 1,000 yards off. This was happening while the 'panic party' were being got on board again, and thus there was every risk of being torpedoed; but *Glen* then proceeded on a northerly course under sail and motor, and at 7.30 p.m. a very large submarine was observed 2 miles away on the starboard beam, heading in about the same direction. After ten minutes this submarine opened fire, then turned to pass astern, and continued firing with both her guns, which *Glen* answered with both of hers. About 8 p.m. the duel ceased; the enemy disappeared to the west on the look-out evidently for a less obstinate ship. If you examine the positions on the chart you will realize that the enemy submarines were evidently concentrated in mid-Channel in order to entrap shipping coming up and down and across the English Channel. They were so placed as to cut the lines of communication to Cherbourg and at the same time have a good chance of bagging some liner bound up along.

This concentration at important centres was noticeable during the submarine campaign; in fact, but a few weeks later *Glen* was again engaged with an enemy in the same vicinity. This was on June 25, the exact position was 14 miles S. by W. of St. Catherine's Point, and the schooner was sailing close hauled on the starboard tack, heading S.W. by S., doing her 2 knots, when she sighted a vessel apparently under sail on her port quarter 4 miles distant. Presently this vessel fired at her, the shot falling 1,000 yards short. This, of course, was a submarine, and it was a not unusual thing to attempt disguise by this means; for obviously a low-lying craft on the surface viewed from a distance would create suspicion. But, parenthetically, it may be mentioned that this sail device was not always carried out with common sense, and I remember on one occasion a submarine giving himself hopelessly away by motoring at good speed in the eye of the wind with his sail of course shaking wildly. Such an unseamanlike act was at once spotted by the nearest patrol, and the submarine had to dive so hurriedly that she left the sail on the water.

In the case of *Glen* the recognition was obvious as soon as the first shot was fired. Several minutes later came another, which fell only 60 yards short, so *Glen* hove-to and 'abandoned' ship, the enemy continuing to fire every few minutes, but the shots fell just over. Her seventh and eighth shots fell much closer, in fact so near that their splash flooded the schooner's deck, and shell splinters struck the sails and bulwarks. *Glen* then opened fire with both guns, but this was a more cautious submarine, who declined to approach nearer than 4,000 yards, fired three more rounds, then submerged and made off.

The activity of the submarines during this week in the neighbourhood of Portland Bill was most noticeable. Submarines were also stationed in the western approaches of the English Channel. The reason for this is not hard to appreciate, for it was on June 26, the day after the above engagement, that the first contingent of U.S.A. troops landed in France on the western coast. Whether the transports would be bound up Channel to Cherbourg or Southampton, the enemy submarines were lying in wait ready for them. And it is significant that also on June 26 the Q-sailing-ship *Gaelic* sighted a submarine at the western entrance of the English Channel and had a short duel with her.

On July 2 *Gaelic* had another indecisive duel, and on the tenth *Glen* (now commanded by Sub-Lieutenant K. Morris, R.N.R.) once more was in action. This time she was further down Channel, about 45 miles S.W. of Portland Bill. In this incident the enemy fired several rifle-shots at the panic party rowing in the boat. An officer appeared at the conning-tower presently, hailed this rowing boat, and in good English ordered her to come alongside. The boat began to do so, but just then something seemed suddenly to startle the officer, and he disappeared into the conning-tower. *Glen* opened fire, and the submarine—one of the UC type—submerged. She was not sunk, but she had been damaged, and Sub-Lieutenant Morris was awarded the D.S.C.

We saw just now that submarines were very fond of hanging about on the approach to Cherbourg. There was a sound reason for this. The coal-fields of France were in the hands of the enemy, consequently it fell to us to keep France supplied. From February, 1917, a system was organized which was the real beginning of the convoy method soon afterwards adopted with such beneficial results to our shipping. This embryonic organization was known as the 'F.C.T.'—French Coal-Trade Traffic. The ships would load coal up the Bristol Channel and then sail independently round to Weymouth Bay. Having thus collected, they were sailed across to Cherbourg together in a group, protection being afforded by trawlers during daylight and moonlight hours only. As one looked at this heterogeneous collection of craft, some of them of great age, lying at anchor off Weymouth Harbour, they seemed distinctly a curious lot; but there was a great dearth of shipping at that time, and any old vessel that could carry coal and go ahead was worth her weight in gold. The system was found most successful, and other group sailings on definite routes, such as Falmouth-Brest and Dover-Dunkirk, were instituted.

The next development was to have one or two Q-ships among the convoys, for the most obvious of reasons, and especially well astern of the convoy, so that the enemy might take them for stragglers and sink them before any of the escort could turn back and help. Then came a still further development, which had been in the minds of many naval officers for a long time. Since there was such a scarcity of tonnage available for general purposes, why not let the Q-ship, instead of carrying ballast, be loaded with a proper cargo? She could easily carry this without interfering with her fighting ability: in fact, she would be trimmed more normally, and rather increase than decrease her power of deception. As to the possibility of secrecy being lost whilst loading in port, the armament was very cleverly concealed and only a little organization was necessary to prevent her true character being bruited about. The main difficulty would be when in the presence of neutral shipping in that particular harbour, but this problem was capable of solution.

Thus it happened now that in many cases the Q-ship became also a trader. Be it noted, her character was not that of an armed merchant ship which is armed only defensively, but a properly commissioned warship carrying cargo as well as her offensive armament. Now, one of these craft was the two-masted 179-ton brigantine *Probus* (alias **Q 30**, *Ready, Thirza, Elixir*). She had been purchased by the Admiralty in 1915, and fitted with an auxiliary motor. Then, based on Granton, she had worked as a decoy in the North Sea.

In May, 1917, having done excellent work as a pure decoy, we find her as a decoy-trader. Having loaded up with coal at Granton, she left there on May 4, and duly arrived at Treguier. From there she proceeded to Swansea with a cargo of pit-props, which were much needed by the Welsh coal mines, seeing that our customary supply from Scandinavia, via the North Sea, was so endangered at that time. From Swansea *Probus*, who was armed with two 12-pounders and two 6-pounders, sailed round to Falmouth, and at 3.30 on the afternoon of June 20 she set sail for Morlaix in company with twelve sailing ships and the one steamship escort, the armed trawler *Harlech Castle*. Think of it in these modern days: a dozen sailing vessels coming out past St. Anthony's Lighthouse! Truly this war has shown how history goes on repeating itself. Who would have thought that sailing-ship convoys, which in other wars used to assemble and leave Falmouth, would ever be witnessed again?

Now, to control a dozen sail you must have sea-room, so the convoy was arranged thus: A mile ahead of the first sailing ship steamed the trawler, then came the twelve ships spread over 3 miles, and then 4 miles astern of the last ship, and looking just as a straggler would be, sailed the *Probus*. There was thus a distance of 8 miles between her and the escort trawler. Most of a day passed before anything occurred. At 2.15 p.m. on June 21 *Probus*, still astern of the convoy, was about 23 miles south-west of the Start and heading on a course S.E. by S. The wind was S.W., force 3, and she was doing about

4 knots through the water, when she observed what appeared to be a ketch-rigged vessel, steering the same course, 4 miles away on the starboard quarter; but from the rapidity with which the bearing altered, it was soon obvious that the ketch was not under sail alone. At 2.30 p.m. the 'ketch' proved her submarine identity by opening fire, the first shot falling 10 yards clear of the brigantine's beam. *Probus* then hove-to, the crew went to action stations, and the boat was got ready to be launched, while the submarine kept up a rapid fire from about 4,000 yards, shells falling unpleasantly close. By now *Probus* was heading about S.W. with fore-yards aback, and, owing to the light wind, was making a stern board. Then her head fell round slowly to the west. The enemy was now bearing about W. to W.S.W., firing rapidly, and heading to the south-east so as to cross the brigantine's bows. It was a beautifully clear summer's afternoon, and you could see the convoy and the smoke from the escorting trawler quite easily. After the submarine had maintained a continuous long-range fire for ten minutes, *Probus* ran up the White Ensign, and at 3,500 yards opened fire with her starboard 12-pounder. The first round fell 500 yards short, but the crew of the submarine's gun hurriedly left their station and made for the conning-tower. The second shot seemed to be a hit, for the enemy, lying across the brigantine's bows, stopped, and a large cloud of smoke went up, and he temporarily ceased fire.

Probus then went about on the other tack, and the enemy took advantage of this to resume firing, while shots began to fall all round; but the port 12-pounder of the British ship now came into action, and the fourth shot was certainly another hit, for it dismantled the German's sails and mast, and raised a cloud of smoke from the fore part of the conning-tower. Shelling continued, and the enemy was compelled to submerge, *Probus's* parting shot hitting him on the top of the conning-tower. It was now about 3.30 p.m., and nothing was seen of the German until a quarter of an hour later, when he was sighted 6 miles away approaching *Probus*. He had probably been stopping his shell-holes, and was now ready to give the sailing ship the knock-out blow; but the armed trawler, with its fishermen crew eager to have a hand in the fight, was by this time making towards the submarine, and this compelled the German to break off the engagement and scurry to the north-east.

Unfortunately this duel demonstrated yet again the great weakness of the sailing ship as a man-of-war. In the olden days, when the swift-moving galley fought the sailing carrack or caravel, the galley was able to press home her attack if the weather fell light, and left the other ship rolling helpless in the calm, with yards and tackle grievously creaking and chafing. The submarine is the modern galley, and the Q-sailing-ship is the carrack's counterpart. As long as there was a good breeze she could be manœuvred, and if there was a hard breeze it would make it difficult for the enemy's gunnery. *Probus* was practically becalmed, so the submarine could run rings round her, and the sailing ship could not be worked up to windward. Of course, on these and similar occasions troubles seldom come singly; for when the brigantine *Probus* made a stern board her starboard propeller had fouled the log-line, so this was out of action. However, *Probus* resumed her original course, followed the convoy, and in spite of the light airs duly arrived at Morlaix on June 25.

Q-SAILING SHIP "FRESH HOPE"

This was a 900-ton three-masted schooner which was requisitioned in the last year of the war. She had previously been the United States "Edith E. Cummins."

Q-SHIP "RECORD REIGN"

This apparently peaceful ketch was one of those armed mystery sailing ships which came into service during the last year of the war.

MORE SAILING-SHIP FIGHTS 189

Although the submarine escaped, *Probus* had succeeded in luring him from the convoy, and had sent him right away. These sailing Q-ships became, in fact, one of the best types of escort for other sailing vessels in convoy, and thus allowed armed steam patrol vessels to be employed elsewhere. Looking in no way different from the rest of the convoy, but fitted with concealed wireless and, later, even with howitzer armament, they had a much better chance than the armed trawler or destroyer of enticing the submarine. Apart altogether from these important considerations, the scheme of carrying freights was a big financial success, and *Probus* paid for herself over and over again. It was nothing unusual for her to earn over £1,000 a month. Naturally enough, then, we find other sailing ships being taken up for this dual work. In November, 1917, the 900-ton three-masted fore-and-aft schooner *Fresh Hope*, lying at Granton, was requisitioned. She had formerly been the United States' *Edith E. Cummins*, and in a fresh breeze could log her 12 knots. Known also as the *Iroquois*, she was fitted out and commissioned by the first week of April, 1918, and served until the Armistice. Other sailing vessels were thus commissioned in 1918, specially selected as being able to carry each at least one 4-inch and two 12-pounders, and to be fitted with auxiliary engines. These were the *Rentoul, Imogene, Viola, Cymric,* and *Elizabeth*. They were actually armed with a 7·5-inch howitzer, in addition to the three guns just mentioned. *Imogene* was a barquentine, and had been carrying china clay from Fowey to St. Malo. *Rentoul* was also a barquentine, *Viola* was a schooner; *Cymric* was a three-masted schooner.

By the end of September there were no fewer than nineteen decoy ships which had been fitted out in the one port of Granton, and nine of these were sailing ships. It will therefore be of interest to show how in this month such vessels were being employed in their double capacity of warship plus freighter. The barquentine *Merops* was discharging a cargo at Runcorn preparatory to loading coal for Cherbourg. The topsail schooner *Dargle* was discharging a cargo at Lerwick, and then loading herrings for Farnborough. The *Fresh Hope* was about to leave Liverpool for Belfast, where she would load with cork ballast for Halifax, Nova Scotia. The *Baron Rose*, another 900-ton schooner, was about to leave Newcastle with cork ballast for Halifax also. The barquentine *Rentoul* was on her way with coal to Cherbourg, the barquentine *Imogene* was on her way with coal for Lerwick. The topsail schooner *Viola* (alias *Vercker*) left Granton with coal for St. Valery-en-Caux. The iron schooner *Cymric* was taking coal from Granton to Cherbourg. Another three-masted schooner was carrying coal from Granton to St. Valery-en-Caux. In addition, there were a dozen steam craft from this same port acting as Q-ships. In another part of the British Isles our old friend *Helgoland* had yet another fight with a submarine. This was on July 11, 1917, in the neighbourhood of the Scillies, and this was another occasion when two ships with sails shelled each other, but unfortunately it was another of those calm days, and hazy. At the outset the enemy's shells passed over the *Helgoland's* fore-t'gallant yard as the latter was just drifting with the tide. Then the motors were started, and at 500 yards both guns and the Lewis guns gave the submarine a warm time, so that she was seriously damaged and had to escape by submerging.

Thus, all round our coasts, in the North Sea, Eng-

Q-SAILING SHIP "RENTOUL"
This barquentine was commissioned as a Q-ship in March, 1918, was well armed, but was also employed simultaneously in carrying coal to France.

Q-SAILING SHIP "LOTHBURY"
The midship gun.

lish Channel, Irish Sea, and Atlantic: from as far north as the Orkneys and Shetlands to as far south as the Bay of Biscay, and as far west as the coast of North America, these Q-sailing-ships were doing their job of work. The fitting out, the manning of these craft and of their guns, put a great strain on our manhood, already greatly diminished by the demands of our Armies abroad and munition makers at home. Nor could the Navy proper and the Auxiliary Patrol Force afford to be weakened. On the contrary, destroyers and light cruisers were being built and commissioned at a rapid rate: whilst more minesweepers, more trawlers and drifters, were daily consuming scores of men. Add to this the fact that other men as gunners were required in great numbers —for practically every British merchant ship became defensively armed—and one can see how important to our island nation and the overseas Empire is the existence of peace-time shipping, with all that it connotes—steamships, liners, tramps, colliers, trawlers, drifters, yachts, fishing smacks, it does not matter. From all these, and from the few full-rigged ships and sailing coasters, we had to draw our supplies of personnel, and it still takes longer to train a man into a sailor than into a military unit.

Never before, not even in Armada days, and probably never again, could such a call come from the fleet in being to the fleet of merchantmen. The sailing ship has had many centuries of usefulness as a fighting ship and a cargo carrier, and if she is being gradually killed by the mechanical ship she is dying hard. Apparently in neither capacity has she quite finished her fascinating and illustrious history.

CHAPTER XIV

THE SUMMIT OF Q-SHIP SERVICE

It was on February 17, 1917, that Commander Gordon Campbell, still in command of *Farnborough*, now named Q 5, again sank a submarine, but in circumstances which, hid from publication at the time, sent a thrill through the British Navy and especially among those who had the good fortune to be serving in that area. The scene was again off the south-west Irish coast, and the enemy at the beginning of the month had commenced the unrestricted warfare portion of their submarine campaign. The Germans, as we have since learned, possessed at this date ninety-five submarines in addition to eight in the Baltic and thirty-one in the Mediterranean. The orders to their submarine captains were very drastic and left no uncertainty, and one of these commanding officers informed one of my friends after the war that unless they were successful in sinking plenty of shipping they soon were removed from their command.

Every Allied merchant ship was to be attacked without delay. 'This form of warfare is to force England to make peace and thereby to decide the whole war. *Energetic* action is required, but above all rapidity of action.' 'Our object is to cut England off from traffic by sea, and not to achieve occasional results at far-distant points. As far as possible, therefore, stations must be taken up near the English

THE MASTER OF THE COLLIER "FARNBOROUGH"

Commander Gordon Campbell, V.C., D.S.O., R.N., taken on the bridge of the "Farnborough" (Q.-5), disguised as a master mariner.

Q.-SHIP "FARNBOROUGH"

The above picture shows her just as she appeared when she destroyed the U.-83. The position of the after gun's crew can just be seen abaft of where the sea is breaking over the stern.

To face p. 192

THE SUMMIT OF Q-SHIP SERVICE

coast, where routes converge and where divergence becomes impossible.' If ever there was a chance of attacking by night, this was to be done. When a ship had been abandoned by her crew the submarine was to sink her by gunfire, and approach the ship from aft. Owing to the activity of the British Q-ships, every ship, even sailing vessels, should be suspected, and both captain and engineer of merchant ships were to be taken prisoners.

Of the above numbers of submarines available this month not less than twenty-five and not more than forty-four could actually be at work on any given date, for the reasons given in another chapter. The first stages of this unrestricted warfare were most marked, for whereas the number of merchant ships sunk by submarines in all waters during December and January had been respectively thirty-six and thirty-five, in February the total suddenly rose to eighty-six—these sinkings occurring in the western approaches, especially off the south coast of Ireland. On February 14 the sailing ship *Eudora* (1,991 tons) had been sunk 30 miles S.S.W. of the Fastnet, and three days later the S.S. *Iolo* 40 miles S. by W. of the Fastnet, so orders from Germany were being carried out to the letter. The seventeenth of February was the Saturday before Ash Wednesday, and Captain Campbell had taken *Farnborough* into the locality just mentioned, the exact position being Lat. 51.34 N., Long. 11.23 W. It was a quarter to ten in the forenoon and the steamer was steering an easterly course at 7 knots, when a torpedo was seen approaching. And then occurred a supreme instance of Q-ship bravery. In his Order Book Captain Campbell had laid it down that 'Should the Officer of the Watch see a torpedo coming, he is to increase or decrease speed as necessary to ensure it hitting.' This order was read and signed by all his officers, so that there could be no misunderstanding. The intention was deliberate, premeditated self-immolation for the greater object of fooling the submarine and then sinking him. The Q-ship's company had all been warned that the intention would be thus, and every man was given an opportunity to leave the ship before sailing. Not one man left. Therefore to-day, when a long way off the torpedo was seen approaching, it could easily have been avoided, but instead, the helm was put hard aport only at the last minute, and only so that it should strike the ship elsewhere than in the engine-room. On came the steel fish and struck the ship abreast of No. 3 hold, wounding an Engineer Sub-Lieutenant, R.N.R., causing a terrific explosion, and making a huge hole in the ship's side.

In the meantime 'Action' had been sounded and all hands went to their stations, the ship being abandoned by every available man with the exception of those required on board. Thus two lifeboats and one dinghy full of men were sent to row about, and the fourth boat was partially lowered. Captain Campbell was lying concealed at one end of the bridge, watching and waiting in his great isolation. Up through the voice-pipe came the chief engineer's report that the engine-room was filling: back came the captain's orders that he was to hang on as long as possible and then hide. This was done. In the meantime *Farnborough's* captain saw the submarine appear on the starboard quarter a couple of hundred yards away, submerged, but cautiously making a thorough scrutiny of the ship through his periscope. Then the German—U 83 was her name—came past the ship on the starboard side only 13 yards away and

Q-SHIP "FARNBOROUGH"

With White Ensign still flying, after her arrival at Berehaven in a sinking condition.

THE SUMMIT OF Q-SHIP SERVICE 195

about 5 yards from the boats. She was so close, in fact, that Captain Campbell, looking down, could see the whole shape of the submarine below the water quite distinctly.

Here was the big crisis. Was this the psychological moment? Was this the right time to make the final gamble? For Captain Campbell the temptation to open fire was almost unbearable, yet the opportunity was not yet: he must wait a little longer and live minutes which were like days. The submarine passed along, then close round *Farnborough's* bows, finally breaking surface about 300 yards on the port bow. It was now five minutes past ten and U 83 motoring along the surface came past the port side, continuing the scrutiny with less caution born of satisfaction. The concealed figure on *Farnborough's* bridge was waiting only until all his guns would bear, and as soon as the enemy thus bore came the great onslaught. It was point-blank range, and the 6-pounder opened the battle, whose first shot hit the conning-tower and beheaded the German captain.

The surprise had been instant and effective, for the submarine never recovered from the shock, but remained on the surface whilst *Farnborough's* guns shattered the hull to pieces, the conning-tower being continually hit, and some of the shells going clean through. Over forty rounds had thus been fired, to say nothing of the Maxim gun. U 83 was beaten, finished, smashed: and she finally sank with her conning-tower open and her crew pouring out. About eight of her crew were seen in the water, and one of *Farnborough's* lifeboats went to their assistance and was in time to pick up one officer and one man, and then rowed back to the ship through sea thick with oil and blood and bubbles. U 83 was satisfactorily disposed of, but what about the decoy ship herself? It was now time to inspect her, and she was clearly in a stricken state. The engine-room and boiler-rooms and both Nos. 3 and 4 after holds were all filling

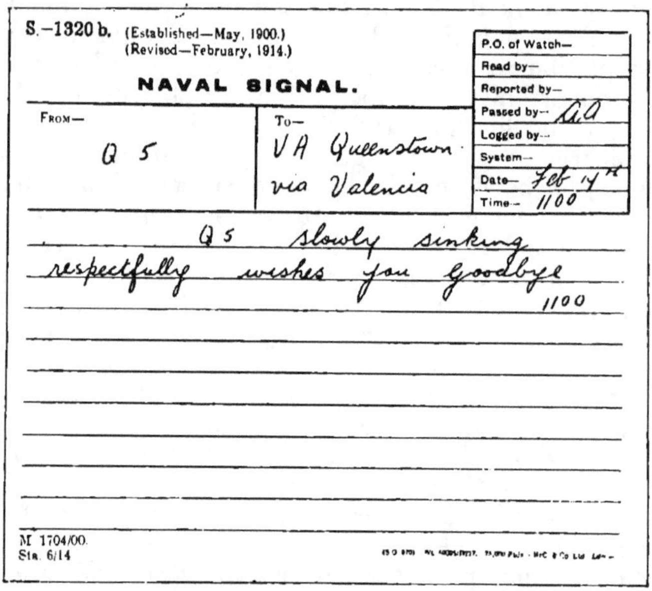

S.–1320 b. (Established—May, 1900.) (Revised—February, 1914.)

NAVAL SIGNAL.

P.O. of Watch—	
Read by—	
Reported by—	
Passed by—	A.A.
Logged by—	
System—	
Date—	Feb 17th
Time—	1100

FROM— Q 5

TO— VA Queenstown via Valencia

Q 5 slowly sinking respectfully wishes you goodbye 1100

M 1704/00.
Sta. 6/14

FIG. 13.—'FARNBOROUGH'S' FAREWELL.

When Q 5 (*Farnborough*) had succeeded in sinking U 83, but was herself in a sinking condition and apparently doomed, Captain Campbell despatched the above wireless signal to Vice-Admiral Sir Lewis Bayly, Commander-in-Chief, Queenstown. It was one of the most pathetic and dramatic messages which ever flashed out of the Atlantic, but happily Q 5 was salved.

rapidly, and she was sinking by the stern: the end could not be far away. Captain Campbell therefore sent a wireless signal for assistance and placed nearly all his hands in the boats, keeping only a few men on

Q-SHIP "FARNBOROUGH"
Brought safely into Berehaven after her famous fight and beached in Mill Cove, with a heavy list.

S.S. "LODORER"
Having served magnificently as a warship under the names of "Farnborough" and Q-5, and having been salved, this ship is here seen ready to be returned to her owners.

THE SUMMIT OF Q-SHIP SERVICE

board, and destroying all confidential books and charts. His signal was picked up, and before noon a British destroyer arrived, and as by this time *Farnborough* was in a critical condition most of the crew were transferred to her.* Presently H.M. sloop *Buttercup* steamed up, and as there seemed a chance of saving the ship Captain Campbell with twelve officers and men then went back on board his ship. She seemed now to have settled to a definite position, and the water, though rising, was gaining but slowly.

At length *Buttercup* got her in tow, but there is nothing so hard to steer as a sinking ship, and the tow parted. At 5 p.m. the sloop again got her in tow, but it was a disappointing business with the water steadily gaining below and the Atlantic swell breaking over the after deck, and thus the ships went on through the night. At 2 a.m. on the Sunday *Farnborough* suddenly took an alarming list and the water gained rapidly, so the crew had to be ordered into the boats once again. The sloop *Laburnum*, which had also arrived, was ordered to close her an hour and a half later, but just as Captain Campbell was walking aft off went one of the depth charges with such an explosion that *Buttercup*, thinking it was a submarine's torpedo, slipped her tow. After remaining aboard *Laburnum* until daylight, Captain Campbell went back to his ship, and then *Laburnum* got her in tow. A course had been set for Bantry Bay, and as she approached she was an amazing spectacle, listing over to the extent of twenty degrees and her stern nearly 8 feet under water. However, the

---

* Twelve officers and men were selected from a host of volunteers to try and get the ship in tow. These were placed in a motor-boat, whilst the Captain boarded the escort to arrange for towage if possible.

armed trawler *Luneda* and the tug *Flying Sportsman* had been sent out to her, and by their assistance she was brought up the fjord and beached at Mill Cove, Berehaven, by half-past nine that Sunday night. Next morning, and for long after, this very ordinary-looking steamer lay among a number of other wounded ships, a strange and impressive sight. *Farnborough* had fought both submarine and adversity, and had won both times: still, had it not been for sound seamanship and her holds being packed with timber she would never have been saved.

There was much work to be done and there were too few salvage experts and men to cope with the results of the submarines' attacks: so for the present *Farnborough* had to reman idle. Months later she was repaired temporarily, refloated, taken away from Berehaven and properly reconditioned, but she had ended her days as a warship. She has now gone back to the Merchant Service as a cargo carrier, and if you ever go aboard her you will find a suitable inscription commemorating her truly wonderful career. As for Commander Campbell, as soon as he had got his ship safely into Berehaven he was summoned to see his Commander-in-Chief, Admiral Sir Lewis Bayly. After that he was received by the King, who conferred on him the highest of all awards for heroes. No details appeared in the Press; only this announcement from the *London Gazette*:

'The King has been graciously pleased to approve of the grant of the Victoria Cross to Commander Gordon Campbell, D.S.O., R.N., in recognition of his conspicuous gallantry, consummate coolness and skill in command of one of His Majesty's ships in action.'

Press and public were greatly puzzled, but secrecy

Q-SHIP "PARGUST"
One of Captain Gordon Campbell's famous commands.

Q-SHIP "SARAH JONES"
This craft did not come into the service until about three months before the end of the war. Her alias was "Margaret Murray."

was at this time essential. 'This,' commented a well-known London daily, 'is probably the first time since the institution of the V.C. that the bestowal of this coveted honour has been announced without details of the deed for which it was awarded.' The popular press named him 'the Mystery V.C.,' and the usual crop of rumours and fantastic stories went round. And while these were being told the gallant commander was busy fitting out another Q-ship in which to go forth and make his greatest of all achievements.

This ship was the S.S. *Vittoria*, a collier of 2,817 gross tons. She was selected whilst lying at Cardiff, whence she was sent to Devonport to be fitted out as a decoy. Commander Campbell superintended her alteration, and she began her special service on March 28, 1917. She was armed with one 4-inch, four 12-pounders, two Maxim guns, and a couple of 14-inch torpedo tubes. She was a slow creature, $7\frac{1}{2}$ knots being her speed, but she looked the part she was intended to play. When Commander Campbell took over the command he was accompanied by his gallant crew from *Farnborough*. She had been fitted with wireless, and down in her holds the useful timber had been stowed. On leaving Devonport she changed her name to *Pargust*, but she was variously known also as the *Snail*, *Friswell*, and *Pangloss* at later dates.

She again came under the orders of Sir Lewis Bayly at Queenstown, and then, being in all respects ready to fight another submarine, *Pargust* went cruising. She had not long to wait, and on June 7 we find her out in the Atlantic again, not very far from the scene of her last encounter. The month of April had been a terrible one for British shipping;

no fewer than 155 of our merchant craft had been sunk by submarines, representing a loss of over half a million of tonnage. In May these figures had dropped slightly, but in June they were up again, though in no month of the war did our losses ever reach the peak of April again. Nor was it only British ships that so suffered, and I recollect the U.S.S. *Cushing* two days previously bringing into Bantry Bay thirteen survivors, including three wounded, from an Italian barque. At this time, too, the enemy submarines were laying a number of dangerous minefields off this part of the world, and as one patrolled along the south-west Irish coast pieces of wreckage, a meat-safe or a seaman's chest, would be seen floating from some victimized steamer.

On the morning, then, of the seventh, picture *Pargust* in Lat. 51.50 N., Long. 11.50 W., jogging along at her slow speed. At that time there was scarcely a steamer that was not armed with some sort of a gun; therefore, if a Q-ship did not display one aft, she would have looked suspicious. *Pargust* kept up appearances by having a dummy gun mounted aft with a man in uniform standing by. I well remember that day. There was a nasty sea running, and the atmosphere varied from the typical Irish damp mist to heavy rain. At 8 a.m. out of this thickness *Pargust* descried a torpedo, apparently fired at close range, racing towards her starboard beam. When about 100 yards off it jumped out of the water and struck the engine-room near the waterline, making a large tear in the ship's side, filling the boiler-room, engine-room, and No. 5 hold, and blowing the starboard lifeboat into the air.

Captain Campbell then gave the order to abandon ship, and the panic party went away in three boats,

Q-SHIP "DUNRAVEN."
Showing forward well-deck and bridge.

THE SUMMIT OF Q-SHIP SERVICE 201

and just as the last boat was pushing off a periscope was sighted 400 yards on the port side forward of the beam. It then turned and made for the ship, and submerged when close to the lifeboat's stern, then came on the starboard quarter, turned towards the ship and, when 50 yards away, partially broke surface, heading on a course parallel, but opposite, to

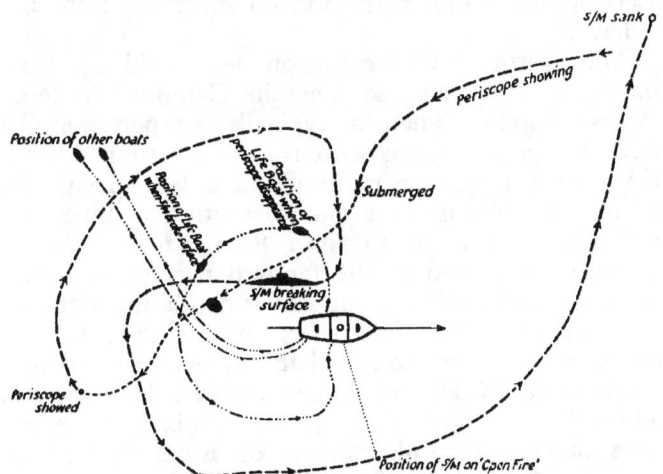

Fig. 14.—Diagram to Illustrate Approximate Movements of 'Pargust' and UC 29 on June 7, 1917.

that of *Pargust*, the lifeboat meanwhile pulling away round the steamer's stern. The submarine followed, and a man was seen on the conning-tower shouting directions. The lifeboat then rowed towards the ship, and this apparently annoyed the Hun, who now began semaphoring the boats; but at 8.36 a.m. the submarine was only 50 yards off, and was bearing one point before the beam, so all *Pargust's* guns were able to bear nicely. Fire was therefore opened, the first shot from the 4-inch gun hitting the base of the conning-tower and removing the two periscopes. Nearly forty more shells followed, most of them being hits in the conning-tower, so that the submarine quickly listed to port, and several men came out of the hatch abaft the conning-tower. She was already obviously in a bad way, with her heavy list and her stern almost submerged, and oil squirting from her sides.

The Germans now came on deck, held up their hands, and waved; so Captain Campbell ordered 'Cease Fire.' Then a typically unsportsmanlike trick was played, for as soon as *Pargust* stopped firing the enemy began to make off at a fair speed. So there was nothing for it but to resume shelling her, and this was kept up until 8.40 a.m., when an explosion occurred in the forward part of the submarine. She sank for the last time, falling over on her side, and 3 feet of her sharp bow end up in the air, 300 yards off, was the last that was ever seen of her. So perished UC 29, and thus one more submarine was added to the score of this gallant captain and crew. One officer (a sub-lieutenant of Reserve) and an engine-room petty officer were picked up. The former had come on to the submarine's deck with a couple of men to fire the 22-pounder, but owing to the heavy sea knocked up by the fresh southerly wind they had been all washed overboard before reaching the gun.

The captain of UC 29 had been killed by *Pargust's* fire. This class of submarine carried besides her 22-pounder and machine-gun eighteen mines and three torpedoes. She had left Brunsbüttel on May 25, calling at Heligoland, and the routine was usually first to lay the mines and then operate, sinking ships

BRIDGE OF Q-SHIP "DUNRAVEN"

Captain Gordon Campbell, V.C., D.S.O., R.N., inspecting the damage by the submarine's shells to his ship.

THE SUMMIT OF Q-SHIP SERVICE 203

with gun or torpedo. As to her mines, it is quite possible that she laid the three mines I recollect sinking on June 12 in the approach to Valentia Harbour, Dingle Bay, and she may have laid three others off Brow Head, one of which I remember on June 4, for it was customary for these craft to lay their 'eggs' in threes. With regard to her three torpedoes we know that one had penetrated *Pargust*, another had sunk a sailing ship—probably the Italian barque already mentioned—and the third had been fired at a destroyer, but passed underneath.

As to *Pargust*, she fortunately did not sink, thanks to her cargo of timber. At 12.30 p.m. another of Admiral Bayly's alert sloops, who always seemed to be at hand when wanted, arrived. This was H.M.S. *Crocus*, who took *Pargust* in tow. The sloop *Zinnia* and the United States destroyer *Cushing* arrived also, and escorted her to Queenstown, which she reached next afternoon. The prisoners had been already transferred to *Zinnia*, and in *Pargust* the only casualties had been one stoker petty officer killed and the engineer sub-lieutenant wounded. For *Pargust's* splendid victory further honours were awarded. Captain Campbell, already the possessor of the V.C. and D.S.O., now received a bar to his D.S.O. To Lieutenant R. N. Stuart, D.S.O., R.N.R., was given the V.C., and Seaman W. Williams, R.N.R., also received this highest of all decorations. These two, one officer and one man, were selected by ballot to receive this distinction, but every officer and every man had earned it.

Before *Pargust* could be ready for sea again much would have to be done to her at Devonport, so Captain Campbell proceeded to look for a new ship, and this was found in the collier *Dunraven*. She was fitted out at Devonport under his supervision, just like her predecessor, and her crew turned over *en bloc* from *Pargust*. She was commissioned on July 28, and within a fortnight Captain Campbell, now already promoted to post-captain at an age which must certainly be a record, was engaged in the most heroic Q-ship fight of all the long series of duels only a few days after leaving Devonport.

Just before eleven on the forenoon of August 8 *Dunraven* was in the Bay of Biscay, about 130 miles west of Ushant, doing her 8 knots and disguised as a defensively armed British merchantman, for which reason she had a small gun aft. In order to conform further with merchant-ship practice of this time, she was keeping a zigzag course. On the horizon appeared a submarine, about two points forward of *Dunraven's* starboard beam. The German was waiting, you see, in a likely position for catching homeward-bound steamers making for the western British ports, and on sighting this 'tramp' he must have felt pretty sure she was bringing home a cargo of commodities useful for winning the war. Pursuing the more cautious tactics of the time, the enemy, having apparently ascertained the 'tramp's' speed and mean course, submerged, but at 11.43 she broke surface 5,000 yards off the starboard quarter and opened fire. In order to maintain the bluff, Captain Campbell replied with his defensive gun, made as much smoke as possible, reduced to 7 knots, and made an occasional zigzag in order to give the enemy a chance of closing. *Dunraven* was now steaming head to sea, and the enemy's shots were falling over, but after about half an hour of this the submarine ceased firing, came on at full speed, and a quarter of an hour later turned broadside on, and reopened fire.

AFTER THE BATTLE

Forebridge of Q-ship "Dunraven" and captain's cabin as the result of the submarine's shells.

In the meantime the decoy was intentionally firing short, and sent wireless signals *en clair* so that the enemy could still further be deceived. Such messages as 'Submarine chasing and shelling me,' 'Submarine overtaking me, help, come quickly . . . am abandoning ship,' were flashed forth just as were sent almost daily by stricken ships in those strenuous days. *Dunraven's* next bluff was to pretend his engines had been hit; so Captain Campbell stopped his ship, which now made a cloud of steam. The next step was to 'abandon ship,' and the 'tramp' had enough way on to allow of her being turned broadside on and let the enemy see that the vessel was being abandoned. Then, to simulate real panic, one of the boats was let go by the foremost fall, an incident that somehow seems to happen in every disaster to steamers. Thus, so far, everything had been carried out just as a submarine would have expected a genuine 'tramp' to behave. Not a thing had been omitted which ought to have been seen by the enemy, who had already closed and continued his shelling. From now ensued a most trying time. To receive punishment with serene stoicism, to be hit and not reply, is the supreme test; but these officers and men were no novices in the Q-ship art, and none had had greater or more bitter experience. However, not all the tactics and devices could prevent the enemy's shells hitting if the German insisted, and this had to be endured in order that at length the submarine might be tempted inside the desired range and bearing.

Thus it happened that one shell penetrated *Dunraven's* poop, exploding a depth charge and blowing Lieutenant C. G. Bonner, D.S.C., R.N.R., out of his control position. This was rather bad luck, and two more shells followed, the poop became on fire, dense clouds of black smoke issued forth, and the situation was perilous; for in the poop were the magazine and depth charges, and it was obvious that as the fire increased an explosion of some magnitude must soon occur. But the main consideration was to sink the submarine, and it mattered little if the Q-ship were lost; so Captain Campbell decided to wait until the submarine got in a suitable position. It was exactly two hours to the minute since the submarine had been first sighted when, just as he was passing close to *Dunraven's* stern, a terrific explosion took place in the poop, caused probably by a couple of depth charges and some cordite. The result was that the 4-inch gun and the whole of its crew were blown up into the air, the gun vaulting the bridge and alighting on the well deck forward, while the crew came down in various places, one man falling into the water, and 4-inch projectiles being blown about the ship in the most unpleasant manner.

That this explosion should have happened at this moment was a misfortune of the greatest magnitude, for it spoilt the whole tactics. Captain Campbell was watching the enemy closely, and the latter was coming on so nicely that he had only to proceed a little further and *Dunraven's* guns would have been bearing at a range of not more than 400 yards. As it was, the explosion gave the whole game away, for firstly it frightened the submarine so that he dived, secondly it set going the 'open fire' buzzers at the guns. Thus the time had come to attack. The only gun in the ship that would bear was the one on the after bridge, and this began to bark just as the White Ensign was hoisted. One shot was thought to have succeeded in hitting the conning-tower just as the enemy was submerging, but if he was damaged it

"DUNRAVEN" DOOMED

This picture shows the Q-ship in her last hours. She has been through an historic duel; she has been torpedoed and shelled, her poop has been blown up, and the Atlantic seas are breaking over her deck.

To face p. 206

was not seriously, and Captain Campbell realized that the next thing to expect was a torpedo. He therefore ordered the doctor to remove all the wounded, and hoses were turned on to the poop, which was now one mass of flames, the deck being red-hot. So gallant had been this well-disciplined crew that even when it was so hot that they had to lift the boxes of cordite from off the deck the men still had remained at their posts.*

The position now was this: a ship seriously on fire, the magazine still intact but likely to explode before long with terrible effects, a torpedo attack imminent, and the White Ensign showing that this was a 'trap-ship' after all. The submarine would certainly fight

* Captain Campbell has been good enough to furnish me with the following details of this heroic episode:

'Lieutenant Bonner, having been blown out of his control by the first explosion, crawled into the gun-hatch with the crew. They there remained at their posts with a fire raging in the poop below and the deck getting red-hot. One man tore up his shirt to give pieces to the gun's crew to stop the fumes getting into their throats, others lifted the boxes of cordite off the deck to keep it from exploding, and all the time they knew that they must be blown up, as the secondary supply and magazine were immediately below. They told me afterwards that communication with the bridge was cut off, and although they knew they would be blown up, they also knew they would spoil the show if they moved, so they remained until actually blown up with their gun. Then, when as wounded men they were ordered to remain quiet in various places during the second action, they had to lie there unattended and bleeding, with explosions continually going on aboard and splinters from the shell-fire penetrating their quarters. Lieutenant Bonner, himself wounded, did what he could for two who were with him in the wardroom. When I visited them after the action, they thought little of their wounds, but only expressed their disgust that the enemy had not been sunk. Surely such bravery is hard to equal. The strain for the men who remained on board after the ship had been torpedoed, poop set on fire, cordite and shells exploding, and then the enemy shell-fire, can easily be imagined.'

now like the expert duellist, and it would be a fight to the finish, undoubtedly. Realizing all this, and full well knowing what was inevitable, Captain Campbell made a decision which could have been made only by a man of consummate moral courage. To a man-of-war who had answered his call for assistance

```
S.-1320 b.  (Established—May, 1900.)
            (Revised—January, 1917.)

                NAVAL SIGNAL.

From—                    To—
  Dunraven                 H.M. Ships

                                    P.O. of Watch —
                                    Read by —
                                    Reported by—
                                    Passed by— AA
                                    Logged by—
                                    System— W.T.
                                    Date— Aug 8th
                                    Time— 12 50 p

  Keep  away  for the  present




                    Coded


M. 1704/00.
Sta. 6/14.
Sta. 596/15.
```

FIG. 15.— THE GREAT DECISION.

Captain Campbell's famous wireless signal refusing assistance when the Q-ship *Dunraven* was already crippled and about to be attacked again.

when the explosion occurred he now sent a wireless signal requesting him to keep away, as he was already preparing for the next phase, still concentrating as he was on sinking the submarine.*

* See illustration above.

Q-SHIP "DUNRAVEN"

Her duel with the submarine being ended, the crippled "Dunraven" is taken in tow by H.M. Destroyer "Christopher," who is seen endeavouring to get her into port.

THE SUMMIT OF Q-SHIP SERVICE

It was now twenty minutes since that big explosion, and the expected torpedo arrived, striking *Dunraven* abaft the engine-room. The enemy was aware of two facts: he had seen the first 'abandon ship' party and this he now knew was mere bluff, and that there were others still remaining on board. In order, therefore, to deceive the German, Captain Campbell now sent away some more of his crew in boats and a raft. It would then look as if the last man had left the ship. From 1.40 to 2.30 p.m. followed a period of the utmost suspense, during which the periscope could be seen circling around scrutinizing the ship to make *quite* sure, whilst the fire on the poop was still burning fiercely, and boxes of cordite and 4-inch shells were going off every few minutes. To control yourself and your men under these circumstances and to continue thinking coolly of what the next move shall be, this, surely, is a very wonderful achievement: more than this could be asked of no captain.

At half-past two the submarine came to the surface directly astern (where *Dunraven's* guns would not bear) and resumed shelling the steamer at short range, and used her Maxim gun on the men in the boats. This went on for twenty minutes, and then she dived once more. Captain Campbell next decided to use his torpedoes, so five minutes later one was fired which passed just ahead of the submarine's periscope as the enemy was motoring 150 yards off on the port side; and seven minutes afterwards *Dunraven* fired a second torpedo which passed just astern of the periscope. The enemy had failed to see the first torpedo, but evidently he noticed the second. It was obvious that by now it was useless to continue the contest any further, for the submarine would go on torpedoing and shelling *Dunraven* until she sank: so Captain

22nd August, 1917.

Dear Captain Campbell

It is with very great pleasure that I convey to you, by the directions of the War Cabinet, an expression of their high appreciation of the gallantry, skill, and devotion to duty, which have been displayed through many months of arduous service by yourself and the officers and men of His Majesty's ship under your command.

In conveying to you this message of the War Cabinet, which expresses the high esteem with which the conduct of your officers and men is regarded by His Majesty's Government, I wish to add on behalf of the Board of Admiralty, that they warmly endorse this commendation.

Will you please convey this message to all ranks and ratings under your command?

FIG. 16.—LETTER OF APPRECIATION FROM THE FIRST LORD OF THE ADMIRALTY TO CAPTAIN GORDON CAMPBELL AFTER THE HISTORIC ACTION FOUGHT BY Q-SHIP 'DUNRAVEN.'

THE SUMMIT OF Q-SHIP SERVICE 211

Campbell signalled for urgent assistance,* and almost immediately the U.S.S. *Noma* arrived and fired at a periscope seen a few hundred yards astern of *Dunraven*. Then came the two British destroyers *Attack* and *Christopher*. *Dunraven* then recalled her boats and the fire was extinguished, but it was found that the poop had been completely gutted and that all depth charges and ammunition had been exploded. From *Noma* and *Christopher* doctors came over and assisted in tending the wounded, a couple of the most dangerously injured being taken on board *Noma* to be operated on and then landed at Brest.

At 6.45 p.m. *Christopher* began towing *Dunraven*, but this was no easy matter, for there was a nasty sea running, the damaged ship would not steer; her stern went down, the sea broke over it and worked its way forward. In this way the night passed, and at 10.15 the next morning *Christopher* was able to report that she was now only 60 miles west of Ushant and bringing *Dunraven* towards Plymouth at 4 knots. By six that evening the ship was in so bad a condition that she might sink any moment, so Captain Campbell transferred sixty of his crew to the trawler *Foss*. About 9 p.m. two tugs arrived, took over the towing, and carried on during the night until 1.30 a.m. of August 10. It was time then for the last handful of men to abandon her in all true earnestness, so the *Christopher* came alongside, in spite of the heavy sea running, and the last man was taken off. It was only just in time, for almost immediately she capsized, and was finally sunk by *Christopher* dropping a depth charge and shelling her as a dangerous derelict soon

* In the meantime he arranged for a further 'abandon ship' evolution, having only one gun's crew on board.

after 3 a.m. Thus the life of *Dunraven* as a man-of-war had been both brief and distinguished.

As to the officers and men, it is difficult to imagine greater and more persistent bravery under such adverse circumstances, and the King made the following awards: Captain Gordon Campbell, V.C., D.S.O., received a second bar to his D.S.O.; Lieutenant C. G. Bonner, D.S.C., R.N.R., received a V.C., as also did Petty Officer E. Pitcher. To Assistant-Paymaster R. A. Nunn, D.S.C., R.N.R., was awarded a D.S.O. Three other officers received a D.S.C., whilst Lieutenant P. R. Hereford, D.S.O., D.S.C., and two engineer officers, all received a bar to their D.S.C.

Such is the story of Captain Campbell's last and greatest Q-ship fight, for after this he was appointed to command a light cruiser at Queenstown. In these duels we reach the high-water mark of sea gallantry, and the incidents themselves are so impressive that no further words are necessary. Let us leave it at that.

Q-SHIP "DUNRAVEN"

This photograph was taken shortly before she finally sank. Already the stern is awash.

CHAPTER XV

LIFE ON BOARD A Q-SHIP

In history it is frequently the case that what seems to contemporaries merely ordinary and commonplace is to posterity of the utmost value and interest. How little, for example, do we know of the life and routine in the various stages and development of the sailing ship! In a volume entitled 'Ships and Ways of Other Days,' published before the war, I endeavoured to collect and present the everyday existence at sea in bygone years. Some day, in the centuries to come, it may be that the historical student will require to know something of the organization and mode of life on board one of the Q-steamships, and because it is just one of those matters, which at the time seemed so obvious, I have now thought it advisable here to set down a rough outline. As time goes on the persons of the drama die, logs and diaries and correspondence fall into unsympathetic hands and become destroyed; therefore, whilst it is yet not too late, let us provide for posterity some facts on which they can base their imagination of Q-ship life.

Elsewhere in the pages of this book the reader will find it possible to gather some idea of the types, sizes, and appearances of the ships employed. The following details are chiefly those of one of the most distinguished Q-ships, the famous *Penshurst*, and as such they have especial interest as showing the organization of a tiny little tramp into a valiant and successful man-of-war that sank several powerful enemy submarines; and it is through the courtesy of her gallant late commanding officer, Captain F. H. Grenfell, D.S.O., R.N., that I am able to present these facts.

Penshurst was a three-masted, single-funnelled, single-screw steamer, owned by a London firm. She had been fitted out as a decoy at the end of 1915 by Admiral Colville at Longhope. Her length between perpendiculars was 225 feet, length over all 232 feet, beam 35 feet 2 inches, draught 14 feet 6 inches, depth of hold 13 feet 7 inches. Her tonnage was 1,191 gross, 740 registered, displacement 2,035 tons. Fitted with four bulkheads, the ship had the maximum amount of hold, the engines being placed right aft. The crew were berthed in the forecastle, the engineers' mess and cabins being aft, whilst the captain's and officers' mess and cabins were adjacent to the bridge just forward of midships. The engine-room pressure was 180 pounds, and the maximum speed, with everything working well and a clean bottom, was 10 knots. Her armament consisted of five guns. A 12-pounder (18 cwt.) was placed on the after hatch, but disguised in the most ingenious manner by a ship's boat, which had been purposely sawn through so that the detached sections could immediately be removed, allowing the gun to come into action. Originally there were mounted a 3-pounder and 6-pounder on each side of the lower bridge deck. These were hidden behind wooden screens such as are often found built round the rails in this kind of ship. These screens were specially hinged so that on going into action they immediately fell down and revealed the guns. Thus

Q-SHIP "DUNRAVEN"

Showing the damage done to her poop after the action with submarine. The after-deck is already well awash and presently she foundered.

To face p. 214

LIFE ON BOARD A Q-SHIP 215

it was possible always to offer a broadside of three guns. In the spring of 1916 *Penshurst* was transferred from Longhope to Milford and Queenstown, and Admiral Bayly had the arrangement of guns altered so that the 3-pounders were now concealed in a gunhouse made out of the engineers' mess and cabins, the intention being to enable both these guns to fire right aft. The 6-pounders were then shifted forward into the positions previously occupied by the 3-pounders on the lower bridge deck. How successful this arrangement was in action the reader is able to see for himself in the accounts of *Penshurst's* engagements with submarines. The ship was also supplied with depth charges, rockets, and Verey's lights.

The crew consisted of Captain Grenfell and three temporary R.N.R. officers, an R.N.R. assistant-paymaster, thirteen Royal Navy gunnery ratings, eight R.N.R. seamen, a couple of stewards, two cooks, a shipwright, carpenter's crew, an R.N.R. chief engine-room artificer, an engine-room artificer, and R.N.R. stokers, bringing the company up to forty-five.

In arranging action stations in a Q-ship the difficulty was that internally the vessel had to be organized as a warship, while externally she must necessarily keep up the character of a merchantman. In *Penshurst* Captain Grenfell had arranged for the following signals to be rung from the bridge on the alarm gong. One long ring meant that a submarine was in sight and that the crew were to stand by at their respective stations; if followed by a short ring it denoted the enemy was on the starboard side; if two short rings the submarine was on the port side. Two long rings indicated that the crew were to go to panic stations; three long rings meant that they were to go to action stations without 'panic.' 'Open fire' was ordered by a succession of short rings and whistles.

With regard to the above, in the case of action stations the look-out men on the bridge proceeded to their gun at the stand-by signal, keeping out of sight, while the crews who were below, off watch, went also to their guns, moving by the opposite side of the ship. In order to simulate the real mercantile crew, the men under the foc's'le now came out and showed themselves on the fore well deck. If 'panic' was to be feigned, all the crew of the gun concealed by the collapsible boat were to hide, the signalman stood by to hoist the White Ensign at the signal to open fire, and the boat party ran aft, turned out the boats, lowered them, and 'abandoned' ship, pulling away on the opposite bow. The signal for standing-by to release the depth charge was when the captain dropped a red flag, and all guns' crews were to look out to fire on the enemy if the depth charge brought the U-boat to the surface.

Special arrangements had been made in the event of casualties. Thus, if the captain were laid out a certain officer was to carry on and take over command. Similar arrangements were made in the event of all officers on the bridge becoming casualties, an eventuality that was far from improbable. In fact, Captain Grenfell gave orders that if a shell burst on or near the bridge a certain officer was to be informed in any case; and if the latter did not receive word of this explosion he was to assume that everyone on the bridge was a casualty and he was to be ready to open fire at the right time. One of the possibilities in the preliminary stages of these attacks was always that owing to the hitting by the enemy's shells, or, more likely still, by the explosion of his torpedo against

THE GALLANT OFFICERS AND CREW OF THE Q-SHIP "DUNRAVEN."
Captain Gordon Campbell is in the second row with Lieutenant C. G. Bonner on his right.

LIFE ON BOARD A Q-SHIP

the side of the ship, some portion of the screens or dummy deckhouses might have been damaged, and thus the guns be revealed to the enemy. So, while *Penshurst's* captain was busily engaged watching the movements of the submarine, the information as to this unfortunate fact might have been made known. It was therefore a standing rule that the bridge was to be informed by voice-pipe of such occurrences. Damage received in the engine-room was reported up the pipe to the bridge. Conversely there were placed three men at the voice-pipes—one on the bridge, one in the gunhouse aft, and one at the 12-pounder—whose duty it was to pass along the messages, the first-mentioned passing down the varying bearing and range of the submarine and the state of affairs on the bridge, and when no orders were necessary he was to keep passing along the comforting remark 'All right.' By this means the hidden officers and guns' crews were kept informed of the position of affairs and able to have the guns instantly ready to fire at the very moment the screens were let down. Obviously victory and the very lives of every man in the ship could be secured only if the vessel came into action smartly and effectively without accident or bungling.

Sometimes victory was conditional only on being torpedoed, so that the enemy might believe he had got the steamer in a sinking condition and the vessel was apparently genuinely abandoned. Inasmuch as the submarine on returning home had to afford some sort of evidence, the U-boat captain would approach the ship and endeavour to read her name. It was then that the Q-ship's opportunity presented itself, and the guns poured shells into the German. Special drills were therefore made in case *Penshurst* should be hit by torpedo, and in this eventuality the boat 'panic party' was to lower away and at once start rowing off from the ship, whilst the remainder hid themselves at their respective stations. As for the engineers, their duty was to stop the engines at once, but to try to keep the dynamo running as long as possible so that wireless signals could still be sent out. The engine-room staff were to remain below as long as conditions would allow, but if the water rose so that these were compelled to come up, their orders were to crawl out on to the deck on the disengaged side and there lie down lest the enemy should see them. As these Q-ships usually carried depth charges and the latter exploded under certain conditions of pressure from the sea, it was one of the first duties on being torpedoed that these should be secured.

Now, supposing the Q-ship were actually sunk and the whole crew were compelled *really* to abandon ship, what then? The submarine would certainly come alongside the boats and make inquiries. She would want to know, for instance, the name of the ship, owners, captain, cargo, where from, where bound. That was certain. She would also, most probably, insist on taking the captain prisoner, if the incident occurred in the last eighteen months of the war. All these officers and men would, of course, be wearing not smart naval uniform, but be attired in the manner fitting the *personnel* of an old tramp. The captain would be wearing a peaked cap, with the house-flag of his Company suitably intertwined in the cap badge, while the men would be attired in guernseys, old suits, and mufflers, with a dirty old cloth cap. Now, if the U-boat skipper was a live man and really knew his work he would, of course, become suspicious on seeing so many hands from one sunken tramp. 'This,' he would remark, 'is no

LIFE ON BOARD A Q-SHIP 219

merchant ship, but a proper trap,' and would proceed to cross-examine the boats' crews. It was therefore the daily duty of Q-ship men to learn a suitable lie which would adequately deceive the German. Here is the information which *Penshurst* was, at a certain period of her Q-ship career, ready to hand out to any inquisitive Hun if the latter had sunk the ship.

In answer to questions the crew would reply: 'This is the S.S. *Penshurst*, owned by the Power Steam Ship Company of London. Her master was Evan Davies, but he has gone down with the ship, poor man. Cargo? She was carrying coal, but she was not an Admiralty collier.' Then the enemy would ask where from and to. If it happened that *Penshurst* was in a likely locality the reply would be: 'From Cardiff'; otherwise the name of a well distant coal port, such as Newcastle or Liverpool, was decided upon. For instance, if *Penshurst* were sunk in the neighbourhood of Portland Bill whilst heading west it would be no good to pretend you were from the Mersey or Bristol Channel. When the German commented on the singularly large number of the crew, he would get the reply: 'Yes, these aren't all our own chaps. We picked up some blokes two days ago from a torpedoed ship.' Then in answer to further questions one of the survivors from the latter would back up the lie with the statement that they were the starboard watch of the S.S. *Carron*, owned by the Carron Company, 2,350 tons, bound with a cargo of coal from Barry (or Sunderland) to a French port. In this case Captain Grenfell would pretend to be the master of the *Carron*, and of *Penshurst's* four officers one would pretend he was the first mate of the *Carron*, another the first mate of the collier *Penshurst*, another the *Penshurst's* second mate, whilst the assistant-paymaster, not being a navigator, passed as chief steward. Thus, every little detail was thought out for every possible *contretemps*. To surprise the enemy and yet not to let him surprise you was the aim.

If, by a piece of bad luck, your identity as a Q-ship had been revealed—and this did occur—so that the enemy got away before you had time to sink him, there was nothing for it but to get the other side of the horizon and alter the appearance of the ship. To the landsman this may seem rather an impossible proposition. I admit at once that in the case of the Q-sailing-ships this was rather a tall order, for the plain reason that topsail schooners and brigantines in these modern days of maritime enterprise are comparatively few in number. But the greatest part of our sea-borne trade is carried on in small steamers of more or less standardized type or types. Vessels of the type such as *Penshurst* and *Suffolk Coast* are to be seen almost everywhere in our narrow seas: except for the markings on their funnels they are as much like each other as possible. In a fleet of such craft it would be about as easy for a German to tell one from another as in a Tokio crowd it would be for an Englishman to tell one Japanese from another. The points which distinguish these craft the one from the other are of minor consideration, such as the colour of the hull, the colour of the funnel, the device on the funnel, the number of masts, the topmast, derricks, cross-trees, and so on. Thus, in the case of *Penshurst* there were any amount of disguises which in a few hours would render her a different ship. For instance, by painting her funnel black, with red flag and white letters thereon, she might easily be taken for one of the Carron Company's steamers, such as

Q-SHIP "BARRANCA"

In one form of disguise. Hull painted a light colour, black Loot-top to funnel, funnel painted a light colour, alley ways open. She is here seen in her original colour as a West Indian fruit-carrier.

Q-SHIP "BARRANCA"

Appearance altered by painting hull black and funnel black with white band. She is here disguised as a Spaniard, with Spanish colours painted on the ship's side just forward of the bridge, though not discernable in the photograph.

the *Forth*. By giving her a black funnel with a white V she might be the *Gloucester Coast* of the Powell, Bacon, and Hough Lines, Ltd.; by altering the funnel to black, white, red, white, and black bands she might have been the *Streatham*, owned by Messrs. John Harrison, Ltd. Other similar craft, such as the *Blackburn* and *Bargang*, had no funnel marks; so here again were more disguises. *Penshurst* further altered her appearance at times by taking down her mizzen-mast altogether, by filling in the well deck forward, by adding a false steam-pipe to the funnel, by shortening and levelling the derricks, by removing the main cross-trees, by painting or varnishing the wood bridge-screen, by giving the deckhouses a totally different colour, by showing red lead patches on the hull, and varying the colour of the sides with such hues as black to-day, next time green or grey or black, and adding a sail on the forestay.

If you will examine the photos of Commander Douglas's Q-ship *Barranca*, you will see how cleverly, by means of a little faking, even a much bigger ship could be disguised. In one picture you see her alleyways covered up by a screen, funnel markings altered, and so on; whilst in another the conspicuous white upper-works, the white band on the funnel, and the dark hull make her a different ship, so that, he tells me, on one occasion after passing a suspicious neutral steamer and not being quite satisfied, he was able to steam out of sight, change his ship's appearance, and then overtake her, get quite close and make a careful examination without revealing his identity. To the landsman all this may seem impossible, but inasmuch as the sea is traversed nowadays by steamers differing merely in minute details, distinguished only to the practised eye of the sailor, such deception is possible. I remember on one occasion during the war a surprising instance of this. Being in command of a steam drifter off the south-west Irish coast, I obtained Admiral Bayly's permission at my next refit to have the ship painted green, the foremast stepped, the funnel and markings painted differently, and a Dublin fishing letter and number painted on the bows, a suitable name being found in the Fisherman's Almanack. The 6-pounder gun forward was covered with fishing gear, which could be thrown overboard as soon as the ship came into action. Discarding naval uniform and wearing old cloth caps and clothes, we left Queenstown, steamed into Berehaven, and tied up alongside a patrol trawler with whom we had been working in company for nearly a year. The latter's crew never recognized us until they saw our faces, and even then insisted that we had got a new ship! In fact, one of them asserted that he knew this Dublin drifter very well, at which my Scotch crew from the Moray Firth were vastly amused.

Routine at sea of course differed in various Q-ships, but it may be interesting to set down the following, which prevailed in that well-organized ship *Penshurst*:

SEA ROUTINE.

Time as per Night Order Book.	Call guns' crew of morning watch; 3-pounder crew lash up and stow. Guns' crew close up, uncover guns, unship 6-pounder night-sights. Gunlayers report their crews closed up to officers of the watch.
5.30 a.m.	Call cooks and stewards.
6.0 a.m.	12-pounder crew and one of 3-pounder crew to wash down bridges and saloon-decks.
7.0 a.m.	Call guns' crews of forenoon watch, lash up and stow hammocks. Hands to wash.
7.30 a.m.	Forenoon watch to breakfast.

Q-SHIP "BARRANCA"
Disguised as a different ship with yellow funnel and black boot-top.

Q-SHIP "BARRANCA"
Appearance changed by closing up alley-ways, painting hull, ship's boats, and funnel so as to resemble a freighter of the P. & O. Line.

LIFE ON BOARD A Q-SHIP 223

8.0 a.m.	Change watches. Morning watch lash up and stow hammocks. Breakfast.
9.0 a.m.	Watch below clean mess-deck, etc.
11.30 a.m.	Afternoon watch to dinner.
12.30 p.m.	Change watches. Forenoon watch to dinner.
1.30 p.m.	Cooks clean up mess-deck.
3.30 p.m.	Tea.
4.0 p.m.	Change watches. Afternoon watch to tea.
6.0 p.m.	Change watches.
7.0 p.m.	Supper.
8.0 p.m.	Change watches. Watch below to supper.
Sunset.	Clean guns, ship 6-pounder night-sights. Cover guns. Drill as required.

A few weeks after the war, Lord Jellicoe remarked publicly that in the 'mystery ship' there had been displayed a spirit of endurance, discipline, and courage, the like of which the world had never seen before. He added that he did not think the English people realized the wonderful work which these ships had done in the war. No one who reads the facts here presented can fail to agree with this statement, which, indeed, is beyond argument. Discipline, of course, there was, even in the apparently and externally most slovenly tramp Q-ship; and it must not be thought that among so many crews of 'hard cases' all the hands were as harmless as china shepherdesses. When ashore, the average sailor is not always at his best: his qualities are manifest on sea and in the worst perils pertaining to the sea. The landsman, therefore, has the opportunity of observing him when the sailor wants to forget about ships and seas. If some of the Q-ships' crews occasionally kicked over the traces in the early days the fault was partly their own, but partly it was as the result of circumstances. Even Q-ship crews were human, and after weeks of cruising and pent-up keenness, after being battered about by seas, shelled by submarines while lying in dreadful suspense, and then doing all that human nature could be expected to perform, much may be forgiven them if the attractions of the shore temporarily overpowered them. In the early stages of the Q-ship the mistake was made of sending to them the 'bad hats' and impossible men of the depots; but the foolishness of this was soon discovered. Only the best men were good enough for this special service, and as the men were well paid and well decorated in return for success, there was no difficulty in choosing from the forthcoming volunteers an ideal crew. Any Q-ship captain will bear testimony to the wonderful effect wrought on a crew by the first encounter with an enemy submarine. The average seaman has much in him of the simple child, and has to be taught by plain experience to see the use and necessity of monotonous routine, of drills and discipline; but having once observed in hard battle the value of obedience, of organization and the like, he is a different man—he looks at sea-life, in spite of its boredom, from a totally different angle. Perfect discipline usually spelled victory over the enemy. Presently that, in turn, indicated a medal ribbon and 'a drop of leaf' at home, so as to tell his family all about it. Never again would he overstay his leave: back to the ship for him to give further evidence of his prowess.

This was the kind of fellow who could be relied upon to maintain at sea the gallant traditions of British seamanhood, and in their time of greatest peril the true big-souled character manifested itself, as real human truth always emerges in periods of crisis. I am thinking of one man who served loyally and faithfully in a certain Q-ship. In one engagement this gallant British sailor while in the execution of his duty was blown literally to pieces except for an arm, a leg in a sea-boot, and the rest a mere shattered, indescribable mass, his blood and flesh being scattered everywhere by the enemy's attack. And yet the last words of this good fellow, spoken just before it was too late, did much to help the Q-ship in her success. In a previous engagement this man's gun had the misfortune to start with seven missfires. This was owing to ammunition rendered faulty by having been kept on the deck too long as 'ready-use.' Consequently his gun did not come into action as quickly as the others. This piece of bad luck greatly upset such a keen warrior, and he was determined that no such accident should occur again. Therefore, in the next fight, just as he was crouching with his gun's crew behind the bridge-screen, he was heard to say to his mates: 'Now, mind. We're to be the *first* gun in action this time.' Immediately afterwards a shell came and killed him instantaneously.

Or, again, consider the little human touch in the case of the Q-ship commanded by Lieut.-Commander McLeod, which had been 'done in' and was sinking, so that she had really to be abandoned. When all were getting away in the boats, Lieut.-Commander McLeod's servant was found to be missing. At the last moment he suddenly reappeared, carrying with him a bag which he had gone back to fetch. In it was Lieut.-Commander McLeod's best monkey-jacket. 'I thought as you might want this, sir, seeing you'll have to go and see the Admiral when we get back to Queenstown,' was his cool explanation. Nothing could crush this kind of spirit, which prevailed in the trenches, the air, and on sea until the Armistice was won. It is the spirit of our forefathers, the inheritance of our island race, which, notwithstanding political and domestic tribulations, lies silent, dormant, undemonstrative, until the great hour comes for the best that is in us to show itself. Germany, of course, had her disguised armed ships, such as the *Moewe*, the *Wolf*, and so on, and with them our late enemies performed unquestionably brilliant work all over the world. It is true, also, that a similar achievement was attained in one disguised sailing ship; nor can we fail to admire the pluck and enterprise which enabled them to get through the British blockade. To belittle such first-class work would be to turn one's back on plain truth.

But the Q-ship service was not a short series of three or four spasms, but took its part in the persistent prosecution of the anti-submarine campaign. It remained a perpetual thorn in the enemy's side, and it was a most dangerous thorn. Unlike the U-boat service in its later stages, it continued to be composed of volunteers, and it was certainly the means of bringing to light extraordinary talent and courage. Like other children, the seaman loves dressing up and acting. In the Q-ship he found this among the other attractions, of which not the least was the conscious joy of taking a big share in the greatest of all wars. In one Q-ship alone were earned no fewer than four D.S.O.'s and three bars, five D.S.C.'s and seven bars, one Croix de Guerre, and six 'mentions' among the officers. Among the men this ship earned twenty-one D.S.M.'s and four bars, as well as three 'mentions.' To-day as you pass some tired old tramp at sea, or watch a begrimed steamer taking in a cargo of coals, you may be gazing at a ship as famous as Grenville's *Revenge* or Drake's *Golden Hind*. At the end of the war the Admiralty decided to place a memorial tablet on board each merchant vessel that had acted as a decoy during the war, the tablet being suitably inscribed with details of the gallant ship's service, together with the names of the commanding officer and members of the crew who received decorations. The first of these ships so to be commemorated was the *Lodorer*, better known to us as Captain Campbell's Q-ship *Farnborough*. After hostilities, in the presence of representatives of the owners and the Ministry of Shipping, Vice-Admiral Sir Alexander Duff unveiled *Lodorer's* tablet, and those who read it may well think and reflect.

CHAPTER XVI

Q-SHIPS EVERYWHERE

In the spring of 1917 there was a 2,905-ton steamship, called the *Bracondale*, in the employment of the Admiralty as a collier. It was decided that she would make a very useful Q-ship, so at the beginning of April she was thus commissioned and her name changed to *Chagford*. She was fitted out at Devonport and armed with a 4-inch, two 12-pounders, and a couple of torpedo tubes, and was ready for sea at the end of June. Commanded by Lieutenant D. G. Jeffrey, R.N.R., she proceeded to Falmouth in order to tune everything up, and then was based on Buncrana, which she left on August 2 for what was to be her last cruise, and I think that in the following story we have another instance of heroism and pertinacity of great distinction.

Chagford's position on August 5 at 4.10 a.m. was roughly 120 miles north-west of Tory Island, and she was endeavouring to find two enemy submarines which had been reported on the previous day. At the time mentioned she was herself torpedoed just below the bridge, and in this one explosion was caused very great injury: for it disabled both her torpedo tubes and her 4-inch gun; it shattered the boats on the starboard side as well as the captain's cabin and chart room. In addition, it also wrecked all the voice-pipe connections to the torpedo tubes and guns, and it flooded the engine-room and put the engines out of commission, killing one of the crew. Lieutenant Jeffrey therefore 'abandoned' ship, and just as the boats were getting away two periscopes and a submarine were sighted on the starboard side 800 yards away. As soon as the enemy came to the surface fire was opened on her by the two 12-pounders and both Lewis and machine-guns, several direct hits being observed. The submarine then dived, but at 4.40 a.m. she fired a second torpedo at *Chagford*, which hit the ship abaft the bridge on the starboard side.

From the time the first torpedo had hit, the enemy realized that *Chagford* was a warship, for the 4-inch gun and torpedo tubes had been made visible, and now that the second explosion had come Lieutenant Jeffrey decided to recall his boats so that the ship might genuinely be abandoned. The lifeboat, dinghy, and a barrel raft were accordingly filled, and about 5.30 a.m. the enemy fired a third torpedo, which struck also on the starboard side. Having sent away in the boats and raft everyone with the exception of himself and a lieutenant, R.N.R., two sub-lieutenants, R.N.R., also an assistant-paymaster, R.N.R., and one petty officer, Lieutenant Jeffrey stationed these in hiding under cover of the fo'c'sle and poop, keeping a smart look-out, however, through the scuttles.

Here was another doomed ship rolling about in the Atlantic without her crew, and only a gallant handful of British seamanhood still standing by with but a shred of hope. To accentuate their suspense periscopes were several times seen, and from 9 a.m. until 9 p.m. a submarine frequently appeared on the surface at long range, and almost every hour a periscope passed round the ship inspecting her cautiously. During the whole of this time *Chagford* was settling down gradually but certainly. At dark Lieutenant Jeffrey, fearing that the enemy might attempt boarding, placed Lewis and Maxim guns in position and served out rifles and bayonets to all. Midnight came, and after making a further examination of the damage, Lieutenant Jeffrey realized that it was impossible for the *Chagford* to last much longer, for her main deck amidships was split from side to side, the bridge deck was badly buckled, and the whole ship was straining badly. Therefore, just before half-past midnight, these five abandoned the ship in a small motor-boat which they had picked up at sea some days previously, but before quitting *Chagford* they disabled the guns, all telescopic sights and strikers being removed.

Having shoved off, they found to their dismay that there were no tanks in the motor-boat, so she had to be propelled by a couple of oars, and it will readily be appreciated that this kind of propulsion in the North Atlantic was not a success. They then thought of going back to the ship, but before they could do so they were fortunately picked up at 7.30 a.m. by H.M. trawler *Saxon*, a large submarine having been seen several times on the horizon between 4 and 7 a.m. The trawler then proceeded to hunt for the submarine, but, as the latter had now made off, volunteers were called for and went aboard *Chagford*, so that by 4 p.m. *Saxon* had commenced towing her. Bad luck again overcame their efforts, for wind and sea had been steadily increasing, and of course there was no steam, so the heavy work of handling cables had all to be done by hand. Until the evening the ship towed fairly well at 2 knots, but, as she seemed then to be breaking up, the tow-rope had to be slipped, and just before eight o'clock next morning (August 7) she took a final plunge and disappeared. The *Saxon* made for the Scottish coast and landed the survivors at Oban on the morning of the eighth. In this encounter, difficult as it was, *Chagford* had done real service, for she had damaged the submarine so much that she could not submerge, and this was probably U 44 which H.M.S. *Oracle* sighted in the early hours of August 12 off the north coast of Scotland, evidently bound to Germany. *Oracle* chased her; U 44 kept diving and coming to the surface after a short while. She had disguised herself as a trawler, and was obviously unable to dive except for short periods. *Oracle* shelled and then rammed her, so that U 44 was destroyed and *Chagford* avenged. Nothing more was seen of *Chagford* except some wreckage found by a trawler on August 11, who noticed the word *Bracondale* on the awnings.

After Lieutenant Jeffrey and crew had returned to their base they proceeded to fit out the 2,794-ton S.S. *Arvonian*. This was to be a very powerful Q-ship, for she was armed with three 4-inch guns instead of one, in addition to three 12-pounders, two Maxim guns, and actually four 18-inch torpedo tubes. She was, in fact, a light cruiser, except for speed and appearance, but the *Chagford* crew were destined to disappointment, for this is what happened. The reader will recollect that in her engagement of June 7, 1917, Captain Campbell's famous ship *Pargust* received so much damage that she had to be left in dockyard hands while he and his crew went to sea in the *Dunraven*. Now, at the beginning of October Admiral Sims asked the British Admiralty for a ship to carry out this decoy work, and to be manned by the United States Navy. The Admiralty therefore selected *Pargust*, and Admiral Sims then assigned her to the U.S.N. forces based on Queenstown. Her repairs, however, took rather a longer time than had been hoped; in fact, she was not finished and commissioned again until the following May, so it was decided to pay off *Arvonian* on November 26, 1917, and she was then recommissioned with a United States crew under Commander D. C. Hanrahan, U.S.N., and changed her name to *Santee*. By the time she left Queenstown for her maiden cruise she was a very wonderful ship. Her 4-inch guns had been disguised by being recessed, and by such concealments as lifebuoy lockers, hatch covers, and so on. The 12-pounder gun aft had a tilting mounting, as also had the two 12-pounders forward at the break of the fo'c'sle on either side. Thus they were concealed, but could be instantly brought into position. Her four torpedo tubes were arranged so that there was one on each beam, one to fire right ahead, and one to fire right astern. She also boasted of a searchlight, a wireless set, and an emergency wireless apparatus. She had two lifeboats, two skiffs, two Carley floats, and also a motor-boat. She was thus the last word in Q-ship improvements, and embodied all the lessons which had been learnt by bitter and tragic experience. Two days after Christmas, 1917, she left Queenstown at dusk on her way to Bantry Bay to train her crew, but in less than five hours she was torpedoed. It was no disgrace, but a sheer bit of hard luck which might have happened to any other officer, British or American. Commander Hanrahan was one of the ablest and keenest destroyer captains of the American Navy, and no one who had ever been aboard his ship could fail to note his efficiency. He had been one of

Q-SHIPS EVERYWHERE 233

the early destroyer arrivals when the United States that summer had begun to send their destroyer divisions across the Atlantic to Queenstown, and he had done most excellent work.

But on this night his Q-ship career came to a sudden stop, though not before everything possible had been done to entrap the enemy. It was one of those cloudy, moonlight, wintry nights with good visibility. As might have been expected under such a captain there was a total absence of confusion; all hands went to their stations, the 'panic' party got away in accordance with the best 'panic' traditions, while on board the crews remained at their gun stations for five hours, hoping and longing for the submarine to show herself. No such good fortune followed, for the submarine was shy; so just before midnight Commander Hanrahan sent a wireless message to Admiral Bayly at Queenstown, and very shortly afterwards the U.S. destroyer *Cummings* arrived. At 1 a.m. the tug *Paladin* took *Santee* in tow, escorted by four United States destroyers and the two British sloops *Viola* and *Bluebell*. *Santee* got safely into port and was sent to Devonport, where she was eventually handed back by the U.S.N. to the British Navy, owing to the time involved in repairs. On June 4, 1918, she was once more recommissioned in the Royal Navy and took the name of *Bendish*, the crew having come from the Q-ship *Starmount*. By this date the conditions of submarine warfare had undergone a modification. In home waters it was only the quite small Q-ships of the coaster type, of about 500 tons, which could be expected to have any chance of successfully engaging a submarine. This class would normally be expected to be seen within the narrow seas, and the enemy would not be so shy. But for such vessels as *Bendish* and *Pargust* the most promising sphere was likely to be between Gibraltar and the Azores and the north-west coast of Africa, where German so-called 'cruiser' submarines of the *Deutschland* type were operating. Therefore a special force, based on Gibraltar but operating in the Azores area or wherever submarines were to be expected, was organized, consisting of four Q-ships. These were the *Bendish* (late *Santee*), Captain Campbell's former ship *Pargust* but now named the *Pangloss*, the *Underwing*, and the *Marshfort*, the whole squadron being under the command of Lieut.-Commander Dane in *Bendish*. After being at last ready for sea in May, 1918, *Pangloss*, commanded by Lieutenant Jeffrey, who for his fine work in *Chagford* had received the D.S.O., had then been assigned to serve under the Vice-Admiral Northern Patrols until she was sent south.

Under the new scheme just mentioned these four Q-ships were so worked that they always arrived and sailed from Gibraltar as part of the convoy of merchant ships, from which class they could not be distinguished. But already long before this date Q-ships had been employed in such distant waters. For instance, in the middle of November, 1916, the *Barranca* (Lieut.-Commander S. C. Douglas, R.N.) was sent from Queenstown via Devonport, and proceeded to operate in the neighbourhood of Madeira and the Canaries, based on Gibraltar. This ship, known officially as Q 3 (alias *Echunga*), had been taken over from Messrs. Elders and Fyffes, Ltd. Her registered tonnage was 4,115, and she had a speed of 14 knots, so she was eminently fitted for this kind of work. She had been employed as a Q-ship since June, 1916, and was armed with a 4-inch, two

Q-SHIP TRANSFORMATION
Crew painting funnel while at sea (see pp. 220-1).

Q-SHIP "BARRANCA" AT SEA
The look-out man aft is disguised as one of the Mercantile crew. The dummy wheel, dummy sky-light, and dummy deck-house are seen. The latter concealed a 4-inch gun and two 12-pounders.

Q-SHIPS EVERYWHERE 235

12-pounders, and two 6-pounders, and terminated her service in the following May. Her captain had been one of the earliest officers to be employed in decoy work, having been second in command to Lieut.-Commander Godfrey Herbert when that officer commanded the *Antwerp*. Soon after this date the Q-ship *Dunclutha* left for that part of the Atlantic which is between the north-east coast of South America and north-west coast of Africa. This ship, together with *Ooma*, both of them being vessels of between 3,000 and 4,000 tons, had commenced their special service at the end of 1916 and been sent to work under the British Commodore off the east coast of South America in the hope of falling in with one of the German raiders, such as the *Moewe*. In May, 1918, both these vessels had to be withdrawn from such service, as the shortage of tonnage had become acute, and were required to load general cargo in a Brazilian port. Another of these overseas Q-ships was the *Bombala* (alias *Willow Branch*). She was a 3,314-ton steamer and had left Gibraltar on April 18, 1918, for Sierra Leone. A week later, off the West African coast, she sighted a submarine off the port quarter, and a few minutes later a second one off the starboard bow. Both submarines opened their attack with shells, this class of submarine being armed with a couple of 5·9-inch guns. After about thirty rounds the enemy had found the range, and then began to hit the ship repeatedly, carrying away the wireless and causing many casualties. *Bombala* shortened the range so that she could use her 4-inch and 14-pounder, and the action went on for two and a half hours. By that time *Bombala* was done for, and it was impossible to save the ship; so the crew were ordered into the boats, and then the ship foundered, bows first. However, the Q-ship had not sunk without severely damaging the enemy, for when the submarines came alongside *Bombala's* boats it was found that in one of the submarines there were seven killed and four wounded.

Q-ships were kept pretty busy, too, in the Mediterranean. On March 11, 1917, when *Wonganella* (Lieut.-Commander B. J. D. Guy, R.N.) was on her way from Malta to England via Gibraltar, she was shelled by a submarine, and while the 'panic' party were getting out the boats, a shell wounded the officer and several of the crew in the starboard lifeboat. Another shell went through the bulwarks of the ship, wounding some men and bursting the steam-pipe of the winch, thus rendering unworkable the derrick used for hoisting out the third boat, and the port lifeboat was also damaged. Shells burst in the well deck and holed the big boat, so in this case, as all his boats were 'done in,' the captain had to give up the idea of 'abandoning' ship. There was nothing for it but to open fire, though it was not easy for orders to be heard in that indescribable din when shells were bursting, steam pouring out from the burst winch-pipe, wounded men in great pain, and *Wonganella's* own boiler-steam blowing off with its annoying roar. As soon as fire was opened, the submarine dived and then fired a torpedo, which was avoided by *Wonganella* going astern with her engines, the torpedo just missing the ship's fore-foot by 10 feet. No more was seen of the enemy, and at dusk the armed steam yacht *Iolanda* was met, from whom a doctor was obtained, thus saving the lives of several of the wounded. In this engagement, whilst the White Ensign was being hoisted, the signal halyards were shot away, so the ensign had to be carried up the rigging and secured thereto.

Wonganella was holed on the water-line and hit elsewhere, but she put into Gibraltar on March 13, and on the evening of June 19 of the same year we find her out in the Atlantic west of the south-west Irish coast on her way homeward-bound from Halifax. A submarine bore down on her from the north, and at the long range of 8,000 yards was soon straddling *Wonganella*. Now the Q-ship happened to have on board thirty survivors from a steamer recently sunk, so again it was impossible to attempt the 'abandon ship' deception. She therefore used her smoke-screen —at this time ships were being supplied with special smoke-making apparatus—and then ran down the wind at varying speeds and on various courses, with the hope that the enemy would chase quickly. *Wonganella* would then turn in the smoke-cloud and suddenly emerge and close the enemy at a more suitable range. But the best-laid schemes of Q-ships are subject to the laws of chance, for now there appeared another merchant ship heading straight towards this scene, and thus unwittingly frustrated the further development of the encounter. This 'merchant ship' was the Q-ship *Aubrietia* (Q 13), who did, in fact, receive a signal from *Wonganella* that no assistance was required; but by that time it was too late to withdraw. The submarine, after shelling *Wonganella* through the smoke, abandoned the attack and withdrew without ever scoring a hit.

During all these months the disguised steam trawlers were continuing their arduous work. On August 20, 1916, the *Gunner* from Granton engaged a submarine during the afternoon, but the German subsequently dived. *Gunner* then proceeded on a westerly course whilst she altered her disguise, and then that same evening encountered this submarine again, shelled her, but once more the enemy broke off the fight. The disguised Granton trawler *Speedwell* was also operating in a manner similar to *Gunner*, and in the following March the trawler *Commissioner* began her decoy work. She was a 161-ton ship armed with a 12-pounder, her method of working being as follows: Lieutenant F. W. Charles, R.N.R., was in command of the fighting portion of the crew, but her fishing skipper was otherwise in charge of the ship. *Commissioner* proceeded to join the Granton fishing fleet, looking like any other steam trawler, and then shot her trawl and carried on like the rest of the fleet. When a submarine should appear *Commissioner* would cut away her fishing gear and then attack the enemy. Such an occasion actually occurred the very day after she first joined the fishing fleet, but the submarine was not sunk.

A similar decoy was the Granton steam trawler *Rosskeen*, which left the Firth of Forth to 'fish' about 20 miles east of the Longstone. Three days later she was just about to shoot her trawl when a shot came whistling over her wheelhouse, and a large submarine was then seen 8,000 yards away. After twenty minutes, during which the enemy's shells fell uncomfortably close, *Rosskeen* cut away her gear and 'abandoned' ship. The submarine then obligingly approached on the surface towards the rowing boat, and when the range was down to 1,200 yards *Rosskeen*, who was armed with a 12-pounder and 6-pounder, opened fire from the former and hit the submarine, the conning-tower being very badly damaged by the third shot. Two more shells got home, and by this time the enemy had had enough, and dived.

These trawlers were undoubtedly both a valuable protection to the fishermen (who had been repeatedly

Q-SHIPS EVERYWHERE

attacked by the enemy) and a subtle trap for some of the less experienced submarine captains. During May two more trawlers, the *Strathallan* and *Strathearn*, were similarly commissioned, and even steam drifters such as the *Fort George* (armed with one 6-pounder) were employed in this kind of work. On the thirteenth of June *Strathearn* was fishing 19 miles east of the Bell Rock when five shots were fired at her, presumably by a submarine, though owing to the hazy weather nothing could be seen. The enemy then evidently sighted a destroyer and disappeared. On the following day *Fort George* was fishing about 35 miles east of May Island, when she was attacked by submarine at 2,000 yards. It was ten o'clock at night, and the drifter, after the third round, secured her fishing gear and returned the fire. The enemy was evidently surprised, for after the drifter had fired three shells the German broke off the engagement and submerged, but with his fourth and fifth rounds he had hit *Fort George*, killing two and wounding another couple.

But on the following twenty-eighth of January *Fort George* was about 14 miles east of May Island, with the decoy trawler *W. S. Bailey* (Lieutenant C. H. Hudson, D.S.C., R.N.R.). The two ships were listening on their hydrophones when a submarine was distinctly heard some distance away, and it was assumed that the enemy was steering for May Island, so the *W. S. Bailey* after proceeding for a quarter of an hour in that direction listened again, and the sounds were heard more plainly. For an hour and a half the enemy was determinedly hunted, and just after 9 p.m. the sounds became very distinct, so the trawler steamed full speed ahead in the submarine's direction, dropped a depth charge, listened, and then, as the enemy was still heard on the hydrophone, a second charge was dropped. The trawler then went full speed astern to check her way, and just as she was stopping there were sighted two periscopes not 20 yards away, on the starboard quarter, and going full speed. The trawler then dropped a third depth charge over the spot where the periscopes had disappeared, and nothing further was heard on the hydrophone, but a fourth charge was then let go to make sure, and the position was buoyed, and the disguised craft remained in the vicinity until January 30. A few days later the *W. S. Bailey* swept with her chain-sweep over the position, and on each occasion the sweep brought up in the place that had been buoyed, and a quantity of oil was seen. Local fishermen accustomed to working their gear along this bottom reported that the obstruction was quite new. In short, the *W. S. Bailey* had succeeded in destroying UB 63, a submarine about 180 feet long and well armed with a 4·1-inch gun and torpedoes. For this useful service Lieutenant Hudson received a bar to his D.S.C., while Skipper J. H. Lawrence, R.N.R., was awarded the D.S.C.

Thus, in all waters and in all manner of ships wearing every kind of disguise, the shy submarine was being tempted and sought out, though every month decoy work was becoming more and more difficult: for though you might fool the whole German submarine service in the early stages of Q-ships, it was impossible that you could keep on bluffing all of them every time. The most that could be expected was that as a reward for your constant vigilance and perfect organization you might one day catch him off his guard through his foolishness or lack of experience or incautiousness. But every indecisive action made it

Q-SHIPS EVERYWHERE

worse for the Q-ships, for that vessel was a mark for future attack and the enemy's intelligence department was thereby enriched, and outgoing submarines could be warned against such a trawler or such a tramp whose guns had a dead sector on such a bearing. Thus an inefficient Q-ship captain would be a danger not merely to himself and his men, but to the rest of the force. Nothing succeeds like success, and there was nothing so useful as to make a clean job of the submarine-sinking, so that he could never get back home and tell the news. Surprise, whether in real life or fiction, is a factor that begins to lose its power in proportion to its frequency of use. It was so in the Q-ships, and that is why, after a certain point had been reached, this novel method became so difficult and so barren in results.

CHAPTER XVII

SHIPS OF ALL SIZES

THE unrestricted phase of submarine warfare instituted in February, 1917, had, apart from other means, been met by an increase in the number of Q-ships, so that by the end of May there were close upon eighty steamers and sailing craft either being fitted out as decoys or already thus employed. By far the greater number of the big Q-ships were serving under Admiral Bayly, the other large craft being based on Longhope, Portsmouth, the south-east of England, and Malta. Of the smaller types, such as trawlers and sailing ships, no fewer than one-half were based on Granton, under Admiral Startin, the rest of these little vessels working out of Stornoway, Longhope, Peterhead, Lowestoft, Portsmouth, Plymouth, Falmouth, Milford Haven, and Malta.

One of the moderate-sized Q-steamers was the 1,680-ton *Stonecrop*, alias *Glenfoyle*, which was armed with a 4-inch, a 12-pounder, and four 200-lb. howitzers. She had begun her special service at the end of May, 1917, under Commander M. B. R. Blackwood, R.N. She was very slow, and her captain found her practically unmanageable in anything of a head wind and sea. Her first cruise was in the English Channel, and she left Portsmouth on August 22. Three days later when 15 miles south of the Scillies she saw a large steamer torpedoed and sunk. *Stonecrop* herself was caught in bad weather, and had to run before the gale and sea towing an oil bag astern. Arriving back at Portsmouth she needed a few repairs, and left again on September 11 to cruise off the western approaches of the British Isles. Six days later she was off the south-west coast of Ireland steering a westerly course when a submarine was seen on the surface. This was the U 88, one of the biggest types, over 200 feet long, armed with a 4·1-inch and a 22-pounder, plus torpedoes. It was now 4.40 p.m., and though the enemy was still several miles away he opened fire three minutes later with both guns. *Stonecrop* accordingly pretended to flee from his wrath, turned 16 points, made off at her full speed (which was only 7 knots), made S.O.S. signals on her wireless, followed by ' Hurry up or I shall have to abandon ship '—*en clair* so that the submarine should read it. And in order further still to simulate a defensively armed merchant ship she replied with her after gun.

Thus it went on until 5.15 p.m., by which time the submarine had not registered a hit and was gradually closing: but most of the shells were falling very near to the steamer, so that the German might easily have supposed they were hits. In order to fool the enemy further still Commander Blackwood had his smoke apparatus now lit. This was most successful, the whole ship becoming enveloped in smoke and seeming to be on fire. A quarter of an hour later *Stonecrop* ' abandoned ' ship, sending away also a couple of hands in uniform to represent the men from the deserted defensive gun. The submarine then displayed the usual tactics: submerged, came slowly towards the ship, passing down the port side, rounding the stern, and then came to the surface 600 yards off the starboard quarter, displaying the whole of his length. For three minutes the British and German captains remained looking at each other, the former, of course, from his position of concealment. But at ten minutes past six, as there were still no signs of anyone coming out of the conning-tower hatch, and as the U-boat seemed about to make for *Stonecrop's* boats, Captain Blackwood decided this was the critical moment and gave the order. From the 4-inch gun and all howitzers there suddenly poured across the intervening 600 yards a very hot fire, which had unmistakable effect: for the fourth shot hit the base of the conning-tower, causing a large explosion and splitting the conning-tower in two. The fifth shot got her just above the water-line under the foremost gun, the sixth struck between that gun and the conning-tower, the seventh hit 30 feet from the end of the hull, the eighth got her just at the angle of the conning-tower and deck, the ninth and tenth shells came whizzing on to the water-line between the after gun and conning-tower, whilst the eleventh hit the deck just abaft the conning-tower and tearing it up. Good gunnery, certainly!

This was about as much as the stunned submarine could stand, and forging ahead she suddenly submerged and sank stern first, but a few seconds later she rose to the surface with a heavy list to starboard, and then sank for good and all. For, on submerging, she had found she was leaking so badly that her condition was hopeless, and she was doubtless intending to surrender, but apparently the fourth shot from *Stonecrop* had so damaged the conning-tower hatch that it could not be opened. Thus there perished U 88, but this was more than the sinking of an ordinary submarine, for with her there went to his doom Lieut.-Commander Schwieger, who, when in command of U 20, had sunk the *Lusitania* on May 7, 1915, with the loss of over eleven hundred men, women, and children. Altogether *Stonecrop's* action had been very neat. He had lured the enemy into a short range, utterly fooled him, and then disabled him before he woke up. For this service Commander Blackwood received the D.S.O., and three R.N.R. lieutenants and a naval warrant officer each received a D.S.C. But Q-ship life was always full of uncertainties, for on the very next day *Stonecrop* was herself torpedoed by another submarine at 1 p.m., though fortunately this was in a position a little nearer the coast. Two officers and twenty survivors were picked up by a motor-launch of the Auxiliary Patrol and landed at Berehaven; sixty-four men in one boat and a raft were remaining behind, but all available craft were sent out to rescue them.

The employment of small coasting steamers was, during the last phase of the war, more and more developed. What the Q-ship captain liked was that the enemy should attack him not with torpedoes but with gunfire. Now, even the biggest German submarines carried usually not more than ten torpedoes, and inasmuch as his cruise away from any base lasted weeks, and, in the case of the *Deutschland* class, even months, it was obvious that the U-boat had to conserve his torpedoes for those occasions which were really worth while. From this it follows that a submarine captain who knew his work, and was anxious to make a fine haul before ending his cruise, would not, as a rule, waste his torpedoes on a 500-ton steamer when he might have secured much bigger tonnage by using the same missile against a 20,000-ton liner.

This suggested an avenue of thought, and as early

as January, 1918, the matter was considered by Admiral Bayly and developed. Already there were in existence several small vessels acting as Q-ships, but simultaneously carrying out in all respects the duties of cargo-carriers from port to port, and thus paying their way. It was now decided to look for a little steamer which, based on Queenstown, would work between the Bristol Channel, Irish Sea, and the south coast of Ireland, where even during the height of the submarine campaign it was customary to see such craft. As a result of this decision Captain Gordon Campbell was sent to inspect the S.S. *Wexford Coast*, which was being repaired at Liverpool. Her gross tonnage was only 423, she had a well deck, three masts, and engines placed aft: just the ordinary-looking, innocent steamer that would hardly attract a torpedo. Owned by Messrs. Powell, Bacon, Hough, and Co., of Liverpool, this vessel had already done valuable work in the war; for in 1915 she had been requisitioned for store-carrying in the Dardanelles, where she was found invaluable in keeping the troops supplied, and when that campaign came to an end assisted at the evacuation. Returning to England, she was again sent out as a store-carrier, this time to the White Sea. *Wexford Coast* was now taken up as a Q-ship, her fitting-out being supervised by Lieut.-Commander L. S. Boggs, R.N.R., who had been in command of the Q-ship *Tamarisk*, and from the last ship came a large part of her new crew. She was duly armed, and fitted with a cleverly concealed wireless aerial, to be used only in case of emergency, and was then commissioned on March 13, 1918, as 'Store-Carrier No. 80,' this title being for the purpose of preserving secrecy. She put to sea in her dual capacity, but on August 31 had the misfortune to be run into by the French S.S. *Bidart*, six miles southeast of the Start, at four o'clock in the morning—another instance of this fatal hour for collisions. The Frenchman grounded on the Skerries and capsized, and the *Wexford Coast* had to put in to Devonport. After the sinking of the Q-ship *Stockforce* (to be related presently), Admiral Bayly wished the captain and crew of the latter to be appointed to a coaster similar to *Wexford Coast*, so the *Suffolk Coast* was chosen at the beginning of August whilst she was lying in the Firth of Forth. Before the end of the month she had arrived at Queenstown, where she was fitted out. On November 10 she set out from Queenstown, but on the following day came the Armistice, which spoiled her ambitions. However, in this, the latest of all Q-ships, we see the development so clearly that it will not be out of place here to anticipate dates and give her description.

Suffolk Coast was intentionally the most ordinary-looking little coaster, with three masts, her engines and funnel being placed aft, and the very last thing she resembled was a man-of-war. But she was heavily armed for so small a ship. In her were embodied all the concentrated experience of battle and engineering development. All that could be learned from actual fighting, from narrow escapes, and from defects manifested in awkward moments was here taken advantage of. Instead of a 12-knot 4,000-ton steamer the development had, owing to the trend of the campaign, been in the direction of a ship one-eighth of the size, but more cleverly disguised with better 'gadgets.' In fact, instead of being a model of simplicity as in the early days, the Q-ship had become a veritable box of tricks. It was the triumph of mind over material, of brain over battle.

Coolness and bravery and resolute endurance were just as requisite in the last as in the first stages of the campaign, but the qualities of scientific bluff had attained the highest value. The basic principle was extreme offensive power combined with outward innocence: the artfulness of the eagle, but the appearance of a dove.

In *Suffolk Coast* there was one long series of illusions from forward to aft. On the fo'c'sle head was a quite usual wire reel such as is used in this class of ship for winding in a wire rope. But this reel had been hollowed out inside so as to allow the captain to con the ship. Near by was also a periscope, but this was disguised by being hidden in a stove-pipe such as would seem to connect with the crew's heating arrangements below. Now this was not merely a display of ingenuity but an improvement based on many a hard case. What frequently happened after the 'abandon ship' party pushed off? As we have seen, this was often the time when the real fight began, and the enemy would shell the bridge to make sure no living thing could remain. That being so, the obvious position for the captain was to be away from the bridge, though it broke away from all the traditions of the sea. In *Suffolk Coast* the enemy could continue sweeping the bridge, but the captain would be under the shelter of the fo'c'sle head and yet watching intently. Similarly both he and his men need not, in passing from the bridge or one end of the ship to another, be exposed to the enemy's fire, for an ingenious tunnel was made right into the fo'c'sle through the hold. In a similar manner, if the forward part of the ship had been 'done in,' there was a periscope aft disguised as a pipe coming up from the galley stove.

SHIPS OF ALL SIZES

Now, when a submarine started shelling a Q-ship, the latter would naturally heave-to and then pretend she had been disabled by being hit in the engine-room. This was achieved by fitting a pipe specially arranged to let steam issue forth. The importance of wireless in these death-struggles may well be realized, so not merely was one wireless cabinet placed below, but another was situated in the fo'c'sle. The *Suffolk Coast*, with her two 4-inch and two 12-pounders, was armed in a manner superior to any submarines excepting those of the biggest classes such as voyaged south to the Canaries and north-west African coast. This Q-ship's guns were concealed in the most wonderfully ingenious manner, so that it would have puzzled even a seaman to discover their presence. Thus the forward 12-pounder was mounted in No. 1 hold, the hatch being suitably arranged for collapsing. The first 4-inch gun was placed further aft, covered by a deck, and the sides made to fall down when the time came for action. The second 4-inch was mounted still further aft and similarly concealed, whilst the other 12-pounder was allowed to be conspicuous at the stern so that all U-craft might believe she was the usual defensively armed merchant ship. Without this they might have become suspicious. In this 'mystery ship' everything was done to render her capable of remaining afloat for the maximum of time after injury, and, in addition to having a well-stowed cargo of timber, she had special watertight bulkheads fitted. With a thorough system of voice-pipes, so that the captain could keep a perfect control over the ship's firing—a most essential consideration, as the reader will already have ascertained—and a crew of nearly fifty experienced officers and men, such a small ship represented the apotheosis of the decoy just as the war was terminating. Every sort of scheme which promised possibilities was tried, and many clever minds had been at work, but this represented the standard of success after four long years.

Every new aspect of the submarine advancement had to be thought out and met, and the variations were most noticeable, but during the last few months of the war considerable attention had to be concentrated on the areas of the Azores, the north, south, east, and west of Ireland, the Bristol Channel, and the approaches to the English Channel in the west. But by the spring of 1918 the crews of German submarines had become distinctly inferior. Their commanding officers were often young and raw, there was a great dearth of trained engineer officers and experienced petty officers, and this was shown in frequent engine-room breakdowns. So many submarines had failed to return home, and others reported such hairbreadth escapes, that the inferior crews became nervous and were not sorry to be taken prisoners. The fact was that not only were expert, highly skilled officers hard to find, but the hands he was compelled to go to sea with were no longer chosen by the captain; he had to accept whatever recruits were drafted to his craft. Of the best *personnel* that remained many had lost their nerve and had a very real dread of mines, depth charges, and decoy ships. The institution of our convoy system and of Q-ships as part of the convoy did not add to the pleasures of the U-boat officers. It is true that the often excellent shooting of the submarines was due to the fact that their gun-layers were generally selected from the High Sea Fleet, but as against this many of our Q-ship expert gunners were out of the Grand Fleet. It is true that the cruiser submarines

SHIPS OF ALL SIZES

with their two 5·9-inch guns, plus torpedoes, were formidable foes even for the most heavily armed decoy, but as against this they took a long time to dive, and thus represented a better target.

If we consider these facts in regard to the later tactics of the submarines in contest with our decoy ships, there is much that becomes clear. The excellence of our intelligence system has been shown by various British and German writers since the war, and, as a rule, we were extraordinarily prepared for the new developments with which our Q-ships were likely to be faced. On the other hand, the enemy's supply of intelligence was bad, and if we put ourselves in the position of an inexperienced young U-boat captain we can easily see how difficult was his task toward the end of hostilities. He was sent out to sink ships, and yet practically every British ship was at least armed defensively, and there was nothing to indicate which of them might be a well-armed decoy, save for the fact that he had been informed by his superiors that trap-ships were seldom of a size greater than 4,000 tons. Sailing ships, fishing craft, and steamers might be ready to spring a surprise, so that it was not easy for the German to combine ruthless attack with reasonable caution: thus, in effect, the battle came down to a matter of personality. It was not merely a question of the man behind the gun, nor of the man behind the torpedo, but the man at the periscope of the submarine versus the man peeping at him from the spy-hole of the steamer. They were strange tactics, indeed, to be employed in naval war when we consider the simple, hearty methods of previous campaigns in history, but even as an impersonal study of two foes this perpetual battle of wits, of subtleties, and make-believe, must ever remain both interesting and instructive in spite of the terrible loss of life accompanying it. Life on board one of the small steam Q-ships was, apart from its dangers arising through mines and submarines, distinctly lacking in comfort. The following extracts from the private diary of a Q-ship's commanding officer at different dates afford, in the fewest words, an insight into the life on board :

'The heavy westerly gale was banking up the west-going tide, and made the most fierce and dangerous sea that I have ever seen. The ship made little headway and was tossed about like a small boat. Fortunately we managed to keep end on to the sea, or I think the old tub would have gone slick over. As it was she behaved well, though her movements were pretty violent. Seas broke over the stern and washed away the stern gratings, one big sea broke right over the forward deck, a tumbling mass of foam, into the water on the other side of the ship, carrying away a ventilator and some steam-pipes. I had one spasm of anxiety, when in the middle of all this the wheel jammed for a few seconds, and I feared she would broach-to. If we had done so, I think the ship would at once have been rolled over and smothered. I have never before seen such enormous breakers. . . .'

'Had just finished tea and was sitting at the table yarning with the others when the alarm gong went and we all dashed out. . . . Immediately before the gong went, M——, our young R.N.V.R. signalman, who had never been to sea before, and who was on watch, remarked to W——, the officer of the watch, "What's that funny-looking stick sticking out of the water over there?" W—— cast an eye at the said "funny-looking stick sticking out of the water" 200 yards on our starboard beam, and remarked profanely :

"Good God, man, why, it's a periscope!" and promptly rang the gong.' It was, indeed, a periscope, and presently the submarine opened fire and sent a shell through the ship's engine-room, which disabled the ship, though she was afterwards towed into port, where she was repaired and refitted for her next encounter.

'Completed loading timber at 11 a.m. Total 599 tons. That ought to keep us afloat if we are torpedoed. . . . The ship's behaviour is quite different to what it was with coal ballast. She moves, but with a much easier motion, and without that terrible jerkiness she had before. . . . When off the —— we fell in with a lifeboat under sail, evidently with survivors from a sunk ship. Stopped and took them on board. They turned out to be the captain, 2nd officer, purser, 3rd engineer, and ten men, part of the crew of the S.S. ——, which had been torpedoed at 11.30 a.m. yesterday. . . . Discussing the daily lie for Fritz with S——: To-day we are from Cape Coast Castle with kernels, bound for London. I wonder if it will go down with Fritz. . . .'

And the following entry after successfully sinking a German submarine notwithstanding many months of monotonous uneventfulness:

'I then "spliced the main-brace." We passed the S—— Light at 11.30 p.m., and just before picking up the Examination boat received a wireless message from [the Commander-in-Chief], which reads: "Very well done. A year's perseverance well rewarded." . . . We anchored at midnight, and a boat at once came off with a doctor, who removed the wounded. . . . A tug brought off the armed guard sent . . . to receive our prisoners. . . . We formally mustered the prisoners and handed them over with the signing of receipts for their custody and disposal, etc. It was an impressive moment when I led the officer in charge to the saloon, and handed over to him the commanding officer of the submarine. A couple of bluejackets with rifles fixed promptly closed up at either elbow, and he was marched out. He had the grace to pause at the door, where I was standing, and to thank me for my treatment of him. He was no doubt very much upset by the loss of his ship: we found him extremely glum and did our best to cheer him up. He had lunch with us, and I think he really did find that we were human. Similarly the other officers tendered their thanks (they all went away in a good deal of our clothing), and when it came to the marching off of the men, —— stepped out of the ranks and tendered to me their grateful thanks for the excellent treatment they had received at our hands.'

CHAPTER XVIII

THE LAST PHASE

ONE of the effects of the British blockade on Germany was to prevent such valuable war material as iron reaching Germany from Spain. Now Spanish ores, being of great purity, were in pre-war days imported in large quantities for the manufacture of the best qualities of steel, and it was a serious matter for Germany that these importations were cut off. But luckily for her she had been accustomed to obtain, even prior to the war, supplies of magnetic ore from Sweden, and it was of the utmost importance that this should be continued now that the war would last much longer than she had ever expected.

If you look at a map of Scandinavia inside the Arctic Circle you will notice the West Fjord, which is between the Lofoten Isles and the Norwegian mainland. Follow this up and you come to the Ofoten Fjord, at the head of which is the Norwegian port of Narvik. From here there ran across the Swedish border to Lulea what was the most northerly railway in Europe, and Narvik was a great harbour for the export of magnetic iron ore. Hither German ships came, loaded, and then, by keeping within the three-mile limit of territorial waters, going inside islands, and taking every possible advantage of night, managed to get their valuable cargoes back home for the Teutonic munition makers.

Now it was obviously one of the duties of our

Tenth Cruiser Squadron, entrusted with the interception of shipping in the north, to see that Germany did not receive this ore. But having regard to the delicacy of not violating the waters of a neutral nation, and bearing in mind the pilotage difficulties off a coast studded with islands and half-tide rocks, this was no easy matter. It was here that the small ships came in so useful. We can go back to June, 1915, and find the armed trawler *Tenby Castle* (Lieutenant J. T. Randell, R.N.R.) attached nominally to the Tenth Cruiser Squadron, but sent to work single-handed, as it were, off the Norwegian coast intercepting shipping. As a distinguished admiral remarked, here she lay in a very gallant manner for twenty days, during which time she sank one enemy ship, very nearly secured a second, and was able to hand over to the Tenth Cruiser Squadron a neutral ship with iron ore. It was a most difficult situation to handle, for it required not merely a quick decision and bold initiative, but very accurate cross bearings had to be made, as these offending steamers were on the border-line of territorial waters. That great enemy of all seamen irrespective of nationality, fog, was in this case actually to be a very real friend to our trawler; for in thick weather and the vicinity of a rock-bound coast full of hidden dangers, skippers of the ore ships would naturally be inclined to play for safety and stand so far out from the shore as to be in non-territorial waters. A further consideration was that owing to the effect of the magnetic ore on their compasses they could not afford to take undue navigational risks in thick weather. What they preferred was nice clear weather, so that they could hug the land.

The success of *Tenby Castle* was such that half a

dozen other trawlers were selected and stationed off that coast except in the wild wintry months, and this idea, as we shall presently see, was developed still further, but it will assist our interest if we appreciate first the difficulties as exemplified in the case of the *Tenby Castle*. On the last day of June, 1915, this trawler was about five miles N.E. of the Kya Islet, and it was not quite midday, when she sighted a steamer coming down from Nero Sound; so she closed her and read her name, *Pallas*. Inasmuch as the latter was showing no colours, *Tenby Castle* now hoisted the White Ensign and the international signal to stop immediately. This was ignored, so the trawler came round and saw she was a German ship belonging to Flensburg, and fired a shot across the enemy's bow. The German then stopped her engines, ported her helm, and headed in the direction of the coast, having a certain amount of way on. The trawler closed and ordered her to show her colours, but the German declined; so the latter was then told to steer to the westward, which he also refused to do. Lieutenant Randell, informing him now that he would give him five minutes in which to make up his mind either to come with him or be sunk, sent a wireless signal informing H.M. ships of the Tenth Cruiser Squadron, then went alongside the German and put an armed guard aboard; but the captain of *Pallas* rang down for full speed ahead and starboarded his helm, whereupon *Tenby Castle* fired a couple of shots at the steamer's steering gear on the poop, damaging it. The German stopped his engines once more, but the ship was gradually drawing towards the shore, so that when *Victorian* arrived *Pallas* was about two and a half miles from the land, thus being just within territorial waters, and had to be released. There had been no casualties.

The next incident occurred a week later. At ten minutes to six on the morning of July 7 *Tenby Castle* was lying off the western entrance of the West Fjord, the weather being thick and rainy, when a large steamer was seen to the N.N.W., so *Tenby Castle* put on full speed and ordered her to stop. This was the Swedish S.S. *Malmland*, with about 7,000 tons of magnetic ore. After being ordered to follow the trawler, *Malmland* put on full speed and drew ahead; so she was made to keep right astern at reduced speed, and just before half-past eight that morning was handed over to H.M.S. *India* of the abovementioned cruiser squadron. The day passed, and it was a few minutes after midnight when this trawler, again lying off the West Fjord, sighted a steamer coming down from Narvik. A shot was fired across the steamer's bows, and on rounding-to under the steamship's stern it was observed that she was the German S.S. *Frederich Arp*, of Hamburg. She was ordered to stop, then the trawler closed and ordered the steamer to follow. The German refused to obey and steamed towards the land, so the *Tenby Castle* was compelled to fire a shot into his quarter, and this caused him to stop. After he had several times refused to follow, Lieutenant Randell gave him five minutes and informed him he would either have to accompany the trawler or else be sunk. The five minutes passed, the obstinate German still declined, and two minutes later put his engines ahead and made towards the shore. It was now an hour since the ship had first been sighted, so there was nothing for it but for the trawler to sink her, and she was shelled at the waterline and sunk four and a half miles away from the

THE LAST PHASE

nearest land, her crew of thirteen being handed over a few hours later to H.M.S. *India*. Thus a cargo of 4,000 tons of magnetic ore was prevented from reaching Germany.

Now, it was quite obvious that the information of these incidents would not be long in reaching Germany from an agent via Norway. The German Captain Gayer has stated since the war that news reached Germany that 'an English auxiliary cruiser was permanently stationed' off West Fjord, whose task, he says, was 'to seize and sink the German steamers coming with minerals from Narvik.' Therefore, on August 3, Germany despatched U 22 from Borkum to West Fjord, and this craft had scarcely taken up her position when she saw the armed merchant cruiser *India* enter West Fjord and torpedoed her at long range, so that *India* was sunk. Gayer, who occupied during the war a high administrative position in the U-boat service, adds the following statement: 'It was,' he remarks, 'one of the few instances in which a submarine found with such precision the object of attack really intended for it, when the information had been given by an agent.'

We pass over the intervening years and come to February, 1918. On the nineteenth of that month the Q-ship *Tay and Tyne* had left Lerwick, in the Shetlands, to perform similar work off the Norwegian coast, where she arrived on the twenty-second. This was a little 557-ton steamer, which had been requisitioned at the end of the previous July and fitted out at Lowestoft with a 4-inch gun aft, suitably hidden, and a couple of 12-pounders. She was a single-screw ship, built at Dundee in 1909, having a funnel, two masts, and the usual derricks. In addition to her guns she carried one torpedo tube and also smoke-making apparatus. She was commanded by Lieutenant Mack, R.N., with whom Lieutenant G. H. P. Muhlhauser, R.N.R., went as second in command, both of these officers, as the reader will remember, having served together in the Q-sailing-ship *Result*. Having commissioned the new ship, Lieutenant Mack then took her from Lowestoft to the secluded area of the Wash in order to practise gunnery and the 'panic' party arrangements. Months passed, but on February 22 something of interest happened, for some distance below the Vigten Islands a couple of steamers were sighted, so course was then altered to cut off the one that was bound to the southward. When 1,000 yards away the latter hoisted German colours, so *Tay and Tyne* (alias *Cheriton* and *Dundreary*) hoisted the international signal 'M.N.' to stop immediately. This ship was the *Dusseldorf*, a nine-year-old, typical German flush-decked tramp of 1,200 tons, with 1,700 tons of magnetic ore on board. As she disregarded the signal, a shell was fired across her bows, and this caused her to stop and hoist the answering pennant. Lieutenant Mack then steamed round the stern, keeping her covered all the time with his gun, and now took up station inshore of the German.

Dusseldorf had been completely taken by surprise, and never supposed that this little steamer could possibly be a trap-ship. *Tay and Tyne* lowered a boat containing several of the British crew, under Lieutenant Muhlhauser, armed with revolvers and rifles, and this guard then boarded the enemy, on board whom were found a couple of Norwegian Customs House officials and two Norse pilots. Lieutenant Muhlhauser then ordered the German captain to muster his crew, which he promptly did, and now the terrified crew were given five minutes to collect their clothes. The captain handed over the ship's papers and protested that the ship was in territorial waters. Eleven Germans and the four Norwegians were then transferred to the Q-ship, who landed the four Norwegians in the *Dusseldorf's* boat at Sves Fjord, and this boat they were allowed to keep. The British boarding party had consisted of a dozen men, but Lieutenant Muhlhauser sent three back to the Q-ship, and retained three German stokers and the two German engineers in order to get the prize back to England, these five men working under the supervision of one of the *Tay and Tyne's* crew.

Having received orders to proceed, Lieutenant Muhlhauser then began to take the *Dusseldorf* across the North Sea. I am indebted to him for having allowed me to see his private diary of this voyage, and I think it well illustrates the unexpected and surprising difficulties with which Q-ship officers so frequently found themselves confronted. Having parted company with the *Tay and Tyne*, *Dusseldorf's* new captain proceeded to look for navigational facilities, but in this respect she was amazingly ill-found. The only chart available showed just a small portion of the North Sea, and there was no sextant in the ship. This was a delightful predicament, for with all her magnetic ore it could be taken for certain that the compass would have serious deviation, and, having regard to the number of minefields in the North Sea and the physical dangers of the east coast of Scotland, it was a gloomy prelude to crossing from one side to the other.

Having been round the ship, it was now possible to ascertain her character. She was not a thing of beauty, there was no electric light, the engine-room was in a neglected condition, and round it were the engineers' cabins, the skipper and mate being berthed in a deckhouse under the bridge. However, as the prize dipped to the North Sea swell it was a joy to realize that all the hundreds of tons of ore would not reach Germany. At this late stage of the war she was very short of this commodity, and the loss to her would be felt. The *Tay and Tyne* had certainly made a most useful capture. Fortunately there was found plenty of food in *Dusseldorf*, and enough coal for about three weeks, so if only a few days' fine, clear weather could be ensured, the ship would soon be across and anchored in a British harbour. That, of course, was always supposing there was no encountering of mines or torpedoes.

By dusk of the first day the Halten Lighthouse (Lat. 64.10 N., Long. 9.25 E.) was made out, and then the night set in. For some time the glass had been falling, and before the morning it was blowing a gale of wind with a heavy sea. Loaded with such a cargo *Dusseldorf* made very heavy weather, and was like a half-tide rock most of the time, and during the next day made only 30 miles in twenty-four hours! Strictly speaking, this is not the North Sea but the Atlantic Ocean, and February is as bad a month as you could choose to be off this Norwegian coast in a ship that could make good only a mile an hour. By the afternoon of the twenty-fourth the Romsdal Islands had been sighted, and then, fearing lest the enemy might have received news of the capture and sent out some of his light forces, the ship was kept well out from the shore. The Germans should never get this ore, and arrangements were made to sink her rather than give her up.

With no chart, a doubtful compass, and so few

appliances, was there ever an Atlantic voyage made under more casual circumstances? Bearings were taken of the Pole Star and Sirius in order to get a check on the compass, and the ship proceeded roughly on a W.S.W. course. During the twenty-fifth and twenty-sixth it blew a westerly gale, and the seas crashed over her without mercy. Owing to the cargo being heavy and stowed low, the *Dusseldorf* displayed a quick, lively roll, and already had broken down twice, when for a third time on the evening of the twenty-sixth she again stopped. She was now four days out, and the captain was a little anxious as to his position, but it was impossible to ascertain it. A cast of the lead was taken and bottom was found at thirty fathoms. From this it was assumed that they were now somewhere near the Outer Skerries (East of the Shetlands); and inasmuch as it was believed there was a German minefield, laid this year, not far away, anxiety was in nowise lessened. As soon as the repairs had been effected, course was altered to south-east for 16 miles, then south for the same distance, and north-west in the hope of making the land. This was done, but no land appeared, and it was blowing a gale from the north-west. Whether the ship was now in the North Sea or whether she had overshot the Shetlands and got the other side of Scotland, who could say? Neither the error of the compass nor the error of the log could be known. It was now the twenty-seventh, and they might be north, south, east, or west of the Shetlands, but, on the whole, Lieutenant Muhlhauser believed he was in the North Sea, so decided to run south until well clear of the Moray Firth minefields, and then south-west until the land was picked up.

The twenty-eighth of February passed without land

being sighted, and there was always the horrible possibility that suddenly the ship might strike the shore in the darkness. It was a long-drawn-out period of suspense, aggravated by bad weather and the presence of mines and submarines. But as spring follows winter and dawn comes after night, so at length there came relief. At six in the morning of the first of March a light was picked up on the starboard bow, which, on consulting a nautical almanack, was identified as the Bell Rock (east of the Tay). Continuing further south, two trawlers and an armed yacht were sighted off May Island, so a signal was sent through the yacht to Admiral Startin at Granton reporting the arrival of a prize captured by *Tay and Tyne*, and, in due course, having steamed up the Firth of Forth, *Dusseldorf* at last came to anchor and reported herself. It had been a plucky voyage made under the worst conditions, and many an officer has been decorated for an achievement less than this.

As for *Tay and Tyne*, she, too, had passed through a trying period. After landing the Norwegian pilots and Customs House officials in Sves Fjord she had steamed out to sea and made bad weather of the gale, water even pouring into the engine-room; but she had been saved from foundering by taking shelter in a Norwegian fjord, and next day cruised about the coast looking for more ore ships, but had no further luck, so on February 25 shaped a course for Lerwick, where she duly arrived, and the German prisoners were taken out of the fo'c'sle and handed over to the naval authorities.

In the following month *Tay and Tyne*, accompanied by another Q-ship named the *Glendale*, was again off the Norwegian coast on the look-out for ore ships, just as in Elizabethan days our ancestral seamen

THE LAST PHASE

were in a western sea looking out for the Spanish ships with their rich cargoes. *Glendale* (alias *Speedwell II.* and Q 23) was a disguised trawler of 273 tons belonging to Granton, and armed with a couple of 12-pounders, a 6-pounder, and two torpedoes. On the twenty-first of March, *Glendale* was off the Oxnaes Lighthouse when she captured the German S.S. *Valeria* with 2,200 tons of ore. In vile weather these three ships then started to cross to Lerwick, but, after they had got part of the way across, *Valeria's* small supply of coal gave out, so on the twenty-third she had to be abandoned and then sunk by the shelling from the two Q-ships, the crew having been previously taken off by boats, while both Q-ships poured oil on to the sea. Although *Valeria* never reached a British port this was most useful work; for not only was the ore prevented from reaching Germany, but they were deprived of a brand-new 1,000-ton ship. Her captain, who, together with the rest of the crew, was brought into Lerwick, had only just left the German Navy, and this was his first trip. Incidents such as these show what excellent service can be rendered in naval warfare irrespective of the size of ships and of adverse circumstances, provided only that the officers have zeal and determination. The risks run by these two small ships were very great when we consider the manner in which our Scandinavian convoys had been cut up in spite of destroyer protection. Conversely, seeing how necessary for the prosecution of the war these supplies of ore were to Germany, is it not a little surprising that she did not station a submarine off the Norwegian coast to act as escort, submerged, and then torpedo the *Tay and Tyne* as soon as she began to close the ore ship? One of her smaller submarines could surely have been spared for such an undertaking, and it would have been, from their point of view, more than worth while.

Finally, we have to relate the fight of another small coasting steamer transformed into a Q-ship. This was the *Stockforce* (alias *Charyce*), which had been requisitioned at Cardiff at the beginning of 1918, and then armed with a couple of 4-inch guns, a 12-pounder, and a 3-pounder. Her captain was Lieutenant Harold Auten, D.S.C., R.N.R., who had had a great deal of experience in Q-ships under Admiral Bayly, and had recently commanded the Q-ship *Heather*. On the thirtieth of July, 1918, *Stockforce* was about 25 miles south-west of the Start, steaming along a westerly course at $7\frac{1}{2}$ knots, the time being just before five in the afternoon, when the track of a torpedo was seen on the starboard beam coming straight on for the ship. The crew were sent to their stations, the helm was put hard aport and engines full speed astern, in the hope of avoiding the torpedo; but it was too late. The ship was struck on the starboard side abreast of No. 1. hatch, putting the forward gun out of action, entirely wrecking the fore part of the ship, including the bridge, and wounding three ratings and an officer.

As soon as the torpedo had exploded there came a tremendous shower of timber, which had been packed in the hold for flotation purposes, and besides these 12-pounder shells, hatches, and other debris came falling on to the bridge and fore part of the ship, wounding the first lieutenant, the navigating officer, two ratings, and adding to the injuries of the forward gun. All this had happened as the result of one torpedo. The enemy, perhaps, being homeward bound with a spare torpedo in his tube, had *not* hesitated to use such a weapon on a small coaster instead of employing his guns. *Stockforce* had been

THE LAST PHASE 267

fairly caught and was settling down by the head. The 'abandon ship' party then cleared away their boat and went through their usual make-believe, whilst the ship's surgeon had the wounded taken down to the 'tween deck, where their injuries could be attended to. Here it was none too safe, for the bulkheads had been weakened by the explosion so that the water flowed aft, flooding the magazine and 'tween decks to a depth of three feet, and thereby rendering the work of the surgeon not merely difficult but hazardous.

Whilst the 'panic' party were rowing ahead of the ship, the rest lay at their stations on board, behaving with the greatest equanimity and coolness, while Lieutenant Auten, as the fore-control and bridge were out of action, exercised his command from the after gunhouse. Five minutes later the submarine rose to the surface half a mile distant, and, being very shy, remained there for a quarter of an hour carefully watching *Stockforce* for any suspicious move. In accordance with the training, the 'panic' party then began to row down the port side towards the port quarter so as to draw the enemy on, and this manœuvre succeeded in fooling the German, who now came down the port side as required, being only about three hundred yards away. As soon as the enemy was full on the beam of *Stockforce*, the latter handed him the surprise packet. It was now 5.40 p.m. as both 4-inch guns opened fire from the Q-ship. The first round from the after gun passed over the conning-tower, carrying away the wireless and one of the periscopes, the second shell hitting the conning-tower in the centre and blowing it away, sending high into the air a man who was in the conning-tower.

Stockforce's second 4-inch gun with her first shot

hit the enemy on the water-line at the base where the conning-tower had been, tearing the submarine right open and blowing out many of the crew. A large volume of blue smoke began to pour out of the U-boat, and shell after shell was then poured into the German until she sank by the stern, by which time twenty direct hits had been obtained. The enemy submerged, leaving a quantity of debris on the water, and was never seen again. But in the meantime *Stockforce* was in a critical condition, and every attempt now was made to save her from foundering. Having recalled the 'panic' party, the engines were put full speed ahead in the effort to reach the nearest land and beach her, as she was rapidly listing to starboard and going down by the head. At 6.30 p.m. two trawlers were sighted who closed the ship, and as *Stockforce* was already practically awash forward and along most of the starboard side, all the wounded and half the men were now transferred to one of these trawlers.

With a volunteer crew the Q-ship then went ahead again, but the engine-room was leaking badly, and in the stokehold there were several feet of water, and it was clear that the life of *Stockforce* was a matter of a very short while, for the water in both engine-room and stokehold began now to rise rapidly and the ship was about to sink. But two British torpedo-boats had now arrived, and at 5.15 p.m., when off Bolt Tail, with Plymouth Sound only a few miles off, the *Stockforce's* captain had to send the rest of the ship's company from the sinking ship, while he remained on board with only the first lieutenant. Five minutes later a dinghy from one of the torpedo-boats fetched them also, and after only another five minutes *Stockforce* sank. It had been a plucky fight and a fine endeavour to save the ship, but this was not to be successful. Handsome awards were made in respect of these efforts, the coveted Victoria Cross being conferred on Lieutenant Auten, whilst the Distinguished Service Cross was bestowed on Lieutenant H. F. Rainey, R.N.R., Lieutenant L. E. Workman, R.N.R., Lieutenant W. J. Grey, R.N.R., Sub-Lieutenant G. S. Anakin, R.N.R., Assistant-Paymaster A. D. Davis, R.N.R., and Surgeon-Probationer G. E. Strahan, R.N.V.R.

This last fight represents Q-ship warfare at its highest point of development. We have here the experienced officers of each nation, knowing all the tricks of their highly specialized profession, fighting each other in the most cunningly devised craft. Each of these vessels represented all that could be done by a combination of intellect and engineering skill, so that when the two should meet in the sea arena the fight could not fail to be interesting. After the preliminary moves had been made how would matters stand? The answer is that in the final appeal it was largely a matter of luck. Now, in the duel we have just witnessed the first round of the match was undoubtedly won by the submarine, whose torpedo got home and wrought such damage that the ship was doomed from the first. Round number two, when the 'panic' party succeeded in luring the enemy on to the requisite range and bearing, was distinctly in favour of *Stockforce*. So also was round three, in which she managed to shell him so thoroughly. But here the element of luck enters and characterizes the rest of the day. To all intents and purposes the submarine was destroyed and sunk; whereas, in point of fact, notwithstanding her grievous wounds, she managed to get back home. It was touch-and-go with her, as it had been with von Spiegel's submarine after being shelled by the *Prize*, but good fortune just weighed the scales and prevented a loss. On the other hand, *Stockforce* might have had the luck just to keep afloat a few more miles and get into Plymouth Sound, but as it was she sank a little too soon, and thus the actual result of the encounter might by some be called indecisive, or even in favour of the enemy. This is not so. To us the loss of a small coaster turned temporarily into a man-of-war was of little consequence. A similar ship, the *Suffolk Coast*, would soon be picked up and then turned over to the dockyard experts to be fitted out; but in the case of a submarine there were only limited numbers. That particular U-boat would now have a long list of defects and be a non-combatant for a long time, and her crew would morally be seriously affected by their miraculous escape, and they would not forget to pass on their impressions to their opposite numbers in other submarines.

It was rather the cumulative effect of Q-ships, destroyers, mines, auxiliary patrol craft, depth charges, hydrophones, convoys, and good staff work which broke the spirit of the German submarine menace, so that if the war had continued much longer U-boats would have been thwarted except within certain limits of the North Sea. Every weapon has its rise and fall in the sphere of usefulness; the shell is repelled by armour-plate, the Zeppelin is destroyed by the aircraft, and so on. So it was with the Q-ship. It came into being at a time when no other method seemed likely to deal with submarines adequately. It became successful, it rose into popularity to its logical peak, and then began to wane in usefulness as the submarine re-adapted herself to these new conditions.

THE LAST PHASE

Afterwards came the period when the mine barrages in the Heligoland Bight, in the Dover Strait, and across the northern end of the North Sea, and the hydrophones, in swiftly moving light craft, made the life of any submarine precarious in his going and coming. The hydrophone has made such wonderful developments since the war that in the future within the narrow seas a submarine would find life a little too thrilling to be pleasant.

But for a long period the Q-ship did wonders, and to the officers and men of this service for their bravery and endurance we owe much. They were taking enormous risks, and they turned these risks into successes of great magnitude as long as ever the game was possible. Most, though not all, of the ships and officers and men came from the Mercantile Marine, and in this special force we see the perfect co-operation between the two branches of our national sea service for the good of the Empire. The Royal Navy could teach them all that was to be known about the technicalities of fighting, could provide them with guns and expert gunners, could give them all the facilities of His Majesty's dockyards, whilst at the same time the Mercantile Marine provided the ships and the *personnel* who knew what were the normal habits and appearances of a tramp, a collier, or a coaster. Originally known as special service ships, as decoys, then as Q-ships, these vessels during 1917 and 1918 were known as H.M.S. So-and-So, but it was under the designation of Q-ships that they reached their pinnacle of fame, and as such they will always be known, so it has been thought well thus to describe them in these pages. But whether we think of them as mystery ships or as properly commissioned vessels of His Majesty's Navy, there will ever remain for them a niche in our great sea story, and the valour of all ranks and ratings in all kinds of these odd craft, amid every possible condition of difficulty and danger, should be to those who come after an immortal lesson and a standard of duty to the rising race of British seamanhood. Otherwise these men toiled and endured and died in vain.

INDEX

.˙. The names of Q-ships are in heavy-faced type.

Acton, 164
Alcala. See *Q* 19
Alexander, C. J., Lieutenant, R.N.R., 164
Alyssum, H.M.S., 120, 122-3
Amiral Ganteaume, 7
Anakin, G. S., Sub-Lieutenant, R.N.R., 269
Andalusian, 9
Anglo-Columbian, 26
Antwerp (formerly *Vienna*), 8, 9, 24, 235
Arabic, 20, 32, 132
Armstrong, M., Lieutenant, R.N.R., 67
Arvonian (*Santee, Bendish*), 231-4
Athos. See *Glen*
Attack, H.M.S., 211
Attentive, H.M.S., 7
Aubrietia. See *Q* 13
Aud, 140
Auten, Harold, Lieutenant, R.N.R., 164, 266-9

Bagdale, H.M.T., 64-5
Baralong (*Wyandra*), 20-3, 25, 26-31, 41, 104, 109
Baron Ardrossan, 34
Baron Napier, 33-5
Baron Rose, 190
Barranca. See *Q* 3
Bartel, Leutnant Karl, 116
Bayard, 77
Bayly, Admiral Sir Lewis, 46, 104, 198, 203, 215, 233, 246, 247, 266
Bayonne, 123
Beaton, W. D., Lieutenant, R.N.R., 146
Begonia, 139, 163
Bendish. See *Arvonian*
Berlin, 161
Bernays, Leopold A., Commander, R.N., 161-3
Beryl, H.M.Y., 160
Beswick, W., Lieutenant, R.N.R., 41, 43
Betsy Jameson, 77
Bidart, 247
Blackwood, M. B. R., Commander, R.N., 242, 245
Blair, A. D., Lieutenant, R.N.R., 61
Blessing, 57
Bluebell, H.M.S., 179, 233
Boggs, L. S., Lieut.-Commander, R.N.R., 246
Bolham. See *Sarah Colebrook*
Bombala (*Willow Branch*), 235-6

Bonner, C. G., Lieutenant, R.N.R., 205, 207, 212
Bracondale. See *Chagford*
Bradford City (*Saros*), 31, 101
Bremen, 139
Brewer, Skipper, R.N.R., 145, 149
Brig 10. See *Q* 17
Brig 11. See *Q* 22
Brown Mouse, 77, 78
Buttercup, H.M.S., 197

Camelia, H.M.S., 160
Campbell, Captain Gordon, R.N., 24, 39-46, 109, 161, 192-208, 246
Canadian, 120
Candytuft, 174-6
Capelle, Admiral von, 134
Carrigan Head, 48-9
Casement, Sir R., 140
Cedric, H.M.S., 110
Century. See *Penhallow*
Chagford (*Bracondale*), 228-31
Chancellor, 26
Charles, F. W., Lieutenant, R.N.R., 238
Charyce. See *Stockforce*
Cheero, 55-6
Cheriton. See *Tay and Tyne*
Christopher, H.M.S., 167, 171, 174, 211
Cochrane, W. O'G., Captain, R.N., 174-5
Colville, Admiral Sir Stanley, 13, 214
Commissioner, 238
Crocus, H.M.S., 203
Crompton, Ober-Leutnant, 28, 30
Cullist (*Westphalia, Jurassic, Hayling Prim*), 164, 166-8
Cummings, U.S.S., 233
Cushing, U.S.S., 200, 203
Cymric, 189-90

Daffodil, H.M.S., 165
Dag. See *Result*
Dane, Commander, R.N., 234
Dargle, 77, 177, 190
Davis, A. D., Assistant-Paymaster R.N.R., 269
Deutschland, 139, 234
Donlevon (*Ravenstone*), 159, 160
Doubleday, G. H. D., Sub-Lieutenant, R.N.R., 167
Douglas, S. C., Commander, R.N., 234
Dowie, J. M., Temporary Engineer, R.N.R., 30
Drayton, U.S.S., 165
Dreadnought, H.M.S., 9

Duff, Vice-Admiral Sir Alexander, 227
Dunclutha, 235
Duncombe, 17
Dundreary. See *Tay and Tyne*
Dunois, 107-8
Dunraven, 203-12
Dusseldorf, 260-4

E 13, H.M. Submarine, 23
Echunga. See *Q 3*
Edith E. Cummins. See *Fresh Hope*
Eigler, Ingenieur-Aspirant, 116
Elixir. See *Q 30*
Elizabeth, 189
Else. See *Q 21*
Errington, Lieutenant, R.N.R., 175-6
Eudora, 193

Falaba, 31
Fame. See *Revenge*
First Prize. See *Q 21*
Flying Sportsman, H.M. Tug, 198
Flying Spray, H.M. Tug, 160
Fort George, 239
Foss, 211
Frank, F. A., Lieut. - Commander, R.N.R., 105-6, 164
Frederich Arp, 258
Fresh Hope (*Edith E. Cummins, Iroquois*), 189-90
Friswell. See *Pargust*

G and E, 20
G.L.M. See *George L. Muir*
G. L. Munro. See *George L. Muir*
Gaelic. See *Q 22*
Gayer, Captain, 259
George L. Muir (*G. L. Munro, G.L.M., Padre*), 177
Glen (*Sidney, Athos*), 77-9, 180-4
Glendale. See *Q 23*
Glenfoyle. See *Stonecrop*
Glen Isla, 17
Glitra, 7
Gobo. See *Q 22*
Grenfell, F. H., Captain, R.N., 109-17, 124, 160, 214-6
Grey, W. J., Lieutenant, R.N.R., 269
Gunner, 11, 237
Guy, B. J. D., Lieut.-Commander, R.N., 35-6, 236

Hadziaka, 173
Halcyon, H.M.S., 90
Hallwright, W. W., Lieut.-Commander, R.N., 141
Hannaford, Skipper R. W., R.N.R., 64
Hannah, Lieutenant, R.N.V.R., 150
Hanrahan, D. C., Commander, U.S.N., 232-3
Hansen, Lieut.-Commander, 26, 29

Harlech Castle, H.M. Trawler, 186
Harvey, H. W., Lieutenant, R.N.V.R., 55
Hayes, J., Sub-Lieutenant, R.N.R., 57
Hayling. See *Cullist*
Heather. See *Q 16*
Helgoland. See *Q 17*
Herbert, Godfrey, Commander, R.N., 8, 48-9, 235
Hereford, P. R., Lieutenant, 212
Hermes, H.M.S., 7
Hesione, 26
Hick, Captain Allanson, 30-1
Hobbyhawk. See *Telesia*
Hodson, G. L., Lieut.-Commander, R.N., 33-4
Horley. See *Q 17*
Hudson, C. H., Lieutenant, R.N.R., 239-40
Hughes, E. L., Lieutenant, R.N.R., 57
Hughes, T., Lieutenant, R.N.R., 74-5
Hutchinson, E., Lieutenant, R.N.R., 130

Imogene, 189-90
Ina Williams, H.M. Trawler, 46
India, H.M.S., 258-9
Intaba, 139
Invercauld, 120
Inverlyon, 20
Iolanda, H.M.Y., 236
Iolo, 193
Iroquois. See *Fresh Hope*
Irvine, G., Lieutenant, R.N.R., 178
Island Queen. See *Q 19*

Jeffrey, D. G., Lieutenant, R.N.R., 228-31, 234
Jellicoe, Admiral Viscount, 10, 152, 157 223
Jurassic. See *Cullist*

Kaye, A.B., R.N.R., 40
Kermes, 57
Kerr, J., Lieutenant, R.N.R., 74
Keyes, Adrian, Commander, R.N., 173

Laburnum, H.M.S., 197
Lady Olive. See *Q 18*
Lady Patricia. See *Paxton*
Laggan (*Pladda*), 104, 164
Lammeroo. See *Remembrance*
Lawrence, Skipper, J. H., R.N.R., 240
Lawrie, J., Lieutenant, R.N.R., 69-75
Leonidas, H.M.S., 128
Linsdell, 80
Lisette, 78
Lodorer. See *Q 5*
Lodsen, 49
Louise, 16
Loveless, Engineer-Lieutenant, 43
Luneda, H.M. Trawler, 198

INDEX

Lusitania, 13, 31, 32, 132, 245
Lyons, 9, 25

McClure, Sub-Lieutenant, R.N.R., 33
Mack, P. J., Lieutenant, R.N., 80, 86, 260
McLeod, J. K., Lieut.-Commander, R.N., 164, 225
McLeod, W., Lieutenant, R.N.R., 141
Malachite, 7
Malmland, 258
Manford. See *Q 7*
Maracaio. See *Q 28*
Margit, 32-5
Marshfort, 234
Marx, Admiral, 101, 160
Mary B. Mitchell. See *Q 9*
Mary Rose, *H.M.S.*, 138
Matheson, C. G., Lieut.-Commander, R.N.R., 170-1
Mavis. See *Q 26*
Maxwell, F. N., 13
Meade, Skipper, R.N.R., 146-7
Melville, Lord, 66
Merops. See *Q 28*
Mitchell. See *Q 9*
Moewe, 226, 235
Morris, K., Sub-Lieutenant, R.N.R., 79, 184
Muhlhauser, G. H. P., Lieutenant, R.N.R., 80-2, 86, 260-4
Myosotis, *H.M.S.*, 160

Naylor, Cedric, Lieutenant, R.N.R., 124-5, 128, 130
Nicosian, 22-3
Niger, *H.M.S.*, 7
Noake, Basil S., Lieut.-Commander, R.N., 163
Noma, *U.S.S.*, 211
Noodt, Ober-Leutnant Erich, 116
Nunn, R. A., Assistant-Paymaster, R.N.R., 212
Nyroca. See *Q 26*

Olphert, W., Lieut.-Commander, R.N.R., 164
Ooma, 235
Oracle, *H.M.S.*, 231
Orestes, *H.M.S.*, 171

Padre. See *George L. Muir*
Paladin, *H.M. Tug*, 233
Pallas, 257
Pangloss. See *Pargust*
Pargust (*Vittoria, Snail, Friswell, Pangloss*), 161, 199-204, 231, 234
Paxton (*Lady Patricia*), 104
Penhallow (*Century*), 31
Penshurst. See *Q 7*
Périère, Arnauld de la, 93

Pet, 20
Phillips, Lieutenant, R.N.R., 175
Pitcher, E., Petty Officer, 212
Pladda. See *Laggan*
Powell, Commander Frank, 139
Prevalent, 78
Prim. See *Cullist*
Primo, 7
Prince Charles, 13-16
Princess Ena, 24
Privet. See *Q 19*
Prize. See *Q 21*
Probus. See *Q 30*
Purdy, James, Engineer Sub-Lieutenant, R.N.R., 49

Q 3 (*Barranca, Echunga*), 221, 234
Q 5 (*Lodorer, Farnborough*), 24, 40-7, 109, 192-9, 227
Q 7 (*Penshurst, Manford*), 17, 47, 109-30, 161, 213-22
Q 9 (*Mary B. Mitchell, Mary Y. Jose, Jeannette, Brine, Neptun, Marie Thérèse, Eider, Arius, Cancalais*), 67-74
Q 12 (*Tulip*), 138
Q 13 (*Aubrietia*), 101, 139, 160, 237
Q 15 (*Salvia*), 98-101, 139, 164
Q 16 (*Heather*), 17, 139, 141, 164, 266
Q 17 (*Helgoland, Horley, Brig 10*), 59-64, 78, 190
Q 18 (*Lady Olive*), 104
Q 19 (*Privet, Island Queen, Swisher, Alcala*), 170-1
Q 21 (*Else, First Prize, Prize*) 77, 144
Q 22 (*Gaelic, Gobo, Brig 11*), 65-6, 178-9, 183-4
Q 23 (*Glendale, Speedwell II.*), 264-5
Q 25, 104
Q 26 (*Mavis, Nyroca*), 104, 172-4
Q 28 (*Merops, Maracaio*), 77, 190
Q 30 (*Thirza, Ready, Probus, Elixir*), 18, 185-9
Quickly, 11

Rainey, H. F., Lieutenant, R.N.R., 269
Randell, J. T., Lieutenant, R.N.R., 256-8
Ravenstone. See *Donlevon*
Ready. See *Q 30*
Remembrance (*Lammeroo*), 31
Rentoul, 189, 190
Result (*Dag*), 77, 79, 81-6, 260
Revenge (*Fame*), 56
Rival II., *H.M. Drifter*, 150
Rolfe, C. N., Lieut.-Commander, R.N., 164
Rosskeen, 238

Salvia. See *Q 15*
Sanders, W. E. L., Lieut.-Commander, R.N.R., 60, 61, 144, 157

Santee. See *Arvonian*
Sarah Colebrooke (*Bolham*), 77
Sardinia, 70-1
Saros. See *Bradford City*
Saxon, H.M. Trawler, 230-1
Scheer, Admiral von, 133
Schwieger, Lieut.-Commander, 244
Scott, W. F., Lieutenant, R.N.R., 55
Sidney. See *Glen*
Simpson, S. H., Commander, R.N., 164, 167, 168
Sims, Admiral, 231-2
Smart, R. C. C., Lieut.-Commander, R.N., 101
Smith, J. S., Temporary Engineer Sub-Lieutenant, R.N.R., 41, 44
Smith, Skipper W., R.N.R., 64
Snail. See *Pargust*
Soerakarta, 45
Speedwell, 238
Speedwell II. See Q 23
Speedy, H.M.S., 81
Spence, G., Lieutenant, R.N.R., 167
Spencer, J. G., Lieutenant, R.N.R., 14
Spiegel, Lieut.-Commander Freiherr-von, 145-8
Springwell, 35-6
Starmount, 233
Startin, Admiral, 10
Stockforce (*Charyce*), 247, 266-70
Stonecrop (*Glenfoyle*), 242-5
Strahan, G. E., Surgeon-Probationer, R.N.V.R., 269
Strathallan, H.M. Trawler, 239
Strathearn, H.M. Trawler, 239
Strumbles, 57
Stuart, R. N., Lieutenant, R.N.R., 203
Suffolk Coast, 220, 247-9
Sussex, 132
Swisher. See Q 19

Tamarisk, 139, 164, 246
Tay and Tyne (*Cheriton, Dundreary*), 259-62, 264-5
Telesia (*Hobbyhawk*), 53-6
Tenby Castle, 256-8
Thalia, 57
Thirza. See Q 30
Thornhill. See *Werribee*
Torrent, H.M.S., 91
Tremayne, 175
Tulip. See Q 12
Turnbull, R. J., Lieutenant, R.N.R., 79, 180-1
Tweedie, Lieutenant, R.N.R., 33

U 9, 6; U 18, 7; U 20, 245; U 21, 7; U 22, 259; U 23, 10; U 27, 22, 26; U 29, 9; U 34, 172; U 36, 16; U 40, 10; U 41, 26, 28-31, 40; U 43, 145; U 44, 231; U 62, 138; U 68, 42; U 83, 194-6; U 84, 120; U 88, 242-4; U 93, 145-52
UB 4, 20; UB 13, 54; UB 19, 116; UB 37, 119; UB 39, 180-1; UB 48, 155-6; UB 63, 240
UC 3, 56; UC 29, 202; UC 45, 81, 86
Underwing, 284
Urbino, 28, 30

Vala, 16, 17, 47, 161-2
Valeria, 265
Vereker. See *Viola*
Victorian, H.M.S., 257
Vienna. See *Antwerp*
Vindictive, H.M.S., 24
Viola (*Vereker*), 138, 164, 189-90, 233
Vittoria, 7
Vittoria. See *Pargust*

W. S. Bailey, 239-40
Wadsworth, 104
Wardlaw, Mark, Lieutenant, R.N., 14-16
Warrington, U.S.S., 165
Wegener, Lieut.-Commander, 23
Wellholme. See *Werribee*
Werribee (*Thornhill, Wellholme, Wonganella*), 31, 35-6, 236-7
Westmore, G. G., Lieutenant, R.N.R., 62, 64
Westphalia. See *Cullist*
Wexford Coast, 246
Wharton, W. S., Skipper, R.N.R., 53-4
Whitefriars, 174
Wileyside, 111
Williams, J. W., Lieutenant, R.N.R., 139, 164
Williams, Seaman W., R.N.R., 203
Willow Branch. See *Bombala*
Wilmot-Smith, A., Lieut.-Commander, R.N., 26, 29, 30
Wolf, 226
Wonganella. See *Werribee*
Workman, L. E., Lieutenant, R.N.R., 269
Wreford, 90
Wyandra. See *Baralong*

Ziegler, Sub-Lieutenant, 151-3
Zinnia, H.M.S., 203
Zylpha, 24, 47, 164-5

www.ingramcontent.com/pod-product-compliance
Lightning Source LLC
Chambersburg PA
CBHW061931220426
43662CB00012B/1868